GEOProcessing 2022

The Fourteenth International Conference on Advanced Geographic Information Systems, Applications, and Services

June 26th – 30th, 2022

Porto, Portugal

GEOProcessing 2022 Editors

Claus-Peter Rückemann, Westfälische Wilhelms-Universität Münster (WWU) / DIMF / Leibniz Universität Hannover, Germany

Yerach Doytsher, Technion - Israel Institute of Technology, Haifa, Israel

Printed from e-media with permission by:

Curran Associates, Inc.
57 Morehouse Lane
Red Hook, NY 12571

Some format issues inherent in the e-media version may also appear in this print version.

International Academy, Research, and Industry Association (IARIA)
412 Derby Way
Wilmington, DE 19810

Phone: (408) 893-6407
Fax: (408) 527-6351

petre@iaria.org

Additional copies of this publication are available from:

Curran Associates, Inc.
57 Morehouse Lane
Red Hook, NY 12571 USA
Phone: 845-758-0400
Fax: 845-758-2633
Email: curran@proceedings.com
Web: www.proceedings.com

Table of Contents

GEOProcessing 2022

Forward

The Fourteenth International Conference on Advanced Geographic Information Systems, Applications, and Services (GEOProcessing 2022), held in Porto, Portugal, June 26 - 30, 2022, addressed the aspects of managing geographical information and web services.

The goal of the GEOProcessing 2022 conference was to bring together researchers from the academia and practitioners from the industry in order to address fundamentals of advances in geographic information systems and the new applications related to them using the Web Services. Such systems can be used for assessment, modeling and prognosis of emergencies

GEOProcessing 2022 provided a forum where researchers were able to present recent research results and new research problems and directions related to them. The topics covered aspects from fundamentals to more specialized topics such as 2D & 3D information visualization, web services and geospatial systems, geoinformation processing, and spatial data infrastructure.

We take this opportunity to thank all the members of the GEOProcessing 2022 Technical Program Committee as well as the numerous reviewers. The creation of such a broad and high-quality conference program would not have been possible without their involvement. We also kindly thank all the authors who dedicated much of their time and efforts to contribute to the GEOProcessing 2022. We truly believe that, thanks to all these efforts, the final conference program consists of top quality contributions.

This event could also not have been a reality without the support of many individuals, organizations, and sponsors. We are grateful to the members of the GEOProcessing 2022 organizing committee for their help in handling the logistics and for their work to make this professional meeting a success.

We hope that GEOProcessing 2022 was a successful international forum for the exchange of ideas and results between academia and industry and for the promotion of progress in geographic information research. We also hope that Porto provided a pleasant environment during the conference and everyone saved some time for exploring this beautiful city

GEOProcessing 2022 Chairs

GEOProcessing 2022 General Chair
Claus-Peter Rückemann, Westfälische Wilhelms-Universität Münster (WWU) / DIMF / Leibniz Universität Hannover, Germany

GEOProcessing Steering Committee
Thomas Ritz, FH Aachen, Germany
Yerach Doytsher, Technion - Israel Institute of Technology, Haifa, Israel
Francisco Javier Nogueras-Iso, Universidad de Zaragoza, Spain
Alexey Cheptsov, Information Service Center of the University of Stuttgart (TIK)
Roger Tilley, Sandia National Laboratories, USA
Jui-Hsin (Larry) Lai, Ping-An Technology - Research Lab, USA

GEOProcessing 2022 Publicity Chair

Laura Garcia, Universitat Politècnica de València (UPV), Spain
José Miguel Jiménez, Universitat Politecnica de Valencia, Spain

GEOProcessing 2022

COMMITTEE

GEOProcessing 2022 General Chair

Claus-Peter Rückemann, Westfälische Wilhelms-Universität Münster (WWU) / DIMF / Leibniz Universität Hannover

GEOProcessing Steering Committee

Thomas Ritz, FH Aachen, Germany
Yerach Doytsher, Technion - Israel Institute of Technology, Haifa, Israel
Francisco Javier Nogueras-Iso, Universidad de Zaragoza, Spain
Alexey Cheptsov, Information Service Center of the University of Stuttgart (TIK), Germany
Roger Tilley, Sandia National Laboratories, USA
Jui-Hsin (Larry) Lai, Ping-An Technology - Research Lab, USA

GEOProcessing 2022 Publicity Chair

Laura Garcia, Universitat Politècnica de València (UPV), Spain
José Miguel Jiménez, Universitat Politecnica de Valencia, Spain

GEOProcessing 2022 Technical Program Committee

Alia I. Abdelmoty, Cardiff University, Wales, UK
Danial Aghajarian, Georgia State University, USA
Nuhcan Akçit, Middle East Technical University, Turkey
Zaher Al Aghbari, University of Sharjah, UAE
Md Mahbub Alam, Dalhousie University, Canada
Heba Aly, University of Maryland, College Park, USA
Francisco Javier Ariza López, Escuela Politécnica de Jaén - Universidad de Jaén, Spain
Thierry Badard, Centre de Recherche en Géomatique (CRG) | Université Laval, Canada
Abderrazak Bannari, Arabian Gulf University, Bahrain
Fabian Barbato, Ort University of Uruguay, Uruguay
Melih Basaraner, Yildiz Technical University, Turkey
Peter Baumann, rasdaman GmbH Bremen / Jacobs University Bremen, Germany
Lorenzo Carnevale, University of Messina, Italy
Mete Celik, Erciyes University, Turkey
Wei Chen, University of Birmingham, UK
Dickson K.W. Chiu, The University of Hong Kong, Hong Kong
Alexey Cheptsov, Information Service Center of the University of Stuttgart (TIK), Germany
Alexandre Corrêa da Silva, HEX Geospatial Technologies, Brazil
Mehmet Ali Çullu, Harran University, Turkey
Monica De Martino, CNR-IMATI (National research Council, Institute of applied Mathematics and Information technology), Italy
Cláudio de Souza Baptista, University of Campina Grande, Brazil
Subhadip Dey, Indian Institute of Technology Bombay, India

Javier Nogueras-Iso, University of Zaragoza, Spain
Alexey Noskov, Philipps University of Marburg, Germany
Xiao Pan, Shijiazhuang Tiedao University, China
Shray Pathak, School of Geographic Sciences | East China Normal University, Shanghai, China
Kostas Patroumpas, Athena Research Center, Greece
Davod Poreh, Università degli Studi di Napoli "Federico II", Italy
Satish Puri, Marquette University, Wisconsin, USA
Kuldeep Purohit, Michigan State University, USA
Honggang Qi, University of Chinese Academy of Sciences, China
Thomas Ritz, FH Aachen, Germany
Ricardo Rodrigues Ciferri, Federal University of São Carlos (UFSCar), Brazil
Armanda Rodrigues, Universidade NOVA de Lisboa | NOVA LINCS, Portugal
Claus-Peter Rückemann, Westfälische Wilhelms-Universität Münster (WWU) / DIMF / Leibniz Universität Hannover, Germany, Germany
Ibrahim Sabek, University of Minnesota, USA
André Sabino, Universidade Autónoma de Lisboa, Portugal
Markus Schneider, University of Florida, USA
Raja Sengupta, McGill University, Montreal, Canada
Elif Sertel, Istanbul Technical University, Turkey
Shih-Lung Shaw, University of Tennessee, Knoxville, USA
Yosio E. Shimabukuro, Brazilian Institute for Space Research - INPE, Brazil
Spiros Skiadopoulos, University of the Peloponnese, Greece
Dimitris Skoutas, Athena Research Center, Greece
Francesco Soldovieri, Istituto per il Rilevamento Elettromagnetico dell'Ambiente - Consiglio Nazionale delle Ricerche (CNR), Italy
Katia Stankov, University of British Columbia, Canada
Payam Tabrizian, IDEO, San Fransisco, USA
Ergin Tari, Istanbul Technical University, Turkey
Brittany Terese Fasy, Montana State University, USA
Roger Tilley, Sandia National Laboratories, USA
Goce Trajcevski, Iowa State University, USA
Linh Truong-Hong, Delft University of Technology, Netherlands
Taketoshi Ushiama, Kyushu University, Japan
Marlène Villanova-Oliver, Univ. Grenoble Alpes - Grenoble Informatics Lab, France
Massimo Villari, University of Messina, Italy
Tin Vu, Microsoft Corporation, USA
Hong Wei, University of Maryland, College Park, USA
John P. Wilson, University of Southern California, USA
Jianhong Cecilia Xia, Curtin University, Australia
Ningchuan Xiao, The Ohio State University, USA
Daisuke Yamamoto, Nagoya Institute of Technology, Japan
Xiaojun Yang, Florida State University, USA
Zhaoming Yin, Google LLC, USA
Qiangqiang Yuan, School of Geodesy and Geomatics | Wuhan University, China
F. Javier Zarazaga-Soria, University of Zaragoza, Spain
Shenglin Zhao, Tencent, Shenzhen, China
Qiang Zhu, University of Michigan - Dearborn, USA

Copyright Information

Spatio-Temporal Clustering of Polygon Objects and per Object Interventions

Optimizing Remediation of Spatially Dispersed Contaminated Parcels Under an Annual Budget Constraint

Floris Abrams[1,3], Lieve Sweeck[1], Johan Camps[1]
[1]Belgian Nuclear Research Centre (SCK CEN),
Mol, Belgium
e-mail: {Floris.Abrams, Lieve.Sweeck, Johan.Camps}@sckcen.be

Dirk Catrysse[2], Jos Van Orshoven[2]
[2]Katholieke Universiteit Leuven (KU Leuven)
Leuven, Belgium
e-mail: {Dirk.Cattrysse, Jos.Vanorshoven}@kuleuven.be

Abstract — **Polygons provide a natural representation for many types of geospatial objects such as agricultural parcels, buildings, and polluted sites. These polygon-based entities form the smallest units used in decision making of real-world problems. Acting on these dispersed entities could result in a heterogeneous and difficult to perform an action plan. Clustering of parcels in larger homogeneous actionable units can improve feasibility and reduce cost. Therefore, a polygon-based clustering can be beneficial for environmental disaster management, where due to the large impacted area or limited availability of labor and financial resources, setting priorities of where, how and when to act are indispensable. This paper presents a spatio-temporal clustering algorithm under a budget constraint to prioritize clusters of parcels for intervention in space and time. The proposed algorithm returns homogeneous actionable clusters in space and time, trading off between effectiveness and feasibility and cost of intervention.**

Keywords-Spatio-temporal clustering; Budget constraint; Disaster management; Multi-Attribute Decision Making; MADM.

I. Introduction

When dealing with large natural or man-made disasters decision makers are confronted with setting priorities of where, how and when to remediate, because of a limited availability of labor and financial resources. This priority setting is particularly applicable when the impact of actions is costly and has long lasting influences. For spatially distributed sites with variable characteristics, priority setting among the sites and determination of adequate actions are of major importance. The effectiveness of related decisions is typically conditioned by multiple, and often contradicting criteria of economic, social, technical, environmental and human health-related nature. These characteristics of the decision problem make it suitable for the application of a discrete Multi-Attribute Decision Making (MADM) approach. These MADM approaches typically yield a patchwork of sites with different priorities and preferred actions. Because, performing these actions on multiple adjacent sites at the same time, compared to individual sites, is likely to be more feasible and less costly, making clustering of these sites interesting. Although clustering of pixels is quite common for processing and interpreting raster based datasets (e.g., to determine environmental risk areas, like landslides [1]), it is more complicated in polygon-based data datasets. Nonetheless, polygon objects provide a natural representation of real-world geospatial entities. Therefore, it can be more interesting to provide actionable support to decision making based on polygon-based representations of real-world problems. In the field of afforestation multiple MADM approaches where compared to support decision making, when dealing with raster-based datasets for prioritizing afforestation sites [2], [3]. Furthermore, priorities will be conditioned by the resources available at that period, resulting in the need for spreading the actions in time. However, because of this time aspect the initial decision variables, used for prioritization, change due to physical processes in the landscape or due to the decision context. For an afforestation context, the BIOLP model was developed, to determine how a set of land use types should be distributed over space and time in order to optimize the multi-dimensional land performance of a region [4]. However, the used Integer Programming model based on the Balanced Compromise Programming MADM showed the risk of obtaining solutions that are excessively fragmented.

This paper presents a spatio-temporal approach to deal with the clustering of spatially scattered polygon-based parcels, whereby only a set of actions can be performed per year as constrained by annual budgets. The paper explores an innovative extension of the classic region growing principles, adapted to polygon-based data structures and explicitly takes into account the attributes of the polygons to find the optimal compromise solution for the whole cluster. The algorithm is meant to provide actionable and feasible support to decision makers, by proposing a coherent action plan in space and time for the affected region.

The next section provides in depth explanation of the spatio-temporal cluster algorithm. In Section III, the methodology is illustrated for an agricultural region in Belgium, contaminated after a hypothetical accidental release of radionuclides from a nuclear power plant. Finally, Section IV discusses the algorithms and the case study, then Section V draws the conclusions on applicability of the algorithm to help improve decision-making.

II. SPATIO-TEMPORAL CLUSTERING METHOD

In the following section, first the initial priority scores that are the foundation of the algorithm are explained. Second, the temporal aspects of the parcel interventions and third, the different steps in the algorithm are explained.

A. *Distance based multi-attribute decision making*

An MADM method considering distance in the feature space, named Compromise Programming (CP), was used to rank the set of feasible alternatives. For the CP methodology, a set of independent, operational and non-redundant attributes need to be established as criteria. The performance criteria used will vary significantly between different cases. For each criterion a weight reflecting the importance of the criterion is set by the stakeholders [5]. For this set of criteria, the CP methodology determines the optimal point, a vector of performance attribute values corresponding to an alternative with the best observed performance on each criterion separately. The ideal point is normally unfeasible, because multi-criteria decision problems involve conflicting criteria. Therefore, CP determines a compromise solution by searching for a feasible solution that is closest to the ideal point. The definition of 'closeness' requires the formulation of a distance metric (1), where a larger distance equals a less optimal alternative [6].

$$L = \left[\sum_{i}^{n} w_i^p \left[\frac{f_i^+ - f_i(x)}{f_i^+ - f_i^-}\right]^p\right]^{\frac{1}{p}} \qquad (1)$$

- n is the number of criteria under consideration;
- w_i is the relative importance (weight) assigned to performance attribute i;
- p is a parameter that determines the type of distance function, where 2 represents the Euclidian distance;
- f_i^+ is the optimal value for performance criterion i;
- $f_i(x)$ is the value of the ith performance criterion expressed as a function of the decision variables x;
- f_i^- is the anti-ideal corresponding to the ith attribute that is the "worst" value for this attribute.

Distances based on (1), will be standardized within the interval [0-1], where a distance of 0, represents the optimal alternative where no compromise is needed, because it outperforms all other on all criteria. In contrast, a distance of 1 represents an alternative, with the worst score on all criteria simultaneously.

1) Intervention plan of polygon-based parcels

The first question that needs to be answered is: "Where are the sites for which intervention is most urgent situated?". All sites in need for intervention, are identified as feasible alternatives. The CP methodology returns a distance score for each site, representing the priority/urgency of a parcel to be intervened on. From these scores a ranking of the parcels from high priority (small distance) to low priority (large distance) can be made. For the rest of the paper, the scores for the parcels will be referred to as Parcel Priority Scores (PPS).

2) Optimal intervention per parcel

For each parcel, all the feasible intervention actions for that parcel need to be ranked. Once again the ranking of the interventions is based on a distance score, computed by the CP methodology. For the rest of the paper, the scores representing the priority ranking of a remedial action for this specific parcel referred to as the Action Priority Score (APS).

B. *Temporal dynamics in MADM*

In many decision areas the decision information is collected and evaluated at multiple periods overtime. However, most MADM methods only focus on the decision making problem at a particular period [7]. Therefore, it is necessary to use Dynamic Multi-Attribute Decision Making (dMADM) to tackle the changes of the alternative attributes and weights through time [8]–[10]. For the case of large scale interventions on many different sites, the decision making becomes dynamic due to limits in economic resources or availability of labour forces. Because of these limited resources not all sites can be tackled in one period of time, resulting in postponed interventions. When actions are postponed the initial decision variables may alter and the decision problem needs a multi-period MADM. The amount of parcels that can be acted on each year depends on the annual budget constraint. While performing actions on the most urgent polygons first each of the actions comes at a cost. For each intervention the cost can be calculated based on the cost per unit of area and the size of the parcel. The interventions can be done until the total cost of remediation would exceed the yearly budget, if the budget is reached the remaining parcels are candidates for action in the next period.

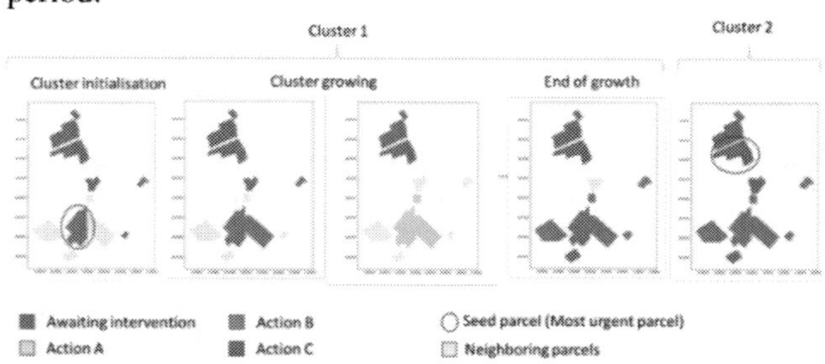

Figure 1. The cluster growing procedure applied on 12 polygon-based parcels, with 3 possible actions. Resulting in 2 homogenous clusters.

C. *Spatio-temporal clustering algorithm with budget constraint*

To determine spatial coherent clusters of parcels with the same intervention action, a spatially explicit clustering algorithm is used. The algorithm operates in a similar fashion as a region growing algorithm, where it consecutively checks if it could add one of the neighboring parcels to the cluster, depending on the similarity between their PPS and RPS. The clustering algorithm is iterative and consists of three phases: The cluster initialisation, followed by the cluster growing procedure and lastly end of growth phase.

1) Cluster initialisation

To optimally allocate resources, the most urgent sites should be treated first. Therefore, the seed parcel is the one with the lowest PPS (smallest distance to the optimal point) and will be selected as the first parcel in the cluster.

2) Cluster growing procedure

After the seed parcel has been determined, the cluster growing procedure attempts to find neighbouring parcels, which can be added to the seed parcel and later the growing cluster. Parcels in a cluster have the same intervention action and are acted on simultaneously. Adding more parcels to the cluster enlarges the cluster, therefore, creating larger actionable units which are preferred from the perspective of reducing the complexity and operational cost of the intervention. But the addition of candidates with a higher PPS or a different optimal APS to the cluster, results in lower performance of the cluster, compared to the set of individual parcels. It is therefore important to find a compromise remediation action between all parcels on the cluster level. The procedure is shown graphically in Figure 1 and pseudo code in Figure 3.

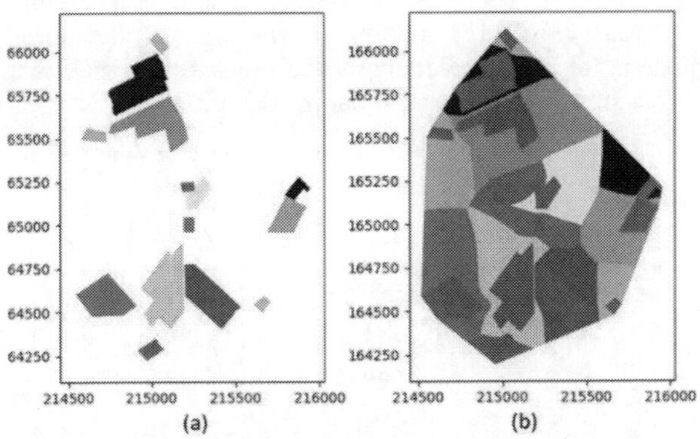

Figure 2. Initial set of distributed parcels (a) and VP computed by the EMT, resulting in a partitioned space (b).

a) Determination of the parcel neighbors

Compared to a raster dataset, where pixels are spatially arranged in a systematic way and neighbours are easy to define, in a vector data set of spatially distributed polygons determining the neighbours is more challenging. To define neighbouring polygons, which are not necessarily sharing a border but rather separated by boundaries such as roads or a small stream, a technique called morphologic tessellation (MT) is used. At the core of MT lies the Voronoi tessellation (VT), a method of geometric partitioning of the 2D space, where a planar set of 'seed points' generate a series of polygons, known as Voronoi polygons (VP). Each VP encloses the portion of the plane that is closer to its seed than to any other polygon [11]. From the partitioned space, the neighbours can be determined by the respected VPs sharing borders. An example of the portioning by VPs is given in Figure 2. Our clustering algorithm makes use of an enclosed tessellation based on the enhanced morphological tessellation algorithm (EMT). EMT allows to set limits to the expansion of the MT, limiting the allowed distance between parcels that can be considered to be neighbours. Further, it allows to set break lines (e.g., larger rivers, administrative boundaries), which the VPs are not permitted to trespass. The VP constructed by the EMT algorithm capture the spatial configuration of all parcels, from which the neighbouring parcels of each parcel can be determined. The EMT algorithm is accessible from an open-source python package (http://docs.momepy.org). Fleischmann (2019, 2020) provide more information regarding the EMT methodology.

Algorithm: Spatio-temporal cluster approach

```
Input: collection of polygon-based parcels, yearly budget (budget), similarity threshold (T)

Create data structure R to store parcels
Add parcels in need for remediation to R

Create data structure S to store remediated parcels
Create data structure RC to store remediation clusters
Create data structure CC to store cluster candidates

Set t to 1
Set BT to budget
Compute PPS for each parcel

While size of R > 0 do

    Select parcel with lowest PPS from R as Seed Parcel (SP)
    Compute APS values for each remedial action
    Select all feasible remediation actions for period t
    Determine the optimal action for seed parcel as action_sp
    Determine neighboring parcels of SP as candidates
    Add candidates to CC

    IF BT - remediation cost action_sp > 0 do
        Set BT to BT - remediation cost action_sp
        Add period to SP
        Add SP to RC
        While CC > 0 do
            Compute composite score (PPS + APS) for all candidate-action combinations
            Select candidate-action_opt with lowest composite score for the whole cluster as CP
            If composite score_sp for action_opt – composite score_sp for action_sp < T do
                If BT - remediation cost CP > 0 do
                    Add period to CP
                    Add CP to RC
                    Determine neighboring parcels of CP as new_candidates
                    Add new_candidates to C
                Else do
                    Set t to t +1
                    Set BT to budget + BT
                    End while
                Endif
            Else do
                End while
            Endif

        End while
        add RC to S
        Remove RC from initial set R

    Else
        Set t to t +1
        Set BT to budget + BT
    Endif
End while
Output: solution set (S)
```

Figure 3. Pseudo code of the spatio-temporal cluster approach, determining the optimal year and remedial clusters.

a) Determining the optimal neighbour

To determine the candidate parcel for growing the cluster, it is necessary to find the parcel and action combination to add to the cluster, with the lowest increase in composite score. The composite score of the cluster is the sum of all PPS scores of the included parcels and their APS scores for the optimal action of the cluster. From this follows, that adding a parcel to the cluster could change the remediation of the whole cluster, resulting in a different compromise solution within the cluster.

This compromise solution is not necessarily the optimal solution for all parcels individually, but from the perspective of the collective composite score of the cluster. When the best parcel is found, it should be checked if it is still similar enough to the seed pixel to be added and that the budget constraint is not exceeded. If for the candidate parcel none of the previous stated thresholds are exceeded, the parcel is added to the cluster and the composite score of the cluster is adapted to the new situation. The growth will continue by the adding the new neighbors and determining the optimal one. This procedure is repeated until the end of growth phase is reached as described in the next paragraph.

3) End of growth

a) Similarity threshold

To determine whether a neighboring parcel can still be added to the cluster, the similarity between the cluster seed and the candidate parcel their composite scores are checked. The difference between both scores cannot exceed the predefined similarity threshold. The threshold is defined by the user, according to its preference to optimality or ease of implementation of the remediation strategy. The reasoning behind the threshold is that when the difference between seed and candidate is large, resources will be used on less urgent parcels or sub optimal interventions will be performed.

b) Budget constraint

The budget constraint limits the amount of resources that can be allocated to intervention in each period. The implementation of a budget constraint in the spatial clustering algorithm, ensures that the cluster cannot exceed the budget for the given period and the clustering is therefore halted once the available budget is reached. Once the budget will be exceeded, the cluster growing is stopped and the polygon's attributes for the new period are determined, then the cluster initialization phase can be started for the new period.

III. Case Study

The results shown in this section are based on a hypothetical accidental radioactive release, affecting 157 polygon-based agricultural parcels in Flanders, Belgium. For a budget of 400.000 euro per year a remediation plan can be designed, that ensures that all parcels are remediated so that after remediation food can be produced in line with the legally set contamination limits.

A. Environmental remediation characterisitcs

A parcel is defined by its on-site characteristics or attributes such as: geographic location, environmental characteristics, agricultural practices. These attributes form the basis for the decision criteria. For the intervention 5 remedial actions are determined, all with a different local and environmental impact and remediation efficiency. The feasibility of the intervention depends on the contamination level and the crop type because some remedial actions are unsuitable for specific agricultural crops or inadequate to reduce the contamination levels below the allowed levels. For example, ploughing actions cannot be performed on parcels with perennial crops. The criteria to assess remedial actions, can vary largely based on the geographical region, contamination type, included stakeholders and data availability.

The reason for including the temporal dynamics in this case study is the altering of certain decision variables in environmental contamination problems. A natural phenomenon, called natural attenuation, causes the mass, toxicity, volume or concentration of contaminants in the soil or groundwater to reduce over time. This implies that the contamination decreases overtime without interference of specific remedial actions. For radioactive contaminations in particular, the reduction of the contaminant is even more strongly determined by radioactive decay, its half-live. For a remedial action to be considered feasible, it should be able to reduce the contamination levels below the legally allowed limits. From the dynamic character of the contamination follows, that after a certain period of time other remedial options can become available, which outperform the previously selected option. Consequently, the remedial actions for each parcel should be revised on a regular basis to ensure they are still optimal for this time period.

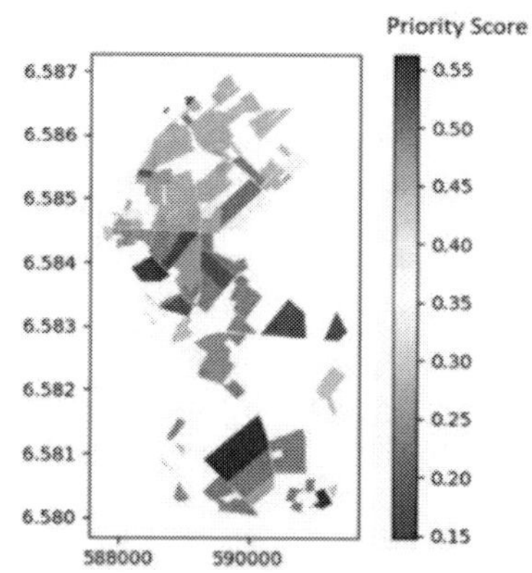

Figure 4. Parcel priority score (PPS) for the affected agricultural parcels, the smaller the more urgent the remediation.

B. Compromise solution on a per parcel basis

The PPS of each parcel is shown in Figure 4, parcels with a low PPS are identified as urgent to remediate. Further, for each specific parcel, the APS for all feasible remediation actions is determined. A specific example for a pasture parcel is shown in figure 5. It is important to acknowledge, that for each parcel, all feasible remedial actions, possess a RPS score, where a lower score represents a more optimal remedial action for that specific parcel.

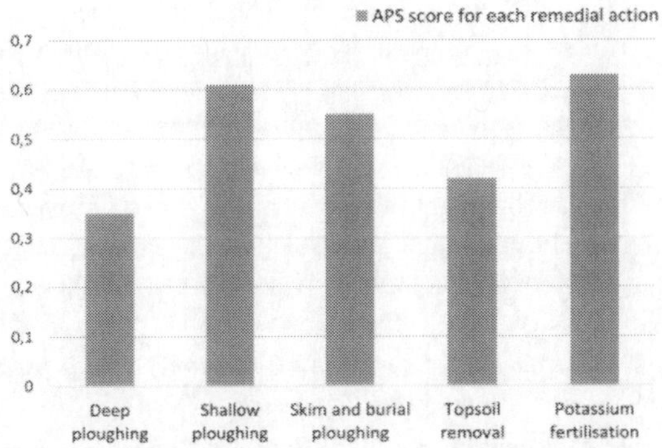

Figure 5. Action Priority Score (APS) for the different candidate remedial actions for an agricultural parcel with cereal cultivation.

C. *Spatio-temporal cluster for the affected region*

A comparison between the action sites per year with similarity threshold = 0 and similarity threshold = 0.25 is shown in Figure 6. A similarity threshold of 0, corresponds to a situation where no candidate parcel will be good enough to add to the cluster, resulting in a remediation plan without clusters. For different values of the similarity threshold a comparison between the remediation plans can be made based on for example: the cost, waste production and time needed for remediation. The comparison between different similarity thresholds is out of the scope of this paper as it relies heavily on characteristics of the contamination and remediation actions.

TABLE 1. THE GROWING PROCEDURE OF A CLUSTER FOR 5 ITERATIONS.

Iterations \ Parcels	A PPS = 0.15	B PPS= 0.17	C PPS= 0.28	D PPS= 0.35	E PPS= 0.41
Iteration I (Seed parcel)	**APS_1: 0.17** APS_2: 0.22 APS_3: 0.33	**APS_1: 0.18** APS_2: 0.23 APS_3: 0.20	APS_1: 0.30 APS_2: 0.24 **APS_3: 0.11**	APS_1: 0.20 **APS_2: 0.11** APS_3: 0.17	**APS_1: 0.15** APS_2: 0.22 APS_3: 0.26
Iteration II (A+B)	**APS_1: 0.35** **PPS: 0.32** **Composite $score_1$: 0.67**				
Iteration III (A+B+C)	**APS_3: 0.64** **PPS: 0.60** **Composite $score_3$: 1.24**				
Iteration IV (A+B+C+D)	**APS_2: 0.80** **APS: 0.95** **Composite $score_2$: 1.75**				
Iteration V (A+B+C+D+E)	**APS_1: 1** **PPS: 1.36** **Composite $score_1$: 2.36**				

D. *Compromise solutions in the clusters*

To highlight the process of finding a compromise between all parcels on the cluster level, five iterations of the growing procedure are shown in Table 1. The growing procedure determines the optimal remediation action for the 5 parcels based on a similarity threshold of 0.25. The yellow cells show the current parcels in the cluster and the remedial action of the cluster is shown based on the subscript number. The APS values in bold show the optimal action per parcel. From Table 1, it becomes clear that while a cluster grows, the optimal remediation for all parcels within the cluster changes based on the clusters compromise solution. In iteration III, the optimal remediation on the cluster level, is the worst performing action for the seed parcel (A), and the second best action for B. Nevertheless, from the perspective of the cluster action 3 is the best compromise solution.

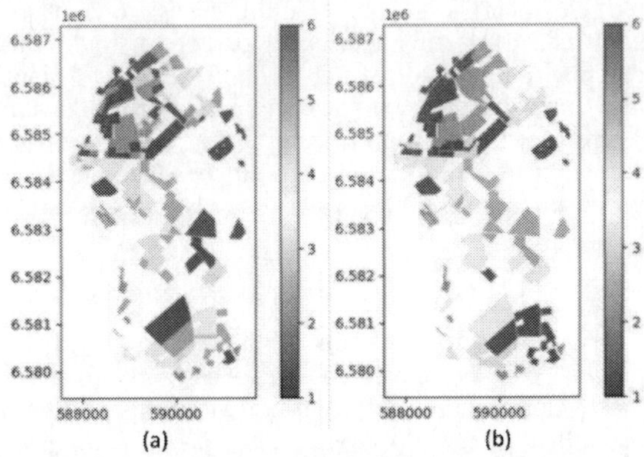

Figure 6. Spatial distribution of the remediated parcels per year after spatio-temporal clustering with a similarity threshold of 0 (a) and a similarity threshold of 0.25 (b). The colors depict the year of remediation per parcel or cluster.

IV. DISCUSSION

Determining the PPS and APS of a parcel, should be done with great care, because it can influence the rest of the process. For the purpose of this research, the CP methodology was used but other distanced based methodologies can replace it. Because of the use of two distance-based metrics, PPS and RPS, the composite distance score still has a physical meaning (distance to the optimal). When other MADM procedures ELECTRE or PROMETHEE are used, this should be done carefully to make sure both scores are still compatible to sum up. Figure 6 shows the clusters that are formed based on the budget constraint and similarity threshold. Reducing the budget, would spread the remediation plan over more years and would interact more with the cluster growing mechanisms, because of more early stops. If the similarity threshold would become bigger, less optimal clusters are allowed and the deviation from the optimal situation of the clusters would grow. The similarity threshold influences the cluster heterogeneity and therefore the compromise solution per cluster becomes more important. Because both values for PPS and APS range between 0 -1, similarity thresholds can range from 0.1 to 0.5. From Table 1, it is clear that more heterogeneous parcels in the cluster result in more changes in the compromise remedial action throughout the growing of the cluster.

When working with polygon-based datasets, topological errors, such as gaps, overlap and sliver polygons occur. Relying solely on these topological relationships, can have major impacts on determining the neighbors. Our approach is not impacted by these errors. The utility of the algorithm was shown based on an environmental remediation case study, where clusters of remediated parcels would reduce cost and effectivity, compared to non-clustered approaches. Nevertheless, other use cases could benefit from a similar approach. For example, when afforesting a large region, not all sites can be afforested at the same time. Further, every plot has a certain suitability and urgency to be afforested. In addition, afforesting connected parcels, with a similar tree composition, would severely reduce the cost of planting and also improve the ecological connectivity of the landscape. Therefore, finding optimal clusters of areas to afforest with similar tree compositions could be facilitated with our proposed algorithm, for raster datasets this was already done [13].

V. Conclusions and Future Work

With the proposed algorithm, dispersed polygon-based parcels can be clustered in space and time for given intervention under an annual budget constraint. In addition, the utility of the algorithm shows promise for many other fields of application. The extension of the region growing principles from a raster data set to polygons is a useful approach for dealing with real-world problems. Further, explicitly taking into account the attributes of all parcels in the cluster, during the cluster growing procedure gives rise to interesting compromise solutions from a cluster perspective. More research on the impact of the similarity threshold is needed and future work should also attempt at defining the similarity threshold in a way, that can more easily be understood by decision makers.

Acknowledgment

This work was supported by a PhD grant for Floris Abrams from the Belgian Nuclear Research Centre (SCK CEN).

References

[1] S. K. Nath, A. Sengupta, and A. Srivastava, "Remote sensing GIS-based landslide susceptibility & risk modeling in Darjeeling–Sikkim Himalaya together with FEM-based slope stability analysis of the terrain," in *Natural Hazards*, vol. 108, no. 3, Springer Netherlands, 2021, pp. 3271–3304.

[2] R. Estrella, W. Delabastita, A. Wijfels, D. Catrice, and J. Van Orshoven, "Comparison of multicriteria decision making methods for selection of afforestation sites," *Rev. Int. géomatique*, vol. 24, no. 2, pp. 143–157, 2014.

[3] R. Estrella, W. Delabastita, A. Wijfels, D. Catrice, and J. Van Orshoven, "Comparison of multicriteria decision making methods for selection of afforestation sites," *Rev. Int. géomatique*, vol. 24, no. 2, pp. 143–157, 2012.

[4] R. Estrella, D. Cattrysse, and J. Van Orshoven, "An integer programming model to determine land use trajectories for optimizing regionally integrated ecosystem services delivery," *Forests*, vol. 7, no. 2, pp. 1–27, 2016.

[5] V. Belton and T. J. Stewart, *Multiple criteria decision analysis: An integrated approach*. 2002.

[6] J. Malczewski and C. Rinner, *Multicriteria Decision Analysis in Geographic Information Science*, no. Massam 1993. 2015.

[7] Z. Xu, "On multi-period multi-attribute decision making," *Knowledge-Based Syst.*, vol. 21, no. 2, pp. 164–171, 2008.

[8] Y. Chen and B. Li, "Dynamic multi-attribute decision making model based on triangular intuitionistic fuzzy numbers," *Sci. Iran.*, vol. 18, no. 2 B, pp. 268–274, 2011.

[9] M. Karatas, "Multiattribute Decision Making Using Multiperiod Probabilistic Weighted Fuzzy Axiomatic Design," *Syst. Eng.*, vol. 20, no. 4, pp. 318–334, 2017.

[10] Q. Dong and Y. Guo, "Multiperiod multiattribute decision-making method based on trend incentive coefficient," *Int. Trans. Oper. Res.*, vol. 20, no. 1, pp. 141–152, 2013.

[11] M. Fleischmann, A. Feliciotti, O. Romice, and S. Porta, "Morphological tessellation as a way of partitioning space: Improving consistency in urban morphology at the plot scale," *Comput. Environ. Urban Syst.*, vol. 80, no. May 2019, p. 101441, 2020.

[12] M. Fleischmann, "momepy: Urban Morphology Measuring Toolkit," *J. Open Source Softw.*, vol. 4, no. 43, p. 1807, 2019.

[13] P. Vanegas, D. Cattrysse, A. Wijffels, and J. Van Orshoven, "Finding sites meeting compactness and on- and off-site suitability criteria in raster maps," in *2nd International Conference on Advanced Geographic Information Systems, Applications, and Services, GEOProcessing 2010*, 2010, pp. 15–20.

A Street Name-Based Summarization Method for Voice Navigation

Tomoya Sukigara
Nagoya Institute of Technology
Aichi, Japan
e-mail: t.sukigara.939@stn.nitech.ac.jp

Yonghwan Kim
Nagoya Institute of Technology
Aichi, Japan
e-mail: kim@nitech.ac.jp

Daisuke Yamamoto
Nagoya Institute of Technology
Aichi, Japan
e-mail: daisuke@nitech.ac.jp

Naohisa Takahashi
Nagoya Institute of Technology
Aichi, Japan
e-mail: naohisa@nitech.ac.jp

Abstract— **While existing voice navigation systems provide simple and easy-to-understand directions, they have a disadvantage in that voice directions tend to be long when the number of left-right turns is large. The objective of this study is to realize a summarization method for voice directions that also provides a geographic image of the route to the destination. The system generates multiple candidate routes and simplifies the voice directions based on street names. Furthermore, we propose a method to evaluate multiple candidate routes and determine the optimal route using evaluation formulas that indicate the degree of summarization of both the route and text of directions. Experimental results showed that the proposed method yielded a higher route recall agreement rate in participants. Although the optimization method was effective, the evaluation formulas did not work well for some paths.**

Keywords-Voice navigation; Road generalization; Turn by Turn; Shortest path problem; Geographic Information System.

I. INTRODUCTION

In recent years, voice navigation systems, such as Google Maps, have become increasingly popular. Many of existing voice navigation systems employ a turn-by-turn style directions method [1], in which 1) a route is determined primarily based on a shortest path algorithm [2], and 2) the distance and direction to the next intersection are repeated by a voice; this enables guidance to a specified destination. While this has the advantage of simple and easy-to-understand guidance, it has the disadvantage of a long voice navigation text if the number of left-right turns is large. It is better to keep voice directions as short and clear as possible, especially when considering the use of voice directions on fixed digital signage, which has become increasingly popular in recent years. For example, the Mei-chan [3] and Shaberu Bus Stop [4] signage-type voice navigation systems, installed at the main gate of our university, allow users to receive voice directions while viewing a route to the required destination on a map on a screen. In other words, when a user prefers a geographical image of a route, detailed voice directions are not necessary, but summarized, short, and easy-to-understand voice directions should be generated.

The objective of this study is to realize a summary of spoken directions that also provides a geographic image of the route to the destination. In order to achieve the above objectives, we previously proposed a method [5] that 1) generate an easy-to-understand route that is not necessarily the shortest route, but is suitable for summarization, and 2) summarize the route so that the voice direction fits within the specified number of characters.

In this study, we adopt the following three approaches: 1) generate multiple candidate routes with fewer right/left turns than the shortest route using the n-Min Stroke Shortest Path (n-MSSP) algorithm; 2) simplify the routes based on street names, considering street names to be key points for generating voice directions; and 3) based on evaluation formulas that indicate the degree of summarization of the route, the best route is determined. We believe that summarizing voice directions will contribute to improved pedestrian navigation and more advanced digital signage-based systems.

In this paper, we describe related studies in Section 2, describe the proposed system in Section 3, discuss the evaluation of the proposed system in Section 4, and summarize in Section 5.

II. RELATED WORK

Although there have been many studies on summarizing natural language sentences and on road generalizations [6-8], few studies have focused on summarizing voice directions.

A road generalization is a method that draws only the major roads in a road network based on the length of road strokes. A stroke is a grouping of road networks based on cognitive psychology [6] [7], and represents a following path. Zhang et al. [8] realized road generalization by selecting distinctive roads based on their connective relationships. Within studies into the applications of road generalizations, methods based on facility search results [9] [10] and in a Fisheye-view format [11] have been proposed. However, road generalization only selects roads based on their geometry and connectivity, and does not consider the implications on voice directions.

There are also several studies on summarization in the Geographic Information System (GIS) field; Kaigun et al. [12] proposed social data and sentence summarization methods for travel route recommendations. Other existing methods include summarizing the structure of a road network in an easy-to-read manner [13], generating customized cognitive turn-by-turn directions based on a user's travel history [14], and summarizing and generating meaningful sentences from travel data [15].

III. Proposed System

The configuration of the proposed system is outlined in Figure 1. First, given a departure point and an arrival point, a set of the n (n=1,2,...) MSSP routes is computed based on the n-min stroke shortest path (n-MSSP) function; these are considered as candidate routes. Then, the candidate routes are simplified based on a street-based path simplifier function. If the simplification of the candidate paths is not sufficient, a Vertex based path simplifier function, based on the number of vertices, is used to further simplify them. Next, the text for the simplified candidate routes' navigation is summarized using on a word count-based text summarization function. Finally, the optimization of voice directions is achieved using the optimal path determination function based on evaluation formulas. This generates a summarized route and the corresponding guidance text. The MMDAgent [16] and MMDAgent EDIT [17] mechanisms were used to generate the voice directions.

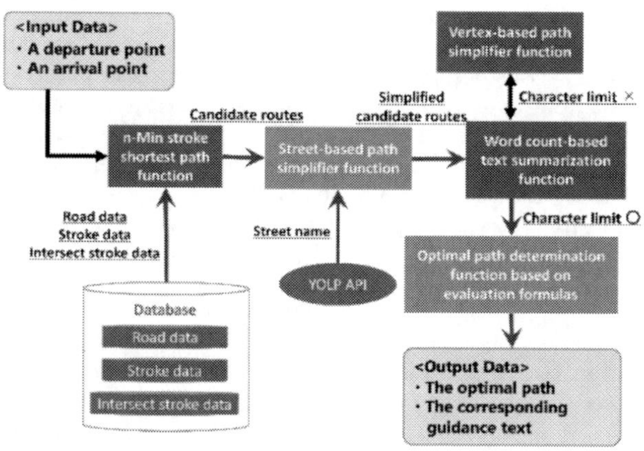

Figure 1. Configuration of the proposed system.

A. n-Min Stroke Shortest Path Function

The n-MSSP search method [18] searches for multiple candidate routes between two points based on given rules, which will be outlined later. The n-MSSP function can obtain the shortest route from the routes that require fewer right or left turns than the shortest route.

Specifically, a road set, stroke set, etc., are obtained from the road database, and the algorithm proposed by Hiura et al. [18] is used to search for and obtain a set of the n-MSSP routes. The definition of the n-MSSP is as follows.

- 1-MSSP

The shortest path among the paths with the fewest number of left or right turns between two points.

- n-MSSP

The path with the smallest amount of left or right turns among the paths shorter than the [n-1]-MSSP route.

B. Street-Based Path Simplifier Function

The street-based path simplifier function simplifies routes by using major roads with street names as key points. In other words, even if there are multiple routes to a major road, the system greatly simplifies route guidance based on the hypothesis that any route can reach the major road if it has a general direction.

The simplification algorithm is shown in Figure 2. First, for every route obtained by the n-MSSP search function, data on the behavior of the current node is stored when progressing to the next node. Next, for each path, the existence of a street name for the next link connected to the current node is checked sequentially in the direction from the end point to the beginning point. If a street name exists, the loop terminates. If there is no street name, the search continues until the next node of the starting point is reached.

```
n_i : The i-th node
a_i : Action at the i-th node
for (i ← 0 to n-1) {
  a_i= next action at the i-th node (go straight : -1, turn left :
0, turn right : 1)
  Store ∞ at the start and end points (a_0,a_(n-1))
}
for(i ← n-2 to 1) {
  if(a_i ≠ −1) {
    Check if there is a street name on the link in the
direction to the end point connected to that node.
    if (Street name ≠null) {
      exit
    }
  }
}
```

Figure 2. Street name-based route simplification algorithm.

C. Word-Based Text Summarization Function

A word-based text summarization function generates an optimal guide text within the specified number of characters. The five key components of a guide text are "minimum information", "time required", "total distance", "distance", and "turning point". "Minimum information" refers to the information expressed only in terms of the direction of the turn, and the other four components are considered to be supplementary information to make the directions easier to understand.

Taking the initial value of each component of the guide consisting of only the "minimum information," we seek a combination that maximizes the sum of values under the condition that the word limit is satisfied. In other words, the problem of generating a guidebook is reduced to the 0-1 knapsack problem, where "number of characters = weight". The value of each component of the guide text is determined based on a hierarchical analysis method [19], as shown in

Figure 3. This allows us to determine the optimal combination for the audio guide text using dynamic programming.

A is more important than B.				A is as important as B.				B is more important than A.
9	7	5	3	1	1/3	1/5	1/7	1/9

A \ B	total distance	time required	distance	turning point	Geometric mean	Weight
total distance	1	1/3	1/9	1/9	$\sqrt[4]{1 \cdot \frac{1}{3} \cdot \frac{1}{9} \cdot \frac{1}{9}} \approx 0.25$	$\frac{0.25}{6.46} \approx 0.04$
time required	3	1	1/5	1/7	$\sqrt[4]{3 \cdot 1 \cdot \frac{1}{5} \cdot \frac{1}{7}} \approx 0.54$	$\frac{0.54}{6.46} \approx 0.08$
distance	9	5	1	1/3	$\sqrt[4]{9 \cdot 5 \cdot 1 \cdot \frac{1}{3}} \approx 1.97$	$\frac{1.97}{6.46} \approx 0.30$
turning point	9	7	3	1	$\sqrt[4]{9 \cdot 7 \cdot 3 \cdot 1} \approx 3.70$	$\frac{3.70}{6.46} \approx 0.57$
				Sum	6.46	1

Figure 3. Value setting for components.

D. *Vertex-Based Path Simplifier Function*

The vertex based path simplifier function uses the Visvalingam-Whyatt algorithm [20] to simplify a path by reducing the number of vertices on the guided path one by one. The Visvalingam-Whatt algorithm is a method that geometrically simplifies Polyline. Although geometrical simplification omits some guidance, such as small turns, we considered it to be sufficient for the purpose of this study, i.e., to grasp the geographical image of the guided route.

Specifically, the Visvalingam-Whyatt algorithm is applied iteratively until the number of vertices within the character limit of the audio guidance text generated by the "minimum information" is reached. For each decrease in the number of vertices, a guide sentence is generated, which is then judged regarding whether it satisfies the termination condition (i.e., the character count limit) or not.

E. *Optimal Path Determination Function*

In the optimal path determination function, all candidate routes are evaluated using the evaluation formulas to determine the optimal route and guide sentences. First, the function obtains the value A_i from the result of the street based path simplifier function, which indicates how well the route is expressed, i.e., how well it concisely captures the main points of the route. The definition of A_i is as follows:

$$A_i = \frac{X}{x_i},$$

where x_i is the number of components in the simplified guide for the i-th candidate route, and X is the number of components in the pre-simplified candidate route directions with the greatest number of right or left turns.

Next, we obtain the value B_i from the vertex-based path simplifier function, which is a measure of how much of the guide text is summarized in the parts that are not related to the main parts of the route. The definition of B_i is as follows:

$$B_i = \frac{n_i}{N_i},$$

where N_i and n_i are the number of vertices of the i-th path before and after applying the vertex based path simplifier function, respectively.

When determining the optimal route for a user, it is necessary to consider the balance between the number of left or right turns and the distance. Therefore, we define C_i and D_i, which are standardized numbers for left/right turns and distances, respectively, as follows:

$$C_i = \frac{c_i - \bar{c}}{\sigma_c},$$

where c_i is the inverse of the number of right/left turns, $\bar{c}$ is the mean of c_i, and σ_c is the standard deviation of c_i, and

$$D_i = \frac{d_i - \bar{d}}{\sigma_d},$$

where d_i is the inverse of the distance, $\bar{d}$ is the mean of d_i, and σ_d is the standard deviation of d_i.

Using these values, we evaluate each path using the following equation, called the evaluation formula (1):

$$E_i = A_i B_i + \omega (C_i + D_i), \qquad (1)$$

where ω is a small value, $A_i B_i$ represents how precisely and clearly the guidance text is expressed, and $C_i + D_i$ represents how well balanced the number of right and left turns and distances are.

IV. EVALUATION

The purpose of our experiment was to verify whether the proposed method of summarizing directions is more effective for users to remember routes and for expressing directions more clearly than the conventional method.

A. *Experimental Condition*

An evaluation experiment was conducted on 12 subjects. Generated directions and map images were presented to the subjects, and 1) the time taken to memorize the route (average measurement time) was recorded; 2) the accuracy of subject' route recall (route matching rate) was analyzed; and 3) a 5-step questionnaire survey was conducted. Table 1 shows the combinations based on the comparison experiments.

Two types of paths (shortest paths and the [n/2]-th n-MSSP) and a combination of three path simplification methods (no summary, vertex based path simplifier, street based path simplifier) were evaluated. The [n/2]th n-MSSP is the [n/2]th path obtained by the n-MSSP algorithm. Subjects performed evaluation experiments on different paths for each method. Methods 1-2, 1-3, 2-2, and 2-3 are the proposed methods.

The character count limit was set to 40 characters, which was considered to be an appropriate length for the voice guidance text based on a preliminary survey. The questionnaire questions, presented on a 5-point scale, were as follows:

1. Is the route easy to remember?
2. Is the guidance easy to understand?
3. Did the voice guidance help ease your anxiety about the road?

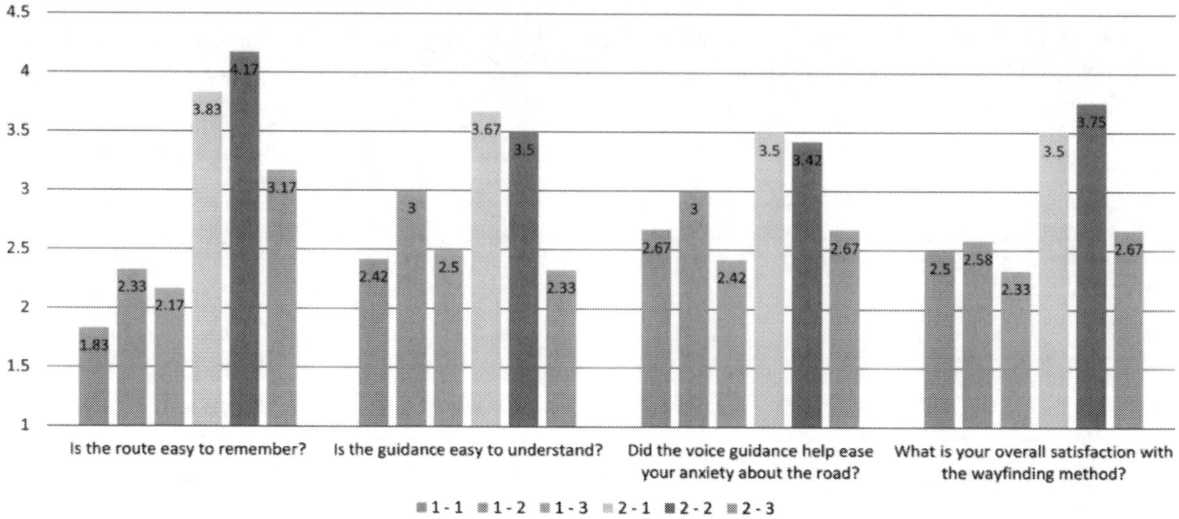

Figure 5. Questionnaire results.

4. What is your overall satisfaction with the wayfinding method?

TABLE I. PATH SEARCH ALGORITHM AND SIMPLIFICATION METHOD.

Method	Path search	Simplification method	Word count
1-1	Shortest path	normal	-
1-2	Shortest path	Vertex based simplifier	40
1-3	Shortest path	Street based simplifier	40
2-1	⌈n/2⌉-th n-MSSP	Normal	-
2-2	⌈n/2⌉-th n-MSSP	Vertex based simplifier	40
2-3	⌈n/2⌉-th n-MSSP	Street based Simplifier	40

B. *Experimental Result*

Figure 4 shows the results of the route matching rate. The route matching rate is the percentage of the actual route that matched the participant's memorized route after they listened to the voice guidance text. The methods based on the ⌈n/2⌉th n-MSSP (2-1, 2-2, and 2-3) yielded higher route matching rates than the methods based on the shortest paths (1-1, 1-2, and 1-3). Since the method based on the ⌈n/2⌉th n-MSSP requires fewer left or right turns than the shortest path, this result suggests that the path with fewer left or right turns is easier for a user to remember.

Table 2 compares the average time taken for a participant to memorize the route by looking at the voice guidance text and route map for each method. Users required less time to memorize the route for Methods 1-2 and 2-2 than for the other methods. This result indicates that the vertex-based path simplifier function is effective in reducing the time required to memorize a route.

Finally, the results of the questionnaire are shown in Figure 5. For the question "Is the route easy to remember?", the summary generated from the vertex-based path simplifier function (Methods 1-2 and 2-2) obtained the highest evaluation for each route. The summary based on the street-based path simplifier function (Method 2-3) did not achieve such a high value. This indicates that there is room for improvement of the street name-based route summarization algorithm. In response to the question "Is the guidance easy to understand?", Method 1-2 received a higher rating when the number of right or left turns was higher.

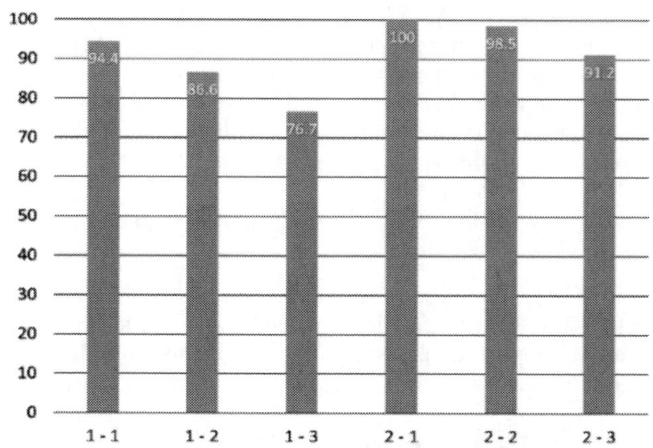

Figure 4. Route matching rate: the degree of agreement between the memorized route and the actual route after listening to the voice guidance text.

TABLE II. TIME TAKEN TO MEMORIZE THE ROUTE.

Method	1-1	1-2	1-3	2-1	2-2	2-3
Mean time	69.6	48.4	65.4	47.3	36.5	51.2

C. Evaluation of Optimization Methods Based on Evaluation Formulas

Next, we evaluated the optimization function based on the evaluation formula (Eq.1). 12 subjects were interviewed about which of the routes between Destinations A and F generated by the following three methods they found easier to understand:

Shortest path The route determined by the shortest path algorithm.

n-MSSP path（proposed method） The route with the fewest number of right/left turns, determined by the n-MSSP algorithm.

Optimal path (proposed method) Overall optimal path generated based on the evaluation equations.

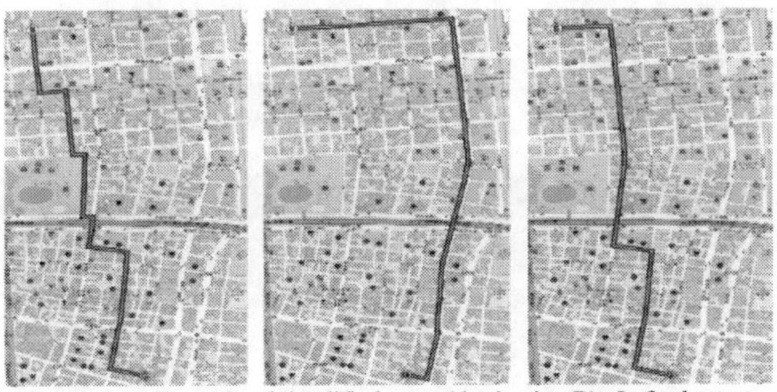

Figure 6. Example of simplified route (destination B). Left: shortest path method. Middle: n-MSSP method. Right: optimal path method.

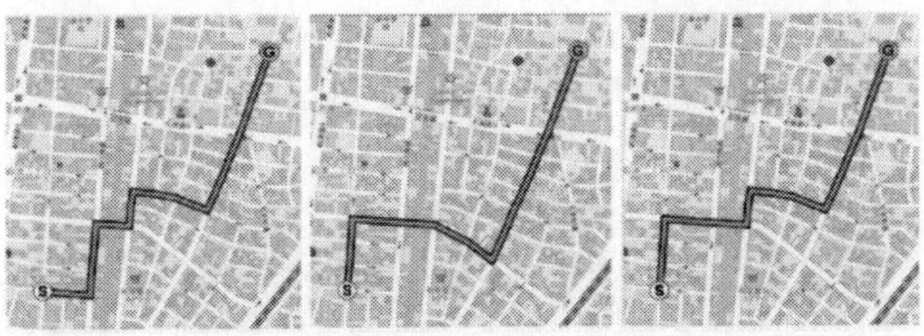

Figure 7. Example of simplified route (destination C). Left: shortest path method. Middle: n-MSSP method. Right: optimal path method.

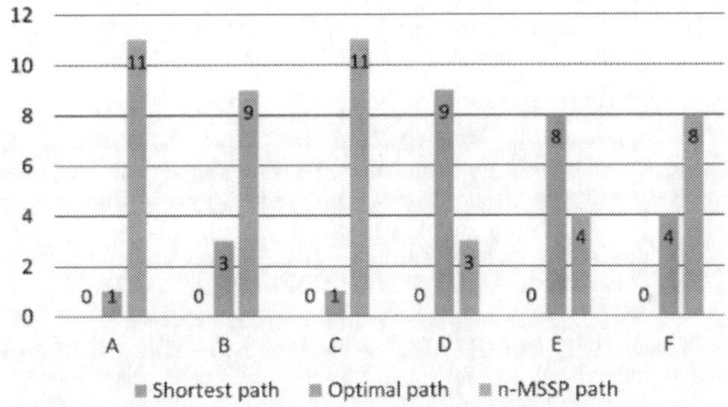

Figure 8. Interviews results regarding optimal routes.

Examples of the paths used in the experiments are shown in Figures 6 and 7, and the experimental results are shown in Figure 8. The n-MSSP path and the optimization path yielded superior results compared with the baseline method, the shortest path. Theoretically, the global optimization method should exhibit the best results, but for some paths, the simpler minimum stroke path was superior. This result suggests that the evaluation formula does not work effectively for some paths, and that improvements can be made.

V. CONCLUSION

In this paper, we proposed a method for summarizing voice directions. Using the n-MSSP (n-min stroke shortest path) algorithm, multiple candidate routes were generated that required progressively fewer right or left turns than the shortest path. We regarded the street names as a key point in generating voice guidance; hence, the routes were simplified based on the street names. Furthermore, the best route and its guide text are determined from multiple candidate routes using the evaluation formula for the degree of summarization of the route.

Through evaluation experiments, a total of six combinations of two different routes and three different guide text generation methods were evaluated. The experimental results showed that the proposed method yielded a higher route recall agreement rate in participants. In particular, the combination of the $\lceil n/2 \rceil^{th}$ n-MSSP and the vertex based path simplifier function was effective. Although the optimization method was effective, the evaluation formulas did not work well for some paths. This suggests that the evaluation formula requires improvements.

In the future, we plan to implement a new summarization method that better combines vertex- and street name-based summarizations, and to improve map rendering to highlight road names and other key points of the route.

ACKNOWLEDGMENT

This work was supported by JSPS KAKENHI Grant Numbers JP19H04115 and JP21K19766.

REFERENCES

[1] C. A. Rizzardo, H. A. Colle, E. A. McGregor, and D. Wylie, "Using a single map display both for navigational planning and for turn-by-turn vehicle guidance: Configural spatial

knowledge acquisition," Journal of Experimental Psychology. Applied, Vol. 19, No. 4, pp. 301-319, 2013.

[2] E. W. Dijkstra, "A note on two problems in connexion with graphs," In Numerische Mathematik, Vol. 1, pp. 269-271. 1959.

[3] K. Oura, D. Yamamoto, I. Takumi, A. Lee, and K. Tokuda, "On-Campus, User-Participatable, and Voice-Interactive Digital Signage," Journal of Japanese Society for Artificial Intelligence, Vol. 28, No. 1, pp. 60-67, 2013. (in Japanse)

[4] D. Yamamoto et al., "Development of talking bus route guidance system and its evaluation by demonstration experiment," DICOMO, Vol. 2018, pp. 1872-1878, 2018. (in Japanese)

[5] R. Hara, (supervisor: D. Yamamoto), "A proposal of voice navigation method by simplifying routes and guidance sentences for a signage-type voice guidance system," Graduation thesis, Nagoya Institute of Technology, 2020. (in Japanese)

[6] R. C. Thomson and R. Brooks, "Efficient generalisation and abstraction of network data using perceptual grouping," Proceedings of the 5th international conference on GeoComputation, pp. 23-25, 2000.

[7] R. C. Thomson and R. Brooks, ""Good continuation" principle of perceptual organization applied to the generalization of road networks," Proceedings of the 19th international cartographic conference, pp. 1215-1223, 1999.

[8] Q. Zhang and P. Fisher, "Road network generalization based on connection analysis," in Proceedings of the 11th Interantional symposium on Spatial Data Handling, pp. 343-353, 2005.

[9] D. Yamamoto, M. Murase, and N. Takahashi, "On-Demand Generalization of Road Networks based on Facility Search Results," IEICE Transactions on Information and Systems, Vol. E102-d, No. 1, pp. 99-103, 2019.

[10] M. Murase, D. Yamamoto, and N. Takahashi, "On-demand generalization of guide maps with RoadNetworks and category-based web search, results," in Proceedings of the 14th international symposium on Web and Wireless Geographical Information Systems (W2GIS 2015), Vol. 19, pp. 53-70, 2015.

[11] D. Yamamoto, S. Ozeki, and N. Takahashi, "Focus+Glue+Context: An improved fisheye approach for web map services," in Proceedings of the ACM SIGSPATIAL GIS 2009, Seattle, Washington, pp. 101-110, 2009.

[12] K. Fu, Y. C. Lu, and C. T. Lu, TREADS: "A safe route recommender using social media mining and text summarization," in Proceedings of the 22nd ACM SIGSPATIAL international conference on Advances in Geographic Information Systems, pp. 557-560, 2014.

[13] A. Asahara, S. Shimada, and K. Maruyama, "Macroscopic structural summarization of road networks for Mobile traffic information services," in Proceedings of the 7th international conference on Mobile Data Management, pp. 42-49, 2006.

[14] Y. Li, H. Su, U. Demiryurek, B. Zheng, K. Zeng, and C. Shahabi, "PerNav: A route summarization framework for personalized navigation," in Proceedings of the 2016 international conference on management of data, pp. 2125-2128, 2016.

[15] H. Su et al., "Making sense of trajectory data: A partition-and-summarization approach," in Proceedings of the 2015 IEEE 31st international conference on Data Engineering, pp. 963-974, 2015.

[16] A. Lee, K. Oura, and K. Tokuda, "MMDAgent—A fully open-source toolkit for voice interaction systems," in Proceedings of the IEEE International Conference on Acoustics, Speech and Signal Processing, Vol. 2013, pp. 8382-8385, 2013.

[17] R. Nishimura, D. Yamamoto, T. Uchiya, and I. Takumi, "Web-based environment for user generation of spoken dialog for virtual assistants," EURASIP Journal on Audio, Speech, and Music Processing, Vol. 2018, No. 1, article number 17, 2018.

[18] Y. Hiura, (supervisor: D. Yamamoto), "Proposal of an efficient nth min stroke shortest path search method," Master's thesis, Nagoya Institute of Technology, 2020. (In Japanese)

[19] T. L. Saaty, "A scaling method for priorities in hierarchical structures," Journal of Mathematical Psychology, Vol. 15, No. 3, pp. 234-281, 1977.

[20] M. Visvalingam and J. D. Whyatt, "Line generalisation by repeated elimination of points," The Cartographic Journal, Vol. 30, No. 1, pp. 46-51, 1993.

A Study of Zero-shot Learning for Visual Search on Satellite and Aerial Images

A. Chuong Dang
Automated Mapping Platform
Woven Alpha, Inc.
Tokyo, Japan
dan.anh.chuong@woven-planet.global

Ion-George Todoran
Automated Mapping Platform
Woven Alpha, Inc.
Tokyo, Japan
george.todoran@woven-planet.global

Srushti Rashmi Shirish
Automated Mapping Platform
Woven Alpha, Inc.
Tokyo, Japan
srushti.rashmishirish@woven-planet.global

***Abstract*—In this article, we present a visual search system based on the latest Deep Learning techniques, which enables users to find images containing similar content as a query image. As many applications battle the dual challenge of limited labelled data that does not cover all the possible classes, we propose to mitigate this issue with an approach we call zero shot learning. We prove the potential of this approach by extensively experimenting on 3 of all time popular aerial imagery datasets. In addition, we show that pre-training the model on top-down imagery improves the final performance of the visual search system.**

***Keywords*—visual search; zero-shot learning; data indexing; deep learning**

I. Introduction

At present there are more than 150 operational satellites equipped with sensors gathering petabytes of data each year for a variety of Earth observations tasks [1]. Usually, this data is ingested and indexed in huge databases considering information like the date of the image, the polygon of the covered area, the number of spectral bands, the image resolution, the number of bits per pixel, the vendor name, and so on. Then it is fairly easy to extract the desired data by employing a query composed of the aforementioned information, e.g., give me all the Maxar WorldView-3 RGB orthorectified imagery acquired after 2017 covering Paris area.

Unfortunately, this type of queries cannot be used for more complex tasks like give me all the images in Africa that contain power plants. In order to enable such a query we need to extract the semantic content of each image. With the Deep Learning revolution, Machine Learning (ML) models based on Convolutional Neural Networks (CNN) proved to be efficient in extracting the semantic content of an image [2]–[4].

Open Street Map (OSM) contains 130 object classes and for many practical applications we could consider they cover all of the use cases. Nevertheless, we identify two practical limitations of this approach. The first one is that the semantic content of many images is too complex to be tagged as belonging to a single class. Labeling such images with more than one classes is difficult and prone to significant errors. In order to exemplify this, consider the image taken from the SpaceNet5 challenge [5] and shown in Figure 1. In this image, one might identify various semantic contents of interest: buildings, beach, road, cars, pools, tennis court and so on. The second limitation is related to the closed-world assumption. In practice we often need to add one or more classes that were not included in the training dataset. In order to solve the above-mentioned problems, researchers considered weak supervision and **zero-shot learning strategies**, i.e., to recognize the objects whose instances were never seen during the training. Since our model has never learnt these additional classes, neither has learnt to classify complex real world scenarios explicitly, we call this approach a zero shot learning.

Figure 1. Example of a satellite image with complex visual content

When the semantic content of an image is complex it is easier to provide a query image and ask for similar images. This is the definition of visual search and it includes the construction of a model that transforms an image into a rich, semantic vector representation, called an embedding. Thus, the model is not trying to directly extract the content of the images but to learn an embedding representation that pulls similar images closer in the embedding space and pushes dissimilar images apart.

Figure 2 shows a visual search service consisting of two parts: the first one extracts an embedding for each image based

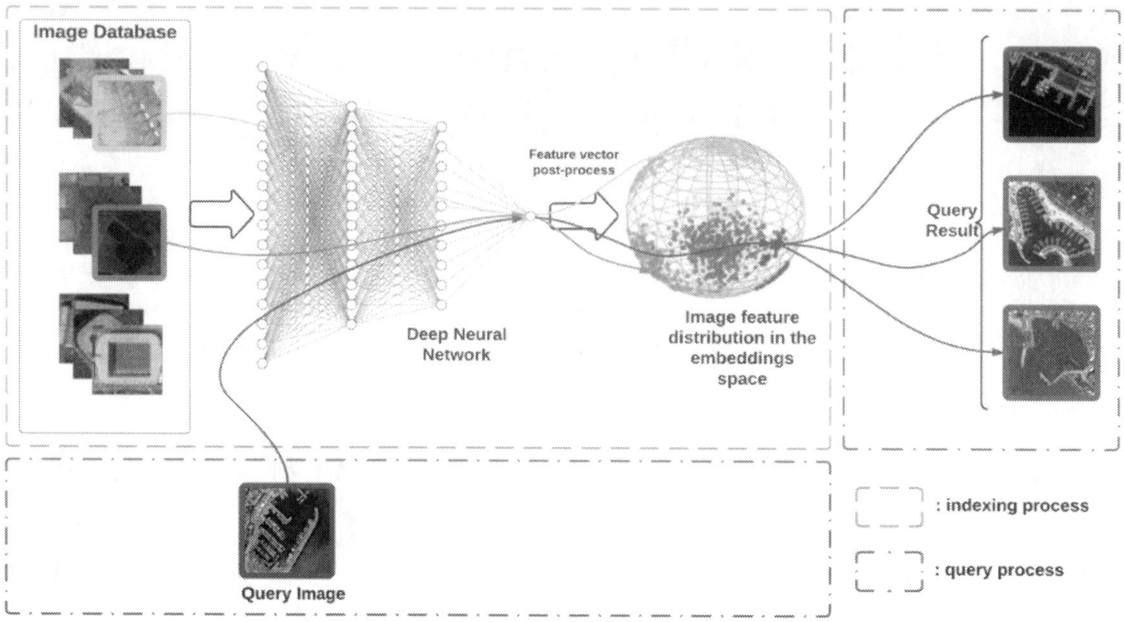

Figure 2. High-level architecture for a visual search system using a deep neural network for learning an image feature vector representation.

on its contents, and the second one deals with the query search in the embedding space. In this paper we mainly focus on the first part and recommend the work published in [6] for the search part.

A visual search service opens new opportunities for improving an existing application or for developing new applications by making use of the right data (inspired from [4]):

- Constructing the training and testing datasets for a new ML-based application, e.g., train an ML model for detecting houses with a pool - for this we need to extract images containing houses with and without pools.
- Better visualisation and understanding of large-scale satellite imagery - it is now possible to easily search and discover similar objects at planetary scale.
- Fast prototyping of a new application - visual search enables us to only extract and use the data that the user really needs for proving the feasibility of a new idea.

This paper is organized as follows. In Section II, we present the prior work related to constructing a visual search system. In Section III, we introduce our solution for constructing a performing visual search system along with the datasets used for doing our experiments. Then, in Section IV, we present the results of various experiences using classic and recent DNN architectures on 3 popular datasets. In Section V, we conduct an ablation study and discuss the importance of feature dimensionality reduction. Finally, we conclude with a summary of future research directions in Section VI.

II. Prior Work

The *classic* solution for extracting embedding vectors for a visual search systems was to aggregate hand-crafted features [7]–[9]. Even though ingenious, these techniques were very difficult to be used on complex imagery at large scale, as it is the case for satellite or aerial imagery.

In the seminal work [10] the authors proved that the representations produced by a deep learning algorithm could be used for image retrieval tasks. Since then, all major work in the domain of visual search focused on extracting the embedding vectors using a deep learning model. We now briefly present the deep learning work for visual search from two aspects:

- *CNN for image retrieval*: Training a CNN model in a supervised manner proved to deliver good results, either by extracting local features (corresponding to some objects of interest) [11] [12] or by extracting global features (corresponding to the entire image). [4]). The main drawback of this technique is the need for huge amounts of manually annotated images with increasing levels of annotation detail.
- *Deep metric learning*: This technique tries to learn the similarity between two images using for example a siamese network [13] or a triplet loss technique [14]. Such models take as input positive samples (corresponding to similar images) and negative samples (not alike images) and it will learn a similarity metric.

III. Method

A. *Visual Search Architecture*

The central purpose of our approach is to learn an embedding function $\mathbf{e} = f_{\boldsymbol{\theta}}(x)$ where $f_{\boldsymbol{\theta}}$ represents a deep neural network (DNN) with parameters $\boldsymbol{\theta}$, mapping an image x to a feature vector $\mathbf{e}$.

In the embedding space, the distance metric $||f_{\theta}(x_i) - f_{\theta}(x_j)||$ gets the particular meaning of the similarity between the 2 images x_i and x_j. Therefore, a good embedding function should map visually similar images closer to each other in the N dimensional space, where N is the size of the feature vector.

In Figure 2 we illustrate a high-level architecture for a visual search system that uses a DNN for learning a feature vector representation for each image in the training dataset.

B. Indexing and query process

In order to train a DNN for learning the embedding function e, we first need to carefully construct a training image dataset making sure it covers all the semantic content of interest. The visual content of these images could then be labeled for supervised training or the unlabeled data could be directly used for unsupervised training. At the end of the training, the learned embedding function will then be applied to all the images we have. If the dimension of the resulting feature vectors is considered too high they could be passed through a dimensionality reduction post-processing step and then stored in a database. We call this the **indexing process**.

With the indexing process finished, it is now possible to take a query image as input, pass it through the same DNN in order to extract its feature vector and then search for similar images in the embedding space (**query process**).

C. Data

For our experiments we used 3 public aerial imagery datasets, having the main properties summarized in Table I. The heterogeneity of these datasets in terms of image resolution, image dimension, and the labeling strategy, allows us to validate that our method works in the general case of any RGB overhead imagery. For example the UC Merced Land Use Dataset [17] corresponds to aerial orthoimagery from USGS National Map of 20 US regions, having a 30 cm resolution.

TABLE I
AERIAL AND SATELLITE IMAGERY DATASETS USED FOR EXPERIMENTS

Dataset	# images	resolution	# classes	image size
UC Merced [17]	2.1k	0.3 m	21	256x256
AID [18]	10k	8 to 0.5 m	30	600x600
RESISC45 [19]	31.5 k	30 to 0.2 m	45	256x256

In the next section, we present multiple experiments using state-of-the-art DNN models, trained using supervised and unsupervised strategies on the 3 aerial imagery datasets.

IV. EXPERIMENTS AND RESULTS

We strongly believe that the key component to have a robust zero-shot visual search system is to improve the process of extracting feature vector representation. This gives us a better latent space for the query process. To verify this hypothesis, we carried out several experiments seeking the optimal method of pre-training DNN, which is then used to extract embedding vectors for aerial/ satellite images. Our experiments range from utilizing DNNs pre-trained on photographic datasets, to investigating the capability of unsupervised pre-training methods, as well as employing more state-of-the-art DNNs' architecture.

For evaluating quantitative performance of the visual search system we use mean Average Precision (mAP) metric as defined in [15] and Recall@K (R@K) metric as introduced in [16]. Experiments and results are detailed in the following paragraphs.

A. Supervised pre-trained DNNs using large photographic imagery datasets

We first investigated the extraction of embeddings for satellite and aerial images using CNN(s) that have been trained on large scale photographic object imagery (e.g., ImageNet1k [20]) and indoor scene datasets (e.g., Places365 [21]). The interesting conclusion was that even though the CNN model trained on photographic images has little prior knowledge of aerial top-down images, it performed relatively well in modeling the feature space for top-down viewed images. To have a fair comparison across all runs, we only adopted ResNet50 [22] as the backbone CNN architecture in this experiment. The results in term of mAP and R@1 for the 3 datasets described in Section III-C are reported in Table II.

TABLE II
PERFORMANCE COMPARISON OF RESNET50 PRE-TRAINED ON PHOTOGRAPHIC DATASETS USING SUPERVISED TRAINING METHOD

Test dataset	Pre-trained dataset	mAP	R@1
UC Merced Land Use	ImageNet1k	***58.9***	***92.9***
	Places365	54.3	90.2
	ImageNet1k & Places365	57.5	92.6
AID	ImageNet1k	***44.6***	***85.4***
	Places365	42.3	83.3
	ImageNet1k & Places365	44.4	84.0
RESISC45	ImageNet1k	34.0	78.7
	Places365	33.2	77.9
	ImageNet1k & Places365	***35.0***	***80.3***

We clearly observed the difference in performance of models pre-trained on different type of datasets. Specifically, the results were better when the model was pre-trained on an object imagery dataset namely ImageNet1k (denoted as bold italic ***numbers***), compared to Places365, an indoor scene dataset. From our perspective, this result is very appealing since it is intuitive to believe that the indoor scenes images may be semantically closer to top-down satellite ones as they both feature complex real world scenes. This observation makes us wonder what kind of performance we would be able to get with a model backbone pre-trained directly on bird eye view imagery. We present our findings in the following section.

B. Supervised pre-trained DNNs using aerial and satellite imagery datasets

Following the setting of previous experiment, we only deployed ResNet50 as the CNN backbone for this experiment. In order to investigate the effectiveness of using bird eye view images, the factor we changed this time was to pre-train the backbone CNN directly on the airborne imagery datasets. We iteratively pre-trained the extractor backbone on one of the satellite imagery datasets, mentioned in section section III-C, then tested its performance on the remaining datasets. However, as the UC Merced Land Use dataset is too small, we skipped using this dataset for pre-training and only adopted it for testing instead. We present the performance comparisons in tables III to V. The best performance metrics are denoted as bold italic ***numbers*** while underline numbers are used for baseline metrics from previous experiments.

TABLE III
PERFORMANCE COMPARISON OF RESNET50 BACKBONE PRE-TRAINED USING SUPERVISED METHOD AND AERIAL IMAGERY DATASETS ON UC MERCED LAND USE DATASET

Pre-trained dataset	mAP	R@1
ImageNet1k	58.9	92.9
AID (x224)	60.0	91.0
AID (x320)	62.7	90.9
RESISC45	***78.6***	***95.9***

TABLE IV
PERFORMANCE COMPARISON OF RESNET50 BACKBONE PRE-TRAINED USING SUPERVISED METHOD AND AERIAL IMAGERY DATASETS ON AID DATASET

Pre-trained dataset	mAP	R@1
ImageNet1k	44.6	85.4
RESISC45	***69.3***	***89.2***

TABLE V
PERFORMANCE COMPARISON OF RESNET50 BACKBONE PRE-TRAINED USING SUPERVISED METHOD AND AERIAL IMAGERY DATASETS ON RESISC45 DATASET

Pre-trained dataset	mAP	R@1
ImageNet1k	34.0	78.7
AID (x224)	***44.0***	***80.9***
AID (x320)	43.4	79.6

(x224): input image size as 224x224.
(x320): input image size as 320x320.

Looking at the performance tables, it is evident that pre-training the extractor backbone directly on top-down airborne images has a positive affect on the visual search system performance.

C. Unsupervised pre-trained DNNs using aerial satellite imagery datasets

Recently, unsupervised training has become the approach of choice to pre-train DNNs. It is noticeable that many proposed unsupervised pre-training methods [28]–[33] improve the performance of the model in the down-stream tasks with a considerable margin. The technique enables us to train the neural networks on a huge amount of data without having to lable it. This inspired us to carry out the next batch of experiments, in which we investigated the capability of unsupervised pre-training methods.

Among many available unsupervised training methods for DNNs, we selectively picked DINO (self-**di**stillation with **no** labels) [23], a self-supervised training method, popular for its clarity and effectiveness. Adopting similar settings with earlier experiments, we only used ResNet50 as CNN backbone architecture in this experiment for the sake of fairness in the comparison. Results are reported in tables VI to VIII.

TABLE VI
PERFOMANCES OF RESNET50 BACKBONE PRE-TRAINED USING UNSUPERVISED METHOD AND AERIAL IMAGERY DATASETS ON UC MERCED LAND USE DATASET

Pre-trained dataset	mAP	R@1
ImageNet1k	58.9	***94.7***
AID	55.0	93.1
RESISC45	***63.0***	93.8

TABLE VII
PERFOMANCES OF RESNET50 BACKBONE PRE-TRAINED USING UNSUPERVISED METHOD AND AERIAL IMAGERY DATASETS ON AID DATASET

Pre-trained dataset	mAP	R@1
ImageNet1k	46.7	88.6
RESISC45	***52.1***	***90.1***

TABLE VIII
PERFOMANCES OF RESNET50 BACKBONE PRE-TRAINED USING UNSUPERVISED METHOD AND AERIAL IMAGERY DATASETS ON RESISC45 DATASET

Pre-trained dataset	mAP	R@1
ImageNet1k	***36.6***	***84.6***
AID	36.1	84.0

Our experiment demonstrated that feature space of visual search algorithm is enhanced by pre-training CNN backbones using unsupervised training method with a sufficient to large amount of bird eye view images. This shed light on how to effectively utilize an abundant source of aerial and satellite images without labeling.

D. Vision Transformer as extractor backbone

In order to understand the impact of utilizing recent state-of-the-art DNN architecture as the backbone extractor, we carried on our next experiment. We purposely chose to deploy Vision Transformers (ViT) [27] because it is the best performance DNN in many tasks at the present.

In this experiment, we only changed the DNN's architecture, while the other components were kept the same. Specifically, we deployed the ResNet50 and variants of ViT models pre-trained on ImageNet1k dataset using DINO self-supervised training method as the backbone extractor. We intentionally chose two small variances (having 21M parameters, comparable to 23M in ResNet50) in ViT family, the difference between the two are input patch size (16×16 and 8×8), denoting as ViT-S/16 and ViT-S/8 respectively. The results in term of performance are reported in tables IX to XI.

TABLE IX
PERFOMANCES OF DIFFERENT PRE-TRAINED DNNS' ARCHITECTURE ON UC MERCED LAND USE DATASET

Backbone architecture	Pre-trained dataset	Pre-trained method	mAP	R@1
ResNet50	ImageNet1k	unsupervised	58.9	94.7
ViT-S/16	ImageNet1k	unsupervised	63.3	***95.7***
ViT-S/8	ImageNet1k	unsupervised	***67.0***	95.4

TABLE X
PERFOMANCES OF DIFFERENT PRE-TRAINED DNNS' ARCHITECTURE ON AID DATASET

Backbone architecture	Pre-trained dataset	Pre-trained method	mAP	R@1
ResNet50	ImageNet1k	unsupervised	46.7	88.6
ViT-S/16	ImageNet1k	unsupervised	49.8	90.2
ViT-S/8	ImageNet1k	unsupervised	***53.7***	***91.7***

TABLE XI
PERFOMANCES OF DIFFERENT PRE-TRAINED DNNS' ARCHITECTURE ON RESISC45 DATASET

Backbone architecture	Pre-trained dataset	Pre-trained method	mAP	R@1
ResNet50	ImageNet1k	unsupervised	36.6	84.6
ViT-S/16	ImageNet1k	unsupervised	39.7	86.9
ViT-S/8	ImageNet1k	unsupervised	***43.0***	***88.8***

ResNet50: Residual Network with depth of 50 layers.
ViT-S/16: Vision Transformer small, 16-patch variance.
ViT-S/8: Vision Transformer small, 8-patch variance.

From the results, we can clearly observe that by simply replacing ResNet50 backbone with a ViT, we can obtain a significant improvement in terms of performance. This implies that one may consider utilizing better DNN architectures available when wanting to enhance the visual search system's performance.

E. Qualitative results

In this section, we would like to present some qualitative search results from our zero-shot visual search system. These search results, shown in Figure 3, are obtained from our system equipped with a ViT-S/8 as the backbone extractor, which had been pre-trained on ImageNet1k dataset using self-supervised method DINO. Visually the results re-confirmed our observations in this study.

V. ABLATION STUDY

Besides the experiments presented above, we also carried out an ablation study on the visual search system, in which we studied the role of feature dimensionality reduction step, e.g., Principal Component Analysis (PCA) [26], Singular Value Decomposition (SVD) [24], k-reciprocal encoding [25]. We discovered an interesting phenomena that needs to be cautiously considered when building a robust and efficient zero-shot visual search system over billions satellite/aerial images.

A. Impact of removing feature dimensionality reduction step

After the feature extraction procedure, one of the post processing steps is to reduce the dimensionality of feature vectors before indexing. There are many methods for feature dimensionality reduction, but for the sake of brevity we only discuss PCA. However, these methods suffer from low scalability since they need to be trained on extracted feature vectors of the gallery images in the database. This process may be trivial for small-medium datasets, yet can be a potential issue when dealing with huge amounts of data, i.e., building a visual search system over billions airborne images. Therefore, in this experiment we examined the influence of removing feature dimensionality reduction step from the system.

TABLE XII
PERFORMANCES OF VISUAL SEARCH SYSTEM WITH & WITHOUT PCA ON AID DATASET

Backbone architecture$^{(**)}$	Dimension Reduction method	mAP	mAP drop ↓	R@1	R@1 drop ↓
ResNet50	PCA	46.7	5.1 ↓	88.6	0.6 ↓
	None	41.6		88.0	
ViT-S/16	PCA	49.8	4.5 ↓	90.2	0.3 ↓
	None	45.3		88.9	
ViT-S/8	PCA	53.7	4.8 ↓	91.7	1.1 ↓
	None	48.9		90.6	

$^{(**)}$: All backbones had been pre-trained on AID dataset using DINO self-supervised method.

From table XII, we can conclude that the performance of the visual search system dropped by a considerable margin in term of mean Average Precision (mAP) and a small margin for Recall at 1 (R@1) when removing dimension reduction method, specifically PCA in our experiment. This demonstrates the necessity of deploying dimension reduction module in the task where high accuracy is required.

VI. CONCLUSIONS AND FUTURE WORK

In this paper we presented two ideas that could help improve the performance of a zero-shot visual search system applied to satellite or aerial imagery: firstly, the importance of pre-training the model using aerial and satellite imagery and secondly, using a new network architecture of deep learning algorithms, i.e., family of ViT, for better feature vector learning.

As future work, we are envisaging to explore more deeply the capacity of ViT for embedding learning in an unsupervised strategy. We believe that applying such strategy to Visual Search will open new opportunities for better using the continuously increasing satellite and aerial data volumes.

REFERENCES

[1] M. Tarasiou and S. Zafeiriou, "DeepSatData: Building large scale datasets of satellite images for training machine learning models," CoRR, abs/2104.13824, 2021.

Figure 3. Example of search results. The left most image is the query image, and the rest of the row shows the top ten search results of our system.

[2] S.Bell and K. Bala, "Learning visual similarity for product design with convolutional neural networks," ACM Trans. Graph., Vol. 34, No. 4, pp 1–10, 2015

[3] K. Sohn, "Improved Deep Metric Learning with Multi-class N-pair Loss Objective," NIPS, 2016

[4] R. Keisler, S. Skillman, S. Gonnabathula, J. Poehnelt, X. Rudelis, and M. Warren, "Visual search over billions of aerial and satellite images," Comput. Vis. Image Underst. vol. 187, Issue C, pp 1-6, 2019.

[5] The SpaceNet Partners, "SpaceNet5: Automated Road Network Extraction and Route Travel Time Estimation from Satellite Imagery, ," https://spacenet.ai/sn5-challenge/, Accessed May 5th 2022

[6] J. Johnson, M. Douze, and H. Jégou, "Billion-scale similarity search with GPUs," IEEE Transactions on Big Data, vol. 7, No. 3, pp. 535-547, 2019

[7] C. Wengert, M. Douze, and H. Jégou, "Bag-of-colors for improved image search," In ACM Multimedia, pp. 1437–1440, 2011

[8] M. Park, J. Jin, and L. Wilson, "Fast content-based image retrieval using quasi-gabor filter and reduction of image feature dimension," Fifth IEEE Southwest Symposium on Image Analysis and Interpretation, 2002

[9] R. Arandjelovic and A. Zisserman, "Three things everyone should know to improve object retrieval," CVPR, 2012

[10] A. Krizhevsky and G. Hinton, "Using very deep autoencoders for content-based image retrieval," in Proceedings of the European Symposium of Artifical Neural Networks (ESANN), 2011

[11] J. Ng, F. Yang, and L. Davis, "Exploiting local features from deep networks for image retrieval," CVPR Workshops, 2015

[12] G. Tolias, T. Jenicek, and O. Chum, "Learning and aggregating deep local descriptors for instance-level recognition," ECCV, 2020

[13] D. Yi, Z. Lei, S. Liao, and S. Z. Li, "Deep metric learning for person re-identification," 22nd International Conference on Pattern Recognition, 2014

[14] W. Ge, W. Huang, D. Dong, and M.R. Scott, "Deep metric learning with hierarchical triplet loss," ECCV, 2018

[15] M. Everingham, S.M.A. Eslami, L. Van Gool, C.K.I. Williams, J. Winn, and A. Zisserman, "The Pascal visual object classes challenge: A retrospective," International Journal of Computer Vision, vol. 111, no. 1, pp. 98-136, 2015

[16] H. Jégou, M. Douze, and C. Schmid, "Product quantization for nearest neighbor search," In IEEE Transactions on Pattern Analysis and Machine Intelligence, vol. 33, no. 1, pp. 117-128, 2011

[17] Y.Yang and S. Newsam, "Bag-Of-Visual-Words and Spatial Extensions for Land-Use Classification," ACM SIGSPATIAL International Conference on Advances in Geographic Information Systems (ACM GIS), 2010

[18] G.-S. Xia, J.Hu, F. Hu, and B. Shi, "AID: A Benchmark Dataset for Performance Evaluation of Aerial Scene Classification," In IEEE Transactions on Geoscience and Remote Sensing, vol. 55, no. 7, pp. 3965-3981, 2017

[19] G. Cheng, J. Han, and X. Lu, "Remote Sensing Image Scene Classification: Benchmark and State of the Art," In Proceedings of the IEEE, vol. 105, no. 10, pp. 1865-1883, 2017

[20] J. Deng, W. Dong, R. Socher, L.-J. Li, K. Li, and L. FeiFei, "Imagenet: A large-scale hierarchical image database," CVPR, 2009

[21] B. Zhou, A. Lapedriza, A. Khosla, A. Oliva, and A. Torralba, "Places: A 10 million image database for scene recognition," In IEEE Transactions on Pattern Analysis and Machine Intelligence, vol. 40, no. 6, pp. 1452-1464, 2018

[22] K. He, X. Zhang, S. Ren, and J. Sun, "Deep residual learning for image recognition," CVPR, 2016.

[23] M. Caron, H. Touvron, I. Misra, H. Jégou, J. Mairal, P. Bojanowski, and A. Joulin, "Emerging Properties in Self-Supervised Vision Transformers," ICCV, 2021.

[24] G. H. Golub and C. Reinsch, "Singular Value Decomposition and Least Squares Solutions," In: Bauer, F.L. (eds) Linear Algebra. Handbook for Automatic Computation, vol 2. Springer, 1971, pp.134-151.

[25] Z. Zhong, L. Zheng, D. Cao, and S. Li, "Re-ranking Person Re-identification with k-reciprocal Encoding," CVPR, 2017.

[26] K. Pearson, "LIII. On lines and planes of closest fit to systems of points in space," The London, Edinburgh, and Dublin philosophical magazine and journal of science, Series 6, vol. 2, Issue 11, pp.559-572, 1901.

[27] A. Dosovitskiy, et al., "An image is worth 16x16 words: Transformers for image recognition at scale," ICLR, 2021.

[28] K. He, H. Fan, Y. Wu, S. Xie, and R. Girshick. "Momentum Contrast for Unsupervised Visual Representation Learning," CVPR, 2020.

[29] X. Chen, H. Fan, R. Girshick, and K. He. "Improved Baselines with Momentum Contrastive Learning," CoRR abs/2003.04297, 2020.

[30] X. Chen, S. Xie, and K. He. "An Empirical Study of Training Self-Supervised Vision Transformers," ICCV, 2021.

[31] T. Chen, S. Kornblith, M. Norouzi, and G. Hinton. "A Simple Framework for Contrastive Learning of Visual Representations," ICML, 2020.

[32] J.B. Grill, et al., "Bootstrap your own latent: A new approach to self-supervised Learning," NeurIPS, 2020.

[33] X. Chen and K. He. "Exploring Simple Siamese Representation Learning," CVPR, 2021.

Automatic Generation Method for Geographically Accurate Bus Route Maps from Bus Stops

Sogo Mizutani
Nagoya Institute of Technology
Nagoya, Japan.
e-mail: s.mizutani.814@stn.nitech.ac.jp

Yonghwan Kim
Nagoya Institute of Technology
Nagoya, Japan.
e-mail: kim@nitech.ac.jp

Daisuke Yamamoto
Nagoya Institute of Technology
Nagoya, Japan
e-mail: daisuke@nitech.ac.jp

Naohisa Takahashi
Nagoya Institute of Technology
Nagoya, Japan
e-mail: naohisa@nitech.ac.jp

***Abstract-* There are two types of route maps: deformed route maps, which schematically show the locations and connections of stations and bus stops, and geographically accurate route maps, which are drawn on a map based on the actual locations of routes. While there have been many studies on the automatic generation of deformed route maps, only a few studies have focused on the automatic generation of geographically accurate route maps linked to road networks, such as bus route maps. Most conventional geographically accurate route maps are created manually, but mapping road data to bus route data is complicated by various constraints. In particular, it is necessary to draw parallel routes so that they do not overlap, and to consider the order in which they are arranged so that they cross each other minimally when turning right or left. In this study, we propose an automatic estimation method for bus route maps using bus stop coordinate series and strokes. This method generates bus stop nodes on the road network from the bus stop coordinate series. Furthermore, the bus route is estimated as a route with the least number of right/left turns between the bus stop nodes using the road priority search method. In addition, when drawing multiple routes, the order of placement of overlapping segments is dynamically determined so that there are fewer intersections when turning right or left. This enables the drawing of geographically accurate route maps with fewer intersections at right and left turns.**

Keywords-network; bus route map; stroke.

I. INTRODUCTION

When using public transportation, such as trains and buses, we often look at route maps to determine how to reach our destination. There are two types of route maps: deformed route maps that schematically show the locations and connections between stations and bus stops, and geographically accurate route maps that are drawn on a map based on the exact location of routes. Deformed route maps, as shown in Figure 1, do not require geographic accuracy in terms of direction and distance, but only that the relative station locations and connections on the route should be known. As shown in Figure 2, a geographically accurate route map can be drawn on a road map based on accurate location information to provide information on bus stops and facilities along the route. The problem of route placement is quite complex, especially when considering that multiple routes may be drawn on a single road.

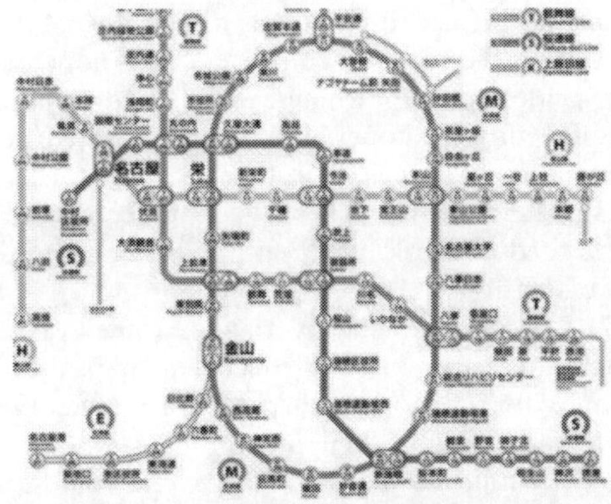

Figure 1. Example of deformed route map. (Cited from the Nagoya City Transportation Bureau.)

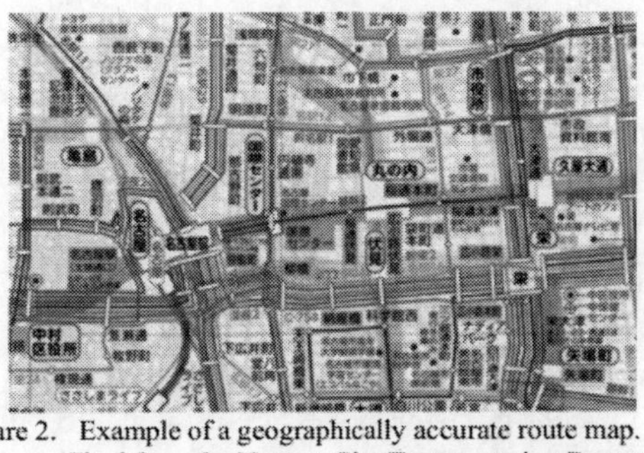

Figure 2. Example of a geographically accurate route map. (Cited from the Nagoya City Transportation Bureau.)

In addition, many web maps, such as Google Maps have become popular in recent years, and it has become necessary to superimpose geographically accurate route maps on them. Furthermore, with the proliferation of the General Transit Feed Specification (GTFS) standard, transit system data for bus and subway routes has been made publicly available;

GTFS includes not only timetable data, but also the latitude and longitude coordinates of bus stops and connection relationships between routes.

The purpose of this study is to propose a method for estimating routes from bus stop coordinates and route system data in the GTFS, and automatically generate highly visible and geographically accurate bus route maps from the estimated results.

Although there have been many studies on the automatic generation of deformed route maps, only a few studies have focused on the automatic generation of geographically accurate route maps in conjunction with road networks, such as bus route maps. Most conventional geographically accurate route maps are created manually, but the task setup is complicated by the need to map the coordinates of roads and bus routes. In particular, it is necessary to draw parallel routes so that they do not overlap. It is also necessary to consider the order in which the routes are arranged to minimize their crossing when turning right or left. The following issues must be addressed to automatically generate geographically accurate bus route maps.

Issue 1) The latitude and longitude coordinates of bus stops published in the GTFS and elsewhere indicate the location of boarding points, which do not necessarily exist on the road. In contrast, a road network consists of nodes indicating intersections and turns and links connecting the nodes, and it is necessary to set starting and ending nodes to estimate routes. Therefore, to estimate a bus route, a bus stop node must be added to the road network based on the location coordinates of the bus stop.

Issue 2) To minimize the overlap of routes, a method to determine the order of placement of routes by brute force for each road link is considered, but such a method would be computation-intensive.

Issue 3) To improve the visibility of the route maps, it is necessary to draw the routes by shifting them from one another, but the order in which the routes are arranged results in a route map with many intersections. Therefore, it is necessary to dynamically determine the order in which the routes with the fewest intersections are placed on the map.

Therefore, we propose a system with the following features.

Feature 1) Route generation function

From the road network and bus stop coordinates, a bus stop node is added to the nearest point on the road link closest to the bus stop. In addition, the routes between adjacent bus stop nodes are estimated by a way-first search and used as bus routes.

Feature 2) Bus stroke/bus stroke fragment generation function

This realizes the function of generating Bus Stroke (BS) using road strokes and bus routes, and generates the overlap between bus routes as a Bus Stroke Fragment (BSF). The BS/BSF model is used to efficiently determine the order of placement.

Feature 3) Route placement function

This function determines the order of placement when drawing multiple routes staggered on a single road link.

In this paper, we describe related studies in Section 2, describe the proposed system in Section 3, discuss the evaluation of the proposed system in Section 4, and summarize in Section 5.

II. RELATED WORK

Many of the existing methods for drawing route maps are intended for train route maps. Onda et al. [1] proposed a method for automatic generation of railroad route maps for Tokyo's train route network. Bast et al. [2] proposed a method for automatic generation of geo-informative railroad route maps with station connectivity and route location as inputs. Other studies [3][4][5] have been conducted to improve the quality of deformed subway route maps.

Wang and Peng [6] proposed an interactive editing system for subway route map layouts; Lloyd et al. [7] proposed a method for color coding subway route maps. Some studies are based on strokes. A stroke is a grouping of road networks based on cognitive psychology and represents a road [8][9] that follows a path. Zhang et al. [10] have realized a total road drawing by selecting distinctive roads based on their connection relations. As for the use of road strokes, studies have been made on total road drawing. Road drawing is a method to draw only major roads in a road network based on the length of road strokes. Methods to realize road drawing from facility search results [11][12] and a method to realize road drawing in the Fisheye view format [13] have been proposed. A stroke-based path finding method [14] has also been proposed.

III. PROPOSED SYSTEM

Figure 3 shows the configuration of the proposed system. In the route generation function, bus stop nodes are generated from bus information and road data published in the GTFS, and routes are generated by routing the bus stop nodes. Next, BS/BSF is generated from the generated route data; BS/BSF is explained in detail in Section C. Next, the route placement function determines the placement order of overlapping BSFs. Finally, the system draws the routes based on the order of placement and provides them to the user.

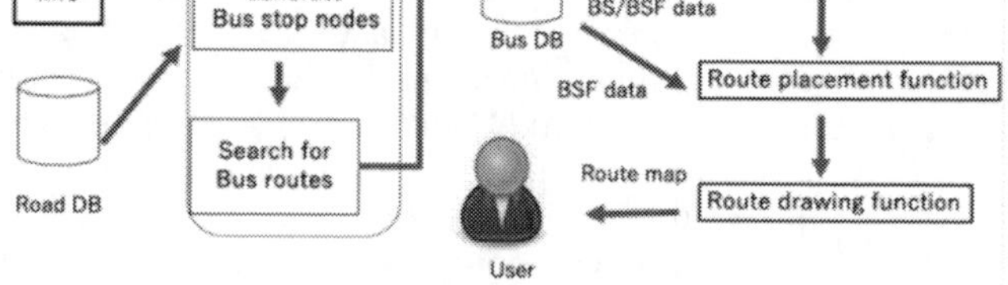

Figure 3. System configuration.

A. Data format

The data and definitions of terms used in this study are described below.

1) Road data format

The road data provided by OpenStreetMap consists of nodes and links. A node represents an intersection on the road network and a road link connects nodes along a point, which is a series of latitude and longitude coordinates. A link connects a start node to an end node, and the road network is a directed graph, given the direction of the road. Road geometry is represented by geometry-type arcs along a point sequence.

OpenStreetMap also provides data representing road types, such as highways, national highways, and pedestrian-only roads, which are stored as road classes.

2) Stroke data format

A stroke is a set of road networks grouped according to cognitive psychology. The example on the left in Figure 4 shows a road network consisting of a set of links between nodes. The example on the right of Figure 4 shows a stroke network consisting of color-coded strokes.

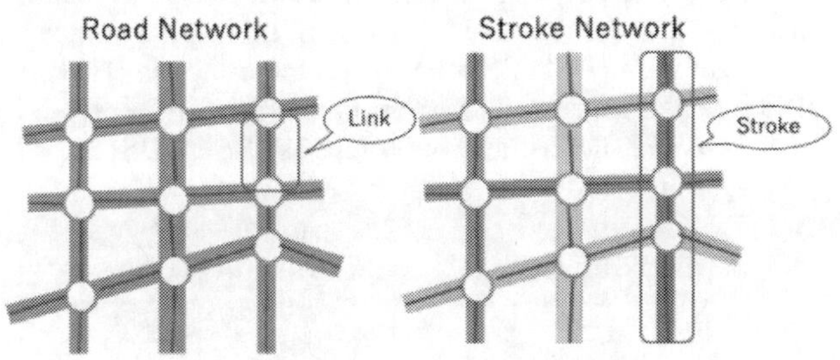

Figure 4. Examples of a road and stroke network.

3) Bus data format

This study uses bus data in the GTFS-JP format, which were released as open data by the Nagoya City Transportation Bureau in 2017. The following three items were used in this study.

Bus stop data

The name, identification (ID), and latitude and longitude coordinates of the bus stop are stored.

System data

The operational data for each system is stored. The system table contains information on the start and end points of the service section within the system, apart from other information. The system data is uniquely identified by system, route code, direction codes.

Bus stop series

The series of bus stops that pass through the system from the start point to the end of the system's service section are stored.

B. Route generation function

The route generation function generates bus route link data from road data, stroke data, and bus information. The main flow generates bus stop nodes from the road network and bus stop series, creates split links, and searches for routes between bus stops.

1) Generation of bus stop nodes

Using the latitude and longitude coordinates of the bus stop, and the road class as inputs, a bus stop node is generated on the road link closest to it in the specified road class.

The method of generating bus stop nodes is shown below. Here, we used PostGIS functions, including ST_DWthin, ST_Distance, ST_LineLocatePoint, and ST_LineInterpolate Point functions.

$L = (l_1, l_2, \cdots, l_i)$: Link set

$Class$: Road class

Bus_{point} : latitude and longitude coordinates of bus stops

Bus_{node} : bus stop node

Step 1) From the link set L, find the nearest link set within a radius of 20 m from Bus_{point} using the ST_DWthin function. However, exclude links whose road class is expressway or a connecting road to an expressway.

Step 2) Find the link with the shortest distance in the set of nearest neighbor links using the ST_Distance function. This link shall be the nearest neighbor link.

Step 3) Find the nearest point in the nearest link from Bus_{point} and get the ratio r of the nearest point to the start and end points of the link using ST_LineLocatePoint function. The obtained ratio r is stored in a table as Bus_{node} using the ST_LineInterpolatePoint function. Table 1 shows the data format of the bus stop nodes.

TABLE1. BUS STOP NODE TABLE

Column name	*Data type*	*Explanation*
id	Integer	Bus stop ID
link_id	Integer	Nearest neighbor road link ID
node_lat	Double	Latitude of bus stop node
node_lng	Double	Longitude of bus stop node
ratio	Double	Percentage on link

2) Creating split links

To perform a route search, it is necessary to split road links using the generated bus stop nodes. In this study, a split link is defined as a set of links in which a road link is divided by a bus stop node. In the example in Figure 5, Link2 of the road link is divided by a bus stop node, increasing the number of links from three to four.

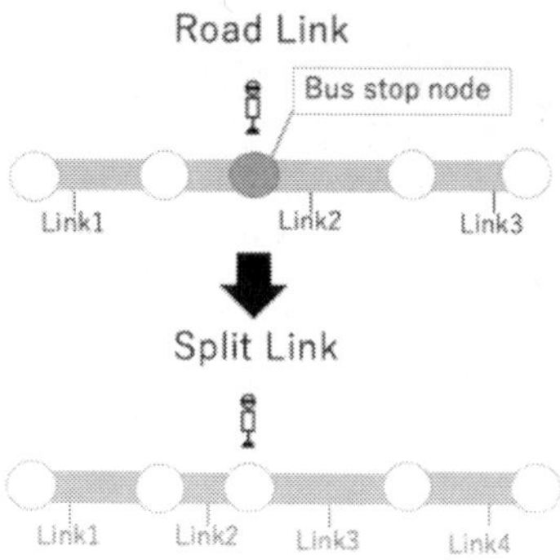

Figure 5. Split link.

3) Route estimation

The variables used for route estimation are defined below, followed by the route search procedure.

$ID = (id_1, id_2, \cdots, id_n)$: List of bus stop IDs for the route to be estimated
$Node = (N_1, N_2, \cdots, N_n)$: Node ID list
$V \ni (s, g)$: Combination of start and end points
$R = (r_1, r_2, \cdots, r_n)$: Route data list

Step 1) Obtain the IDs for the specified system, route, and direction code from the bus stop database.
Step 2) Obtain the bus stop node corresponding to the ID from the bus stop database and add it to the Node.
Step 3) In $v = (N_i, N_{i+1}) \in V$, checks if there is a record, $(s, g) = (id_i, id_{i+1})$ or (id_{i+1}, id_i) in the route table.
Step 4) If it exists, the acquired route data is assumed to be r_i.
Step 5) If not, a min stroke shortest path search in v is performed to find r_i.
Step 6) If all routes are found, R is stored in the route table.

In step 3, by checking whether a route is already in the table, the search time can be reduced by finding sections where a route search is not needed.

In step 5, a min stroke shortest path search is performed. Min stroke shortest search is a method that searches for a route with the shortest distance among routes with the fewest number of left-right turns.

C. Bus stroke/bus stroke fragment generation function

1) Bus stroke

In general, bus routes are often set up on routes with few left-right turns. Therefore, expressing them as a set of strokes requires less data and computation. In particular, when considering the determination of whether multiple routes are running side by side, it is possible to reduce the number of calculations if the determination is made on a stroke-by-stroke basis rather than on a road-by-road basis. Figure 6 shows an example of converting a link set into a BS set. In this example, the red bus routes are represented as {BS1, BS2, BS3}.

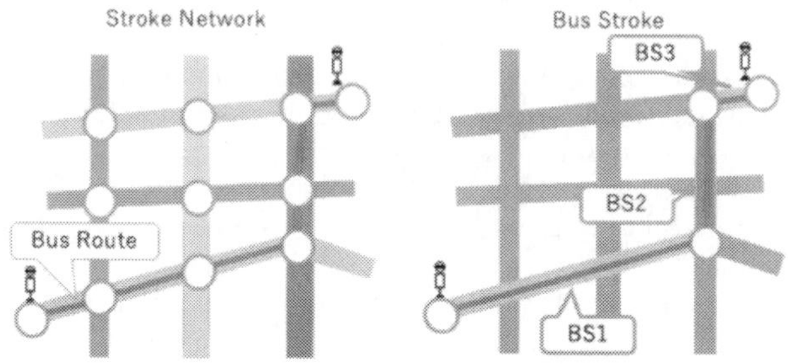

Figure 6. Example of bus stroke generation.

2) Bus stroke fragment

To generate bus strokes for multiple parallel bus routes, some strokes need to be divided into shorter strokes. The divided strokes are called BSFs. Figure 7 shows an example of the division of two routes into BSFs. In this example, BS1 in red is broken down into BSF1 and BSF2. BS2 in blue also includes BSF2. When expressed in BSs, blue routes are represented as {BS1, BS2, BS3} and red routes as {BS1, BS2, BS3}. When expressed in BSFs, blue routes are expressed as {BSF5, BSF2, BSF6} and red routes as {BSF1, BSF2, BSF3, BSF4}. Some BSFs are shared by each route.

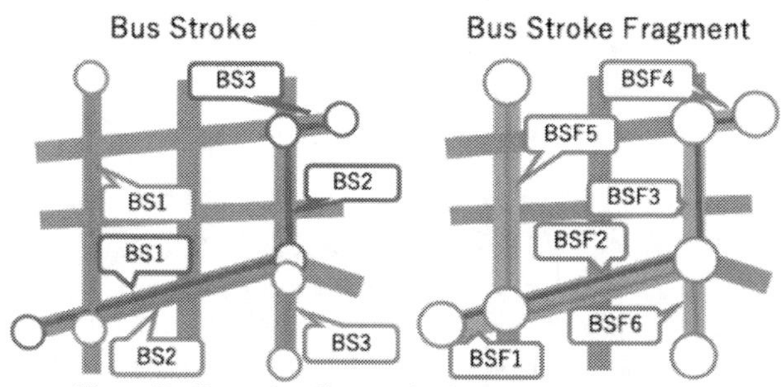

Figure 7. Example of bus stroke fragment generation.

D. Route placement functions

1) Route placement function

The route placement function determines the order of placement when drawing multiple routes staggered on a single road link. This section describes a method for determining the placement order of multiple routes using route BSFs as an input. The procedure is as follows.

Step 1) First, BSF series are obtained from two routes.
Step 2) From the origin side of the routes, determine the order of BSF placement according to Rules 1 and 2 described below. However, if

necessary, the previous placement order can be reused.

Step 3) Next, to add one unprocessed line to the current result, obtain the placement order according to Rules 1 and 2 described below, as in Step 2.

Step 4) Repeat Step 3 until there are no more unprocessed routes.

In Steps 2 and 3 above, the following two rules are applied to determine the placement order.

Rule 1) The placement order of the target BSF is based on the angle formed by the target BSF and the previous BSF, as shown in Figure 8.

Rule 2) For routes where the placement order is not uniquely determined, the BSFs are determined backward until the placement order is determined.

Figure 8 shows an example of route placement. In Rule 1, the order of placement of routes is determined by the angle between the previous BSF and the target BSF on the start point. The PostGIS functions ST_Azimuth and degree were used to calculate the angles: the ST_Azimuth function returns the rightward radians with respect to north, and the degree function converts radians to degrees. These are used to calculate the angle between the previous BSF and the target BSF (Base). In the example in Figure 8, (Route_a, Route_b, Route_c, Base) = (0°, 270°, 225°, 90°). Here, sorted in a descending order based on the angle with the target BSF, the result is (Base, Route_a, Route_b, Route_c). Therefore, the order of placement of the target BSF is Route_a, Route_b, and Route_c.

In the example on the right of Figure 8, both the previous BSF of the blue route and the previous BSF of the yellow route have the same angle. Therefore, Rule 1 cannot be applied as it is in the example on the left side of Figure 8. Therefore, in Rule 2, the placement order of one more previous BSF is directly used as the placement order of the target BSF.

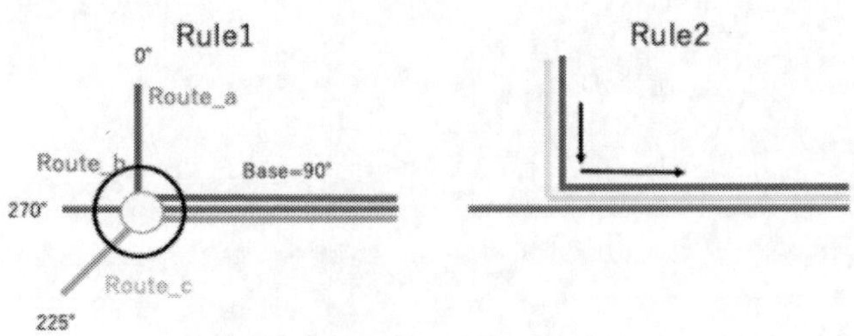

Figure 8. Rules for route placement.

2) Route draw function.

The route draw function draws a route on a web map. In this study, OpenStreetMap was used as the map data and Leaflet was used as the map control library.

The drawing procedure is as follows. First, the result of the route placement function and the geometry of the routes are stored in a GeoJSON format file, and the Leaflet library draws the route on the web map based on the GeoJSON format file. Here, to prevent the overlapping of routes, the Leaflet Polyline Offset is used to shift and draw the overlapping sections of the routes.

IV. EXPERIMENTAL RESULTS

A. Route estimation based on bus stop series

The proposed system estimates routes on the road network from a bus stop series. Therefore, we evaluated the accuracy of the route estimation function by comparing actual bus routes and routes estimated by the proposed system. The evaluation measure is the matching ratio M with the actual route map, and the following evaluation formula (1) is used. Forty bus route maps of the Nagoya City Transportation Bureau were used for the evaluation.

$$M = \frac{Number\ of\ matched\ routes}{Number\ of\ actual\ routes} \times 100 \qquad (1)$$

Table 2 shows the results of the evaluation experiments. The overall estimation accuracy was 93.2%. The results show that the proposed system can estimate bus routes with a high accuracy. The most common example of estimation failure was an estimation error near a bus terminal. This is because bus terminals have many bus stops, with different entrances and exits, which causes the system to generate bus stop nodes on the wrong road links.

TABLE2. RESULTS OF EVALUATION EXPERIMENTS

Total number of routes	***Matched routes***	***Matching ratio M (%)***
890	838	93.2

B. Qualitative evaluation in the results for 30 routes

In this evaluation, the automatically generated routes were evaluated qualitatively. The evaluation criterion was visibility of the route map, which was performed visually by the authors.

Figure 9 shows the results of drawing 30 routes. In this example, all routes were drawn correctly. However, there are some issues, as described below. Although the route drawing function distinguishes routes by color coding, the visibility is reduced because many routes have similar colors. In particular, adjacent routes should be drawn in different colors whenever possible. In addition, BSFs with many overlapping routes and those near bus terminals may be drawn at a distance from the actual road. When there are more overlapping routes near bus terminals, it is necessary to build a drawing function that maintains better visibility.

V. Conclusion

In this study, we proposed a method for automatic generation of bus route maps using bus stop series and strokes. This method generates bus stop nodes from the coordinates of the bus stop series and the road networks and estimates bus routes using a min stroke shortest path search method that minimizes the number of right/left turns between bus stop nodes. The estimation accuracy was 93.2%. We also proposed an efficient method for determining the order of placement by generating BSFs. This method dynamically determines the placement order of overlapping segments when drawing multiple routes and realizes map drawing of routes with fewer right/left turn crossings. Future works can include the construction of a drawing function that maintains visibility near bus terminals and when there are several overlapping routes.

Acknowledgment

This work was supported by JSPS KAKENHI Grant Numbers JP19H04115 and JP21K19766.

References

[1] M. Onda, M. Moriguchi, and K. Imai, "Automatic Drawing for Metro Maps in Tokyo," IEICE-COMP / IPSJ-AL, 2017-AL-163, Vol.13, pp.1-8, 2017.

[2] H. Bast, P. Brosi, and S. Storandt, "Efficient Generation of Geographically Accurate Transit Maps," In Proceedings of the 26th ACM SIGSPATIAL International Conference on Advances in Geographic Information, pp.13-22, 2018. DOI: 10.1145/3337790

[3] J. Stott, P. Rodgers, J. C. Martinez-Ovando, and S. G. Walker, "Automatic metro map layout using multicriteria optimization," IEEE Transactions on Visualization and Computer Graphics, 17(1), 101-114, 2010. DOI: 10.1109/TVCG.2010.24

[4] S. H. Hong, D. Merrick, and H. A. Do Nascimento, "The metro map layout problem," In Proceedings of the International Symposium on Graph Drawing 2004, pp. 482-491, Springer, 2004. DOI: /10.1007/978-3-540-31843-9_50

[5] J. M. Stott and P. Rodgers, "Metro map layout using multicriteria optimization," In Proceedings of the Eighth International Conference on Information Visualization, pp. 355-362, 2004. DOI: 10.1109/IV.2004.1320168

[6] Y. S. Wang and W. Y Peng, "Interactive metro map editing," IEEE transactions on visualization and computer graphics, Vol 22, No. 2, pp. 1115-1126, 2016. DOI: 10.1109/TVCG.2015.2430290

[7] P. B. Lloyd, P. Rodgers, and M. J. Roberts, "Metro map colour-coding: Effect on usability in route tracing," In Proceedings of the International conference on theory and application of diagrams, pp. 411-428, Springer, 2018. DOI: 10.1007/978-3-319-91376-6_38

[8] R. Thomson and R. Brooks, "Efficient generalisation and abstraction of network data using perceptual grouping," In Proceedings of the 5th International Conference on GeoComputation, pp. 23–25, 2000.

[9] R. Thomson and D. Richardson, "'Good continuation' principle of perceptual organization applied to the generalization of road networks," In Proceedings of the 19th International Cartographic Conference, pp. 1215–1223, 1999.

[10] Q. Zhang, "Road network generalization based on connection analysis," In Proceedings of the 11th International Symposium on Spatial Data Handling, pp. 343–353, 2005. DOI: 10.1007/3-540-26772-7_26

[11] D. Yamamoto, M. Murase, and N. Takahashi, "On-Demand Generalization of Road Networks based on Facility Search Results," IEICE Transactions on Information and System, Vol. E102-D, No. 1, pp. 99-103, 2019. DOI: 10.1587/transinf.2017EDP7405

[12] M. Murase, D. Yamamoto, and N. Takahashi, "On-demand Generalization of Guide Maps with Road Networks and Category-based Web Search, Results," In Proceedings of the 14th International Symposium on Web and Wireless Geographical Information Systems, Vol. 19, pp. 53-70, 2015. DOI: 10.1007/978-3-319-18251-3_4

[13] D. Yamamoto, S. Ozeki, and N. Takahashi, "Focus+Glue+Context: An Improved Fisheye Approach for Web Map Services," In Proceedings of the ACM SIGSPATIAL GIS 2009, pp.101-110, 2009. DOI: 10.1145/1653771.1653788

[14] Yuki Hiura, (supervisor: Daisuke Yamamoto), "Proposal of an efficient nth min stroke shortest path search method," Master's thesis, Nagoya Institute of Technology, 2020. (In Japanese)

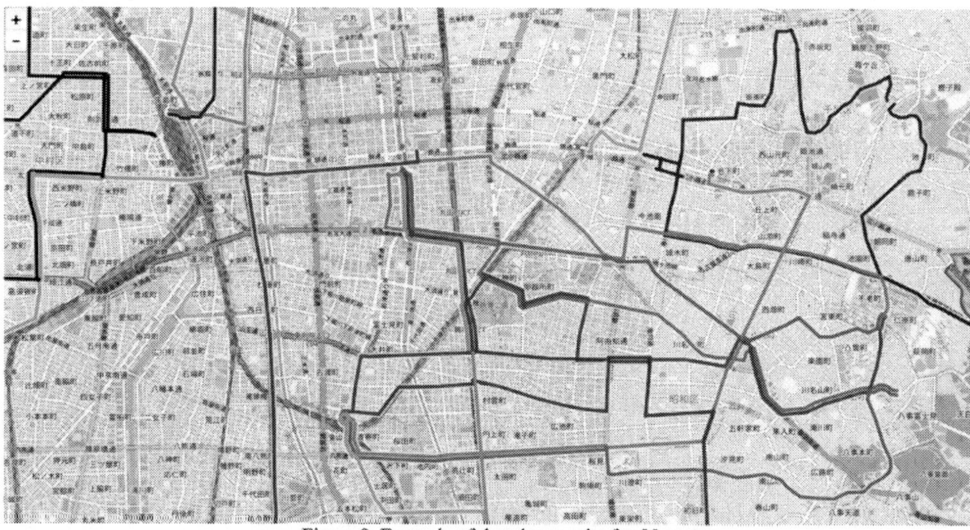

Figure 9. Example of drawing results for 30 routes.

A DEM Quality Dashboard

Ariza-López, Francisco Javier; García-Balboa, José Luis.
Dpto. Ingeniería Cartográfica, Geodésica y Fotogrametría
Universidad de Jaén
Jaén, Spain
Email: fjariza@ujaen.es, jlbalboa@ujaen.es

Reinoso-Gordo, Juan Francisco.
Dpto. Expresión Gráfica Arquitectónica y en la Ingeniería
Universidad de Granada
Granada, Spain
Email: jreinoso@ugr.es

***Abstract*—A more holistic and applied view of data quality is considered and to better communicate it, the use of dashboards is proposed. The use of dashboards is very common in business management and quality management, but not for communicating quality of geospatial data. The definition of the use case, the establishment of the key performance indicators and how to make their graphic representation in the dashboard are key processes to achieve this objective. This paper presents our considerations and progress focused on the development of this proposal.**

Keywords-Quality dashboard; data quality; fitness for use; DEM.

I. Introduction

There are several directly related digital models such as Digital Terrain Models (DTMs), Digital Surface Models (DSMs) and Digital Elevation Models (DEMs). Although the proposal made here may be valid for all of them, it will focus on the case of DEMs. A DEM is a bare-earth terrain void of vegetation and man-made features [1]. DEMs are a key data type for many applications domains because they provide the height component in Geographic Information System (GIS) analysis, the geomorphological description of the land, a reference surface for all hydrological applications (water cycle, erosion, floods, etc.), the basis for the development of forestry models, the base for agricultural parcel rating and are useful in every analysis task related to civil engineering.

The most usual way to evaluate the quality of a DEM is through Positional Accuracy Assessment Methods (PAAMs) (e.g., the National Standard for Spatial Data Accuracy). The use of PAAMs is the data quality approach preferred by official data producers. This is a datacentric perspective (internal quality). But this perspective does not adequately communicate the quality of a DEM data set when it is used in very common applications, such as the calculation of slopes, aspects, drainage networks, etc. This situation means that the data about the quality of a DEM supplied by producers is not understood by a large majority of users [2]. There are many references that indicate the existence of this handicap [3].

We believe that a more holistic view of the quality of a dataset is needed. But this holistic view must also be more applied, more focused on fitness for use. From the statistical point of view, a holistic perspective means a multivariate approach, as opposed to the univariate perspective (positional accuracy only). A more holistic view means considering all those aspects that define the whole, which is really complex. For this reason, the problem must be centered, and what the whole is must be well defined. In order to reach a more fitness for use orientation, we consider that the definition of use cases can be an adequate tool to define the framework of interest (the partial whole of interest). Basically, a use case is the description of an action or process with a certain level of formalization (e.g., using Unified Modelling Languages —UML— diagrams, or any other language). In addition, to better communicate quality, it may be appropriate to use graphic tools, which offer the user a friendlier view. In this sense, we are not referring to the representation of uncertainty (for example, in a terrestrial communication network using buffers of a certain width), but to the graphic expression of all the variables that are of interest to better communicate all the aspects the quality of a data set as a whole.

The above situation, where there is a need to communicate objective information about a complex situation as a whole, is not unique to the field of data quality. For example, in the field of business management it is very common to use numerous variables to define the operation or behavior of a company. In this case, it is usual to resort to the so-called "dashboards". A dashboard is a type of graphical interface which often provides at-a-glance views of Key Performance Indicators (KPIs).

In the geomatics field, dashboards are used in business management, but there are few references related to data quality [4][5]. More common initiatives are related to the use of stars as a rating system (e.g., five stars for open data [6]). Recent DEM quality reviews [7][8] do not indicate the use of graphical elements (e.g., dashboards) to report DEM data quality. On the other hand, there are numerous works [2][3] indicating that users of DEM data do not have a good understanding of quality aspects. For all these reasons, there is a need to make communication regarding the quality of DEM data more understandable.

In line with all of the above, the objective of this work is to establish a dashboard proposal to offer a multivariate quality assessment control panel for a specific use case of DEM data. Therefore, it is also our goal to establish a specific use case on which to develop the dashboard. First, we will define the use case, and then a dashboard proposal will be made. Therefore, the ultimate purpose of our contribution is to convey in a simple and understandable way the quality of the DEM data when considering a specific use case.

The structure of the paper is as follows: Section II presents major considerations that are needed to stablish a use case, Section III is a short discussion informs about our next steps. Finally, Section IV presents a brief conclusion.

II. Defining a Use Case

Reference [3] recompiles several use cases of DEM data, and also the result of a worldwide survey on the main users and uses of DEM data. From this background, we consider that a use case that may be of great interest is the determination of a hydraulic network. A brief definition of the use case can be the following: given a DEM data product "DEMproduct", a well-defined sequence of known algorithms {A1, A2...} are applied to the DEMproduct dataset to obtain automatically a vector dataset corresponding to the drainage network. It should be noted that no operator intervention is considered. In this case, a multivariate quality assessment can be proposed if an adequate reference dataset exist or is created. The existence of the reference is a critical point for all accuracy assessments, but is out of the scope of this work.

Once the use case has been defined, basically through the set {data, algorithms, processes}, we have to define the content and configuration of the dashboard. In relation to its content, this tool must consider all those variables that are of interest from an applied perspective of the data generated and whose quality could be evaluated. For example, relevant aspects of the hydraulic network generated and that can be considered here are: the planimetric positional accuracy of the sections of the network, the positional accuracy of the nodes, the existence of surplus or missing edges, the accuracy of the altimetric profiles of the channels generated, the classification of the typology of the generated network, etc. We consider that user participation is necessary to decide which of these aspects are the most relevant KPIs. The ISO 19157 data quality model [9] will be applied to these KPIs to establish standardized definitions of quality elements and their measurements. Reference [10] presents an example that can adequately serve as a guide on the use of this geospatial data quality model. This example shows the combined use of "quality elements", "quality measures" and "data quality units" as defined by the ISO 19157 standard. In addition to the above, it must also be defined how the results are presented so that they communicate properly. Here the structure of the dashboard (quality dimensions) is as important as the tools (e.g., traffic lights, stars, histograms, box-plot graphics, etc.) that can be used depending on the type of variable being worked with and how you want to represent it. For example, there are variables that could be represented specialized or summarized in a value or in a graph. Another relevant aspect is to know if you want the dashboard to be simply informative (this is what results from the evaluation), or if it has a quality control perspective (the dataset passes/fails in relation to a specific quality element). In relation to graphical tools there is experience, but not with the perspective that is exposed here. We consider that user participation is also very relevant here.

Figure 1 shows an example of a section of two sections of a dashboard in which several KPIs related to the positional accuracy and the network-type classification have been included as traffic light signals.

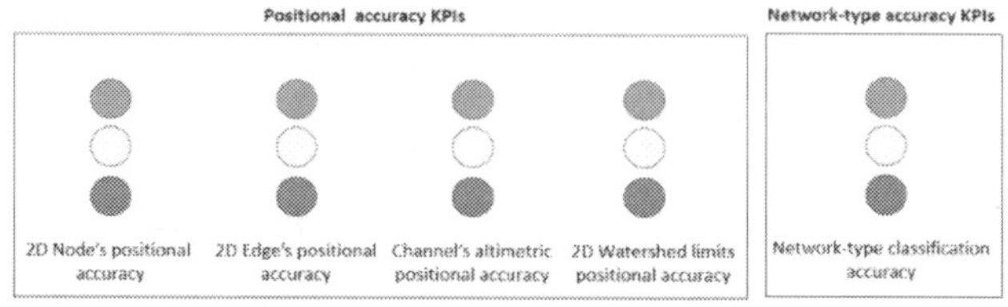

Figure 1. Example of two sections of a dashboard based on traffic light signals.

III. Discussion

The approach of quality to users is a key aspect for the appropriate use of geospatial data. Therefore, the work that has been presented is aligned with a traditional desire in the field of geospatial data, which is to make quality more understandable for users. For this reason, it is very important that the aspects of quality to be considered are those that are really relevant KPIs from a "fitness for use" perspective, but can also be linked to the idea of functional quality (this idea is presented in another contribution of the authors in this congress). The work is just beginning, and the authors are preparing a survey to identify the KPIs for this case, and will subsequently survey various dashboard configurations as well.

The idea has been presented on a single use case, but it can be applied to any use case. Once the most defining use cases of DEM data are available, you can consider developing a complete dashboard for all of them, and such that it offers a holistic view of the quality of a DEM.

An especially critical aspect is the transition from elements of quality, as defined in the ISO 19157 model, to fitness for use, or usability in the jargon of ISO 19157. This is not a specific problem of our proposal, but it is a handicap that affects. The communication capacity focused on the use case would be much greater if this handicap were overcome.

IV. Conclussions

The usefulness of dashboards is unquestionable in the fields of business management and quality management systems. This work presents an idea that already exists but has not received enough attention in the field of geospatial data quality. In order to advance in this line, it has been proposed to link it to use cases, such that they allow to limit the scope of work. The work is in progress, user participation is required to establish the KPIs and the dashboard configuration. We hope that these works will be the basis for offering a standardized communication tool for DEM's quality.

ACKNOWLEDGMENT

This work has been financed by the research project "Functional Quality of Digital Elevation Models in Engineering" of the State Agency Research of Spain. PID2019-106195RB-I00/AEI/10.13039/501100011033 (https://coello.ujaen.es/investigacion/web_giic/funquality4dem/).

REFERENCES

[1] D. F. Maune, Digital Elevation Model Tecnologies and Applications: The DEM Users Manual. ASPRS (2001).

[2] S. P. Wechler, "Perceptions of Digital Elevation Model Uncertainty by DEM Users," Urisa J. vol 15, pp. 57–64, 2003.

[3] F. J. Ariza-López, E.G. Chicaiza-Mora, J. L. Mesa-Mingorance, J. Cai, and J. F. Reinoso-Gordo, "DEMs: An Approach to Users and Uses from the Quality Perspective," Int. J. Spat. Data Infrastruct. vol 13, pp. 131–171, 2018.

[4] E. Folmer and W. Beek, "Data Quality for Use: A Linked Data Approach" The 3rd International Workshop on Spatial Data Quality (SDQ 2020) January 28th- 9th, pp 22-25, 2020.

[5] J. Nogueras-Iso, J. Lacasta, M. A. Ureña-Cámara, and F. J. Ariza-López, "Quality of Metadata in Open Data Portals," IEEE Access 2021, 10.1109/ACCESS.2021.3073455

[6] https://opendatahandbook.org/glossary/en/terms/five-stars-of-open-data/

[7] J. L. Mesa-Mingorance, and F. J. Ariza-López, "Accuracy Assessment of Digital Elevation Models (DEMs): A Critical Review of Practices of the Past Three Decades", Remote Sensing, 12(16):2630 2020, https://doi.org/10.3390/rs12162630

[8] Polidori L, and M. El Hage, "Digital Elevation Model Quality Assessment Methods: A Critical Review", Remote Sensing., 12(21):3522, 2020, https://doi.org/10.3390/rs12213522

[9] International Standardization Association, ISO 19157:2013 Geographic information — Data quality, ISO, 2013.

[10] F.J. Ariza-López, J. Rodríguez-Avi, J. F. Reinoso-Gordo, and I. A. Ariza-López, "Quality Control of As Built BIM Datasets Using the ISO 19157 Framework and a Multiple Hypothesis Testing Method Based on Proportions", ISPRS International Journal of Geo-Information, 8(12):569, 2019, https://doi.org/10.3390/ijgi8120569

Functional Quality:

A Use-case Oriented Data Quality Evaluation

Ariza-López, Francisco Javier
Dpto. Ingeniería Cartográfica, Geodésica y Fotogrametría
Universidad de Jaén
Jaén, Spain
Email: fjariza@ujaen.es

Reinoso-Gordo, Juan Francisco
Dpto. Expresión Gráfica Arquitectónica y en la Ingeniería
Universidad de Granada
Granada, Spain
Email: jreinoso@ugr.es

Abstract—**The current paradigm in geospatial data quality is datacentric (internal quality), but it can be overcome by considering generic use cases that link geospatial data with its processing (algorithms). The new approach proposed by the functional quality supposes an intermediate situation between the user's and producer's perspectives (external and internal quality). This paper defines the functional quality and explains the need for this new perspective.**

Keyords-Data quality; fitness for use; functional quality.

I. INTRODUCTION

The concept of quality is close to everyone, it is used in colloquial language and is universally understood and intuitively accepted. In general, it can be said that a well-done work has quality. The term quality is defined in [1] as the degree to which a set of inherent characteristics of an object fulfils requirements. This definition clarifies that quality does not have to be limited to a single property of the object under consideration, but that several factors may come into play to define quality. On the other hand, what is inherent is what is proper or inseparable from things, and it is worth clarifying that here are factors that are more evident, or explicit, than others that have a more implicit character. Another interesting aspect of this definition is the one that quality refers to the fulfillment of requirements.

In this way, it is interesting to define what fitness for use is. If we go to the American Association for Quality glossary on quality [2], it tells us that fitness for purpose is a «term sometimes used to define the term "quality", to indicate the degree to which a product or service meets the requirements for its intended use». In the Online Browsing Platform of ISO, there is no direct entry for this term, although as a related entry appears «test or usability test», which is defined as «test to determine if an implemented system fulfills its functional purpose as determined by its users». All of the above means that the use of the term "fitness for use" implies having: i) a well-determined purpose of use and ii) the ability to evaluate the performance level. In this work, we will focus on the first aspect of the previous two. In relation to the first component, use cases can be considered. Basically, a use case is nothing more than the description of an action or process with a certain level of formalization (e.g., using Unified Modeling Language diagrams, or any other language). Focused on a specific user requirement, the documentation of a use case must include the actors, actions, inputs, outputs and decisions necessary to achieve the prosed goal. The fitness for use approach supposes the loss of the most transcendent, abstract and general vision of quality to focus on specific use cases. For example, in the automobile sector, there are many possible users, uses and ways of driving a specific vehicle model. Considering that for a user the fuel consumption is a relevant aspect of the quality of a car model, and that it is impossible to adequately inform for all possible situations, standards, such as the New European Driving Cycle (NEDC) [3], and more recently the World Harmonized Light-duty Vehicle Test Procedure (WLTP) [4], have been adopted for dealing in this complex scenario. In the latter, a driving dynamic is adopted that tries to reproduce much better how people drive in the real world [5]. Closer to the geospatial world, there is experience in performing functional tests on web services (semantic services [6], geospatial services [7] such as WFS, WCS, etc.). And, more generally, the OASIS model [8] for web services establishes several quality dimensions on functional aspects.

For all these reasons, we consider that proposing the perspective of functional quality applied to the case of geospatial data is in line with what is already a reality in more advanced fields.

In the case of geospatial data, there are many references (e.g., [9][10]) that indicate that the quality of geospatial data is something that is not really understood by the data users. On the one hand, quality is poorly communicated and on the other, it does not serve the interests of users because quality is typically reported from a producer and data-centric perspective (e.g., ISO 19157) [11], not usage-centric. The functional quality perspective will help avoid this undesirable situation.

The objective of this work is to develop a new perspective of the quality of geospatial data, in which we are guided by the example previously exposed for the automobile sector. We propose that quality be defined and evaluated in specific use cases, which means linking data and processes (algorithms). In this way we get much better approximation to the fitness for use. We call this new perspective functional quality.

The structure of the paper is as follows: Section 2 defines functional quality in more detail. Section III discusses the advantages and disadvantages of this new perspective. Finally, Section IV presents a brief conclusion.

II. Defining the Functional Quality

Given the disaffection that affects users regarding the quality of the data they use due, among other reasons, to the fact that the way in which it is reported does not come close to their real needs, this paper proposes the adoption of a new level of analysis and information on the quality of geospatial data, which we call functional quality. We describe quality with the adjective functional since we propose evaluate how well the data "works" in specific use cases.

Since geospatial data is used in processes, this new level of quality assessment and reporting picks up on this, linking data with algorithms to more fully consider the quality of outputs, which most directly affects to users. Thus, we define functional quality as the consistency, against a reference, of the results generated by a given algorithm when applied to a given geospatial data set (e.g., a given digital elevation model —DEM— dataset that is used for the determination of a hydrographic network).

We understand the functional quality as a new perspective that can be complex and must be defined by various indices (quality measures). For example, for the case of a drainage network determined on a DEM dataset and a given algorithm, some aspects that can help to inform about the functional quality of the DEM are: displacements of the resulting network, completeness of the obtained network, topological problems present in the network, etc. That is to say, aspects that may be of interest to a user who will use that drainage network in their production processes or decision making.

Therefore, functional quality approximates the "fitness for use", but focused on a use case defined as generic and not considering particular requirements of some users or others (for example, for an engineering project, resolution requirements are different for the phases of feasibility study, preliminary design and project). With all this, a certain component of particularity is eliminated, as occurs when applying the NEDC and WLTP methods for assessing the fuel consumption in specific driving scenarios.

So, functional quality can be considered as the middle layer of a three-layer system, each of which brings us closer to quality from a different perspective: internal quality (the data-centric traditional producer's perspective), functional (use-case-centric perspective) and external quality (fitness for use perspective). In this way, a more general approach to use cases can be made without going into the problem of countless users and specific conditions of their applications, which supposes a context that is too rich and broad to be addressed. Basically, we are following the same scheme that has been mentioned previously for the case of the automobile sector with respect to the information on vehicle consumption.

III. Discussion

Before adopting a new perspective, it is worth thinking about whether or not it brings advantages over the previous situation. ISO 19157 establishes the framework for geospatial data quality. In this international standard, the concept that is closest to functional quality is the quality element called "usability". In ISO 19157, this quality element does not have a clear formulation and is not linked to use cases or algorithms, which is a relevant aspect of functional quality. A better explanation is given in ISO 25010, but there is no formal description. Obviously, the above can make difficult to establish a link with a (semi-)formal description of specific use cases as proposed by us.

In our view, the advantages of working with functional quality are several. Functional quality links the data to the essence of the processes (algorithms), and to applied use cases. All this has a more applied vision and vocation than the internal quality reported by the producers. Internal quality is much more data-centric, focused on the data itself, without considering its use. As functional quality remains linked to use cases by means of algorithms, functional quality provides a greater degree of specificity and always refers to the pair: *FQ = Function {given data set, given algorithm}*. That is, the algorithm is always present as a characteristic of the considered use case. In this way functional quality can provide valuable information to producers and users. For the former, it focuses on the applied interests of users and offers producers information so that they can improve their data quality definition and geospatial data, since now they will better understand the impacts on the final results. For the latter, it offers a more user-centric quality, focused on the use problems that they actually have when using the data, which makes it more understandable, interesting and valuable. In addition, this way of reporting quality is a wake-up call to those users who do not pay much attention to the processing algorithms and who consider that every digital result is good in itself. Finally, given that there are very common use cases and algorithms, the definition and evaluation of functional quality could be standardized for these cases, which would offer greater confidence and transparency.

An aspect that is also relevant in the understanding data, their quality and use, is the quality of the metadata. Functional quality could also be assessed in the metadata. In any case, functional quality should be included in the metadata, which would represent a clear improvement in terms of making them more understandable and practical for users.

IV. Conclusion

The main contribution of this work is conceptual and has focused on justifying the need to introduce a new level of quality assessment (functional quality), which is more informative for users but, at the same time, can be applied by producers. Based on what is already being done in other fields (e.g., vehicles and web services), we consider that adopting the perspective of functional quality is a natural evolution for the case of data and its processes.

This new level of evaluation is intermediate between quality, as it is currently understood and materialized by producers, and quality in the sense of "fitness for use". Functional quality links geospatial data with its processes, so it offers a way that is much closer to users and can help producers to be more attentive to user's needs. In the near future we will continue to develop complete illustrative examples and show the advantages of the use of the functional quality.

ACKNOWLEDGMENT

This work has been financed by the research project "Functional Quality of Digital Elevation Models in Engineering" of the State Agency Research of Spain. PID2019-106195RB-I00/AEI/10.13039/501100011033 (https://coello.ujaen.es/investigacion/web_giic/funquality4dem/).

REFERENCES

[1] International Standardization Association, ISO 9000:2015 Quality management systems — Fundamentals and vocabulary, ISO, 2015.

[2] https://asq.org/quality-resources/quality-glossary/f

[3] European Union, Regulation (EC) No 715/2007. Official Journal L 171, 29.6.2007.

[4] European Union, Regulation (EU) 2017/1347. Official Journal L 192, 27.7.2017.

[5] Dirección General de Tráfico, Nuevas mediciones, consumos más reales. https://revista.dgt.es/es/motor/reportajes/2020/1217-WLTP.shtml

[6] A. Tahir, D. Tosi, S. Morasca, "A systematic review on the functional testing of semantic web services", Journal of Systems and Software, Volume 86, Issue 11, Pages 2877-2889, 2013, https://doi.org/10.1016/j.jss.2013.06.064.

[7] G. Giuliani, A. Dubois, P. Lacroix, "Testing OGC Web Feature and Coverage Service performance: Towards efficient delivery of geospatial data", Journal of Spatial Information Science, No. 7, 1-23, 2013, http://dx.doi.org/10.5311/JOSIS.2013.7.112

[8] OASIS, Quality Model for Web Services September 2005 http://cliplab.org/Projects/S-CUBE/papers/oasis05:WSQM-2.0.pdf

[9] S. P. Wechler, "Perceptions of Digital Elevation Model Uncertainty by DEM Users," Urisa J. vol 15, pp. 57–64, 2003.

[10] F. J. Ariza-López, E.G. Chicaiza-Mora, J. L. Mesa-Mingorance, J. Cai, and J. F. Reinoso-Gordo, "DEMs: An Approach to Users and Uses from the Quality Perspective," Int. J. Spat. Data Infrastruct. vol 13, pp. 131–171, 2018.

[11] International Standardization Association, ISO 19157:2013 Geographic information — Data quality. ISO, 2013.

Enriching Georeferenced Environmental Data Using Web Data Extraction to Contribute to Degraded Area Impact Analysis

Clovis Santos
ICEN/UFR
Federal University of Rondonópolis-UFR
Rondonópolis, Brazil
email: clovis@ufr.edu.br

Carina Dorneles
INE/CTC/UFSC
Federal University of Santa Catarina-UFSC
Florianopópolis, Brazil
email: carina.dorneles@ufsc.br

***Abstract*—Data enrichment uses resources to fill gaps in customer data sets, enterprise systems, marketing, product sales, and related applications. Environmental applications have the potential to be enriched by aggregating georeferenced data from external sources. The data available on the Web might be a viable alternative to support data enrichment. Usually, this process is done manually, at a high cost of time and human resources. In this context, georeferenced data enrichment using external datasets is a viable and available resource that can be used to reduce financial costs and improve the geographic localization process, which directly depends on appropriate hardware, such as GPS devices and human availability for data collection. This paper presents two main contributions: (i) a data extraction process, which enriches georeferences in a specific application; and (ii) a data enrichment process, which indicates potential risks in environmental areas with potential soil degradation problems. We validate the extracted data from the Web, using these data in an application to verify the distance between areas classified as degraded and possible points of interest in or near urban areas. Finally, it is essential to point out that the research has an interdisciplinary essence involving information systems and the environment, collaborating with both domains.**

***Keywords*—** Georeferencing, data enrichment, environment, extraction web data, environmental retrieve information

I. Introduction

Environmental mapping of degraded areas is usually created through *in loco* visits. Identifying degraded areas consists of delimiting the geographic coordinates of their respective boundaries. The delineation of areas can be identified in Web repositories, providing alternatives to enriching geo-referenced databases for environmental scenarios. The first step in enriching data is identifying repositories of interest for the area under study. The paper describes the use of geographic coordinates and site identification to identify potential side effects in nearby regions, as described in Section IV.

The main problem in this context is finding georeferenced data on the Web related to delineating degraded areas. Usually, these are data with limited access, but free or non-commercial tools are essential for delineation with good geographic accuracy. Another critical issue is acquiring georeferenced data, which has a high cost and is a barrier for many rural properties. This difficulty leads to obligatory irregularities for small plots associated with family farms. Data sources are made publicly available on the Web as tables of geographic data for a variety of areas, including urban sustainability, transportation networks, policy studies, and health. However, environmental fields are particular, making it challenging to use generic data common in other fields.

Another essential aspect discussed in this paper is eXtensible Mark-up Language, XML, which has been widely used as the standard language for data exchange [18]. The data extraction used in the paper inspects content with Keyhole Markup Language (KML) format, which uses XML as a framework. The content of this type of file stores various data, but the research explores only a subset referring to coordinates for delimiting polygons or locating specific points in geographic areas.

The paper presents an alternative to the enrichment of georeferenced data that contributes to identifying and monitoring environmental impacts in degraded areas and their consequences when detected near urban areas and essential reference points such as river sources. In this context, the georeferenced data were obtained through web extraction in government portals with public access without commercial licenses. It is important to mention that the proposed approach is not restricted to degraded areas. The delimitation in this subarea of the environmental domain has been used to specialize enrichment. However, the enrichment-related approach can be applied to subsets of data from the same domain, such as agriculture, rainfall, and animal control.

The data enrichment process can be classified into six approaches [6]:

- Data fusion: a procedure for unifying data from multiple sources representing the same entity with consistency and valuable presentation.
- Data entity recognition: a process of identifying words in texts, finding and recognizing names of people, companies, organizations, cities, and other predefined entities.
- Data Disambiguation: a method for disambiguation or elimination of ambiguity is the process of identifying the correct data entity in the presence of inconsistent and ambiguous variations in entity names.
- Data Segmentation: a process of grouping data into a set of predefined attributes.
- Data Input: an approach to estimate values for missing or conflicting data items.
- Data Categorization: a procedure for identifying data into different categories based on topics, events, or other features.

The proposal described in this paper uses data entity recognition to identify valuable data for the proposed enrichment. Although researchers have divided web data extraction into different problems based on the modality of the data, they have faced similar problems, such as identifying relevant data for the domain under study using prior knowledge related to the web environment [8]. The extractor used in this paper is a complementary tool to adequately prepare the data for mapping to the selected entity from the target database. This data is essential to generate reports with georeferencing related to environmental information.

Data extraction in web environments does not have a specific domain for data enrichment. The focus is generally on enrichment without a vertical target for the data. In this context, our proposal contributes with an environmental domain approach, which focuses on a practical application for data enrichment in a real scenario related to monitoring degraded environmental areas.

We aim to use a simple application architecture as a tool to identify side effects near degraded areas using georeferenced data obtained through data enrichment from web sources. The metric used to evaluate the results was defined with geographic identification of sites within a predetermined radius in geographic areas. It is essential to see that degradation like erosion scan leads to siltation of springs that cause irreversible environmental impacts depending on the degree of degradation. Therefore, the result of the enriched data identify potentially damaged sites. After the site's indications, a comparison between the resulting information and the regional maps is possible.

Our proposal suggests a viable alternative for enriching georeferenced data. Section III, provides an overview of a computational architecture for extracting, cleaning, and linking external data sources in a web environment to tables in databases.

This paper presents four contributions regarding georeferenced data extraction for enrichment related to the natural environment:

- Web data extraction: objectively and practically shows a viable alternative for web data extraction as an alternative to enrich georeferenced databases.
- Georeferencing: presents how to use georeferenced data as a resource for environmental monitoring of degraded areas.
- Data enrichment: presents web application architecture for data extraction with goals to enrich a georeferenced database.
- Environment: describes a computational solution to assist environmental consultants and technicians in monitoring degraded areas identifying possible impacts in nearby regions.

This paper is organized as follows. In Section II, we describe works related to web data extraction and georeferenced data enrichment. In Section III, we present the proposed architecture for data extraction, cleaning, and association. In Section IV, we present a case study. In Section V, we discuss some conclusions and possibilities for future work.

II. RELATED WORKS

In the context of research, the enrichment of georeferenced data depends on the extraction result. According to [7], data extraction from web pages started in the 2000s. Currently, the proposed solutions are essentially used with wrappers or programs to extract information from the web. Although there are several papers on this topic, this section will cover some works related to the main topics of this paper. This section provides an overview of approaches to extracting data from web content based on the XML structure, such as the KML. We point out the difference we propose related to each work discussed.

According to [2], poor data quality has various causes and is a challenge that should not be underestimated. Sometimes, the data source is in the wrong format or range of values, and data must be cleaned or validated. High data quality is desirable and the main criterion to determine if the enrichment was successful and the statements are correct. Our paper presents an alternative to data enrichment from web extraction. High data quality is possible when the data are suitable for use and meet the objectives set by data users. This definition clarifies that data quality highly depends on context, synergy, needs, uses, and access [1].

The research described by [19] addresses data integration in the biomedical domain. Despite being a different domain from the one addressed in our paper, some similarities, for example, data integration for information generation, can be observed. However, the authors' proposal presents query integration without data extraction. In our research, extraction is one of the steps for using data in georeferencing applications.

The research presented in [20] gives a general analysis regarding techniques for extracting data from the web. Extraction is one of the essential points of the present research, with the differential in data extraction as part of the solution for data enrichment in the environmental domain. This paper referred to some items, such as constructing the micro parse to analyze raw content and structuring it for database storage.

In [21], the authors address data enrichment using web documents as sources, which is the approach we also used in our research. Similar to what was described in [20], the research has the main objective to evaluate improvements in querying the enriched database. Our proposal has no perspective of directly analyzing the enriched data since verifying the data quality is certified by visualizing the data in specific geographical scenarios. Plotting the polygons in environmental preservation areas indicates the accuracy and quality of the enriched data.

The research presented in [22] investigates the domain associated with dictionaries for natural language. In our approach, numerical values represent the data domain, so post-processing for validating the data associated with a specific vocabulary is unnecessary. However, the mentioned research also contributed to constructing the micro parse used to select the relevant numerical values to create georeferenced coordinates.

The paper presented by [17] takes a similar approach. However, it uses generic semi-structured data, while the approach of our proposal is to use structured data in a specific area of the environment.

Analogous to our approach, the authors in [24] also developed research focusing on data enrichment for agricultural policy support. However, the domain is slightly different as we addressed data enrichment for the environmental domain, but they are related or complementary. Other topics that are similar to our needs also relate to the storage and query of the extracted data. Both papers use relational databases as a resource for storing the data arranged in tables for the agility of the queries. We have used the proposal presented in [24] as reference rules for the parse developed in our research. A similar approach identifies georeferenced coordinates storing databases after cleaning them.

Data extraction using the web as a source usually uses applications written specifically for this purpose. Creating a generic application becomes almost unfeasible in the face of the diversity of structures used to build pages that are the public repositories usually used by extractors. In our proposal, we have created a tool with a graphical interface to visualize the extracted data in all stages. A similar approach has been presented in [23], composed of an API and a graphical interface that presents the implementation extraction use. In our approach, the extractor implementation was developed specifically for a dataset with characteristics previously defined for KML files. We highlight that the format used is not restrictive but used as a delimiter for demonstrations presented in the results section.

Finally, the environment targets enriched data, such as the extraction and enrichment of georeferenced data to delineate degraded areas. The paper [5] defines land degradation as a process in which the biophysical state of the environment is affected by a combination of natural or human-induced processes acting on the land. This process can lead to an acceleration of degradation. Plants and animals that generally play a role in restoring the land may not survive. The enriched data can identify the potential environmental impacts of nearby threats.

The information presented at the end of Section IV refers to regional reviews of sites based on data enriched with web extraction and data imported from state datasets. In this scenario, the proposed application is limited to verifying distances between geographic points. The work [7] presents a solution independent of structural changes in the data source. Traditional wrappers rely heavily on structures such as HTML as sources. In this work, syntactic rules identify the content of interest. Other environmental monitoring initiatives are described in [4], where an open-source software called "Free and Open Source Software (FOSS) for land degradation vulnerability assessment" is presented. The idea is to identify different levels of vulnerability using models of Environmentally Sensitive Areas

(ESAs). [3] presents another initiative with "Open Foris", which is a set of free, open-source software tools that facilitate collecting, analyzing, and reporting forest inventory data. It is important to note that the application proposed in the paper covers the extraction, enrichment, and operations with georeferencing of regions in environmental areas. The other works referenced focus on analyzing soils and data related to inventories, so the paper's approach can contribute to different situations.

The biggest challenge is having high-quality georeferenced data, which are usually restricted since they are obtained with expensive equipment or provided through equally expensive private services. Delimiting an area for monitoring with generic datasets, with precision above 30 meters, for example, can compromise results associated with mapping and applications requiring accuracy. In this sense, the article shows a viable and reasonable alternative to aggregate georeferenced data to the integrated database systems for geographic identification and monitoring in the environmental scenario.

III. PROPOSAL

The proposal provides a viable, cost-effective solution for aggregating georeferenced information from external sources into entities in databases. This solution supports applications using environmental georeferencing data. Furthermore, using georeferenced information contributes to regulatory requirements, such as delineating permanently protected areas, river sources, rural headquarters, and property boundaries.

The proposal's development began with identifying the type of data source appropriate for the specific domain. Web sources related to georeferencing for the environment using the standard KML. Next, was developed a prototype for extracting data about selected sources, allowing integration with environmental databases. The final step is to enrich the data with entities from the environmental databases to produce information about secondary impacts in urban areas or at sites of ecological importance near degraded areas.

A. Infrastructure Detail

This section presents an overview of the proposed architecture for extracting, cleaning, and associating georeferenced data in three steps. The first obtains data from external sources from an address (*url*) specified by transferring the content to a local structure. The next step refers to data cleaning. After this step, the captured content is analyzed, and redundant data is removed using a micro-parse to identify relevant content such as territory names and geographic coordinates. The last step refers to the association of the georeferenced data with the data of the target schema. The association is done under user supervision using an intermediate entity. This oversight must show the correspondences between the entity's attribute value and the captured georeferenced coordinates. Section IV presents the use of coordinates for data enrichment in environmental scenarios. Figure 1 shows the structure of the data after extraction without cleaning it.

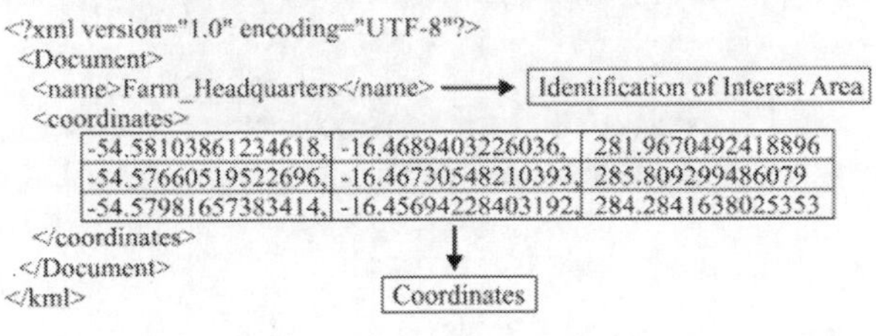

Fig. 1. Remote Data Source Structure.

IV. RESULTS

The most significant value for enriched data is the georeferencing of the natural environment. Environmental georeferencing is essential for water resource identification, rural access, and mapping of degraded areas. In situations where environmental regulations are not respected, such as deforestation in restricted areas, court proceedings verify the development of the regeneration process for the specified area. In this sense, georeferencing is essential for temporal comparisons and tracking. Web data extraction refers to georeferenced data. This data type was chosen for its relevance to the environment, as shown in Figure 2. Figure 2 also shows the data collected at an initial stage without any transformation. The data is not yet usable at this stage, as it is still in the original structure without any modification to make it accessible to external applications and users.


```
< ?xml version="1.0" encoding="UTF-8"?><kml xmlns="http://www.opengis.net/kml/2.2">
<Document><Placemark><name>EmbargadaDesmatamento3</name><ExtendedData><Data name="name">
<value>EmbargadaDesmatamento3</value></Data><Data name="styleUrl"><value>#m_ylw-pushpin</value>
</Data><Data name="styleHash"><value>-5bd746ca</value></Data><Data name="styleMapHash">
<value>[object Object]</value></Data></ExtendedData><Polygon><outerBoundaryIs><LinearRing>
<coordinates>-55.70101499034053,-16.89472397864652,0 -55.69083781135536,-16.91544069960135,0 -55.68711889758733,-1
</LinearRing></outerBoundaryIs></Polygon></Placemark><Placemark><name>EmbargadaDesmatamento1</name>
<ExtendedData><Data name="name"><value>EmbargadaDEsmatamento1</value></Data><Data name="styleUrl">
<value>#m_ylw-pushpin</value></Data><Data name="styleHash"><value>-5bd746ca</value>
</Data><Data name="styleMapHash"><value>[object Object]</value></Data></ExtendedData>
<Polygon><outerBoundaryIs><LinearRing><coordinates>-55.52006081273624,-16.88564309999979,0 -55.51760894219638,-1
```


Fig. 2. Raw Content.

As shown in Section III, the data used came from KML files after extraction. All the tests were performed locally, and the datasets used are also available on the web using the same infrastructure. It is essential to note that this file format is used and shared by many geoprocessing applications. Despite a large amount of data available in this file format, only two data were used. In this case, the name of the georeferenced area or point and the coordinates were used to delineate it. The coordinates are essential for enrichment operations performed with the profit and loss database.

After the data is extracted and cleaned, it is temporarily stored in a local database. The main objective of this temporary database is to have the possibility of structured data storage, during the cleaning step. The use of a temporary database simplifies the association between the database entities for the enrichment and the local data. Both are data organized in entities and attributes, as shown in Figure 3. In a further step of the enrichment, the temporary data is clear for new operations.

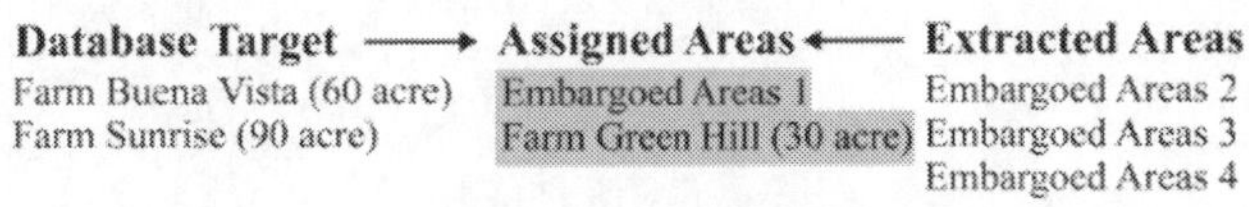

Fig. 3. Area Association.

The contribution of enrichment is the aggregation of georeferenced data on rural properties, which are data related to degraded areas. Erosion and large deforested areas near river sources or urban areas result in significant environmental and urban problems, especially with vertical erosion close to cities.

An important point raised by [12] refers to the classification of the data, which allows comparative analyzes in different regions such as protected areas, national parks, and others. The proposed enrichment process incorporates complementary data, adding resources later used to improve information generation. The application allows manual intervention in the prototype to classify the geographic data extracted and linked to the target database. The areas were classified into six groups according to the specification of an environmental specialist.

A. Information from Enriched Data

An example using the government database is shown to illustrate data enrichment. This database contains the central geographic location of all counties and districts in Brazil. This reference was used to calculate the distance between the center of urban areas or districts and the center of degraded areas, using the equation 2. For illustration, we have used a radius of 100 km from the center of the degraded areas. Figure 4 shows the pseudocode representation of the algorithm used for checking possible affected areas. Figure 5 illustrates a geographic area with localities in the Amazon border zone identified with the criteria data enriched from the extraction. Two equations were used for this calculation. The first identifies the center of the degraded area, and the second calculates the distance between the center of the degraded area and the center of the urban areas according to the Haversine Equation 1. The Haversine formula is a mathematical equation for calculating the distance between two coordinate points. The distance result obtained by Haversine is considered the smallest circular distance on Earth. The formula avoids a significant rounding error compared to other algorithms such as Pythagoras Equirectangular or Euclidean distance, which is also used to calculate the distance between two coordinates [10].

$$hav(\Theta) = hav(\varphi 2 - \varphi 1) + cos(\varphi 2)hav(\lambda 2 - \lambda 1) \qquad (1)$$

In addition, was used an equation for calculating the midpoint for geographic areas of polygons, given in Equation 2. The result defines the first point between the area to be verified and the second point, which is in the middle of the nearby locations.

$$\Delta\sigma = (sin\varnothing_1 sin\varnothing_2 + cos\varnothing_1 cos\varnothing_2 cos(\Delta\lambda)) \qquad (2)$$

As seen in Figure 4, the information generated by calculating distances between damaged areas and points of geographic interest, such as cities and river sources, can help develop preventive measures to restore these areas and prevent further damage nearby. The approach adopted for storing and visualizing the information uses a temporary storage table for display in a graphical user interface. As described earlier, the criterion for determining the distance between the central points of the damaged areas and the geographic points of interest was 100 km. This value was the reference used to search the geographic locations within this radius. The relevant areas included in the specified region are temporarily stored in memory with the data: Description of the location, distances, and State, as shown in Table I.

```
Algorithm ImpactAnalysis(param_Dist)
{  MidPoint(CoordMaxMin.Min_Lat,
            CoordMaxMin.Max_Lat,
            CoordMaxMin.Min_Lon,
            CoordMaxMin.Max_Lon,
            Ret_La, Ret_Lo)
   dist ← Distance(Ret_La, Dataset_Lat,
                   Ret_Lo, Dataset_Lo)
   while Dataset ≠ end_records
   if (dist<param_Dist)
   {
     TableDist ← Dataset_Distance
     TableDist ← Dataset_Location
     TableDist ← Dataset_Type
     TableDist ← Dataset_State
   }
}end-Algorithm
```

Fig. 4. Impact analysis algorithm.

Confirmation of the degree of degradation and the consequences for nearby sites depends on technical criteria established by technicians and environmental consultants. In this sense, technicians can confidently set parameters for the analysis, such as the type of degradation and the appropriate distance between degraded areas and areas of interest. The scenario proposed in this paper is illustrative because any technical criterion was used to determine that the distance of 100 km is technically valid, but the intent is to present a realistic example of the use of enriched data from data extraction. Although the definition of distance-related metrics is a parameter defined by technicians in the environmental field, there is no commitment to the paper's proposal. The test scenario was created flexibly for adjustments in calculating distances that meet environmental requirements.

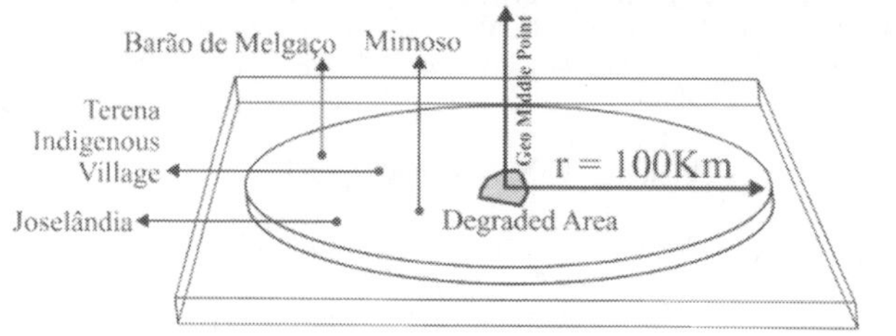

Fig. 5. Search area.

The Table I shows in tabular form the found locations for radius=100km. Although the defined radius is large, it is only illustrative, and values can suit different requirements.

TABLE I
QUERY RESULTS.

Country	Location	Distance	State
Barão de Melgaço	Barão de Melgaço	84 km	MT
Barão de Melgaço	Joselândia	67 km	MT
Santo Antonio	Mimoso	80 km	MT
Santo Antonio	Terena Indigenous Village	61 km	MT

Another important point related to the extracted data analysis is the terrain's surface. These analyses include data on heights for each geographic coordinate, which is generally not obtained from GPS devices or websites that provide open geographic datasets. The Open Elevation API (https:openelevation.com) was used for this type of enrichment, which provides elevation data for geographic coordinates (latitude and longitude).

Figure 6 shows the representation of a degraded area and the elevations for each coordinate. Irregular heights can indicate potential soil erosion. The surface of the degraded region leads to possible rainfall shifts leading to erosion of soil and substrate.

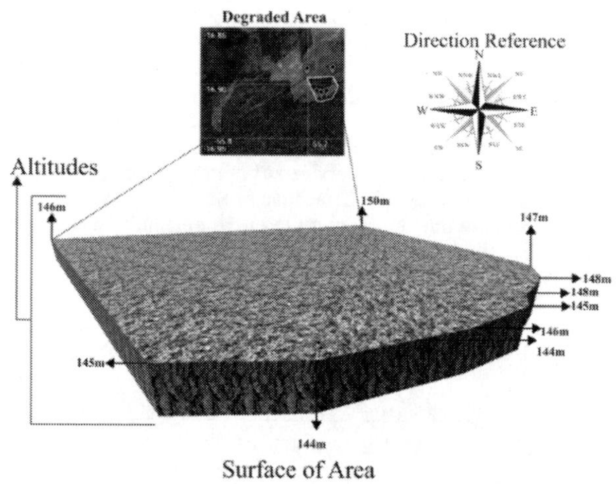

Fig. 6. Map area.

The review of the degraded area contributes directly to the impact that any soil shifts may have on nearby relevant points. With this in mind, an analysis was performed from the lowest elevations of the degraded area to nearby points of interest, according to the potential direction of possible ground shifts. It is important because degraded areas with sloping surfaces to points such as river sources or highways may have more significant impacts depending on the distance between them.

B. Results Considerations

The results obtained were satisfactory and illustrated extension possibilities for other applications. We have found difficulties creating a micro-parse to analyze the captured content due to its heterogeneity. Although the pages follow the same structure, some may have a different structure depending on the tool used to create them.

Data enrichment was performed satisfactorily with only one limitation: creating an intermediate table to link the georeferenced data to the target table. In data enrichment, changes to the data structure are essential in some cases, as it involves adding new data to a structure that was generally not prepared to accommodate it.

The content presented in this paper related to georeferenced data can be used as references for analyzing the distance between different environmental areas. The availability of this data in the web environment is large and promotes essential data sources. Another critical point is the availability of georeferenced data by government agencies, which also serves as an alternative for data enrichment.

Monitoring degraded areas is an ongoing task that presents numerous difficulties. The paper does not deal with this subject in depth but presents a satisfactory solution that contributes to consultants and environmental engineers of governmental regulatory agencies.

V. CONCLUSIONS AND FUTURE WORK

This paper describes an alternative for data extraction in a web environment in the environmental domain, specifically with georeferenced data. We have presented a consistent way to enrich databases with georeferencing to the environment. The proposal does not aim to exhaust the topic but to present an alternative to the growing demand for environmental data. The cost of obtaining this type of data is relatively high, and as shown in the paper, public access tools are feasible. Government interest in monitoring the conservation or restoration of protected areas is constant, and cost-effective alternatives must be analyzed to meet this demand. Two central points are essential in research as contributions. The first refers to the enrichment of environmental data by extracting data available in both government portals and APIs. The second contribution relates to developing tools to assist environmental engineers in monitoring degraded areas and potential impacts on nearby sites. An essential contribution to this research is to extend the import capabilities to other web data sources besides the file structure presented in this paper. This approach will help add more resources to rural properties in an environmental context, leading to essential allies for inspections in various government administrative areas.

REFERENCES

[1] I. Jaya and F. Jaya and I. Ishak and Lilly Affendey and M. Jabar, "A review of data quality research in achieving high data quality within organization, " Journal of Theoretical and Applied Information Technology, vol. 95, No 12, pp.2647–2657, June 2017.

[2] O. Azeroual and M. Jha, "Without Data Quality, There Is No Data Migration, " Big Data Cogn. Comput., Special Issue Educational Data Mining and Technology, vol. 5(2), 2021.

[3] Open Foris. http://openforis.org/, (retrieved: October/2021)

[4] V. Imbrenda and G. Calamita. and R. Coluzzi and M. D'Emilio and M. Lanfredi and A. Perrone and M. Ragosta and T. Simoniello, "Free and Open Source Software for land degradation vulnerability assessment, " EGU General Assembly Conference Abstracts, vol. 15, pp.11153–, 2013.

[5] B. Boer and I. Hannam, "Chapter 21: Land Degradation Law, " in Jorge Viñuales and Emma Lees (eds), Oxford Handbook on Comparative Environmental Law, 2019.

[6] S. Azad and S. Wasimi and A. Ali, "Business Data Enrichment: Issues and Challenges, " 2018 5th Asia-Pacific World Congress on Computer Science and Engineering (APWC on CSE), 2018, pp. 98-102, 2018.

[7] J. Lloret-Gazo, "A Browserless Architecture for Extracting Web Prices", SAC'20: Proceedings of the 35th Annual ACM Symposium on Applied Computing, pp. 2193–2200, March 2020.

[8] X. Dong and H. Hajishirzi and C. Lockard and P. Shiralkar, "Multi-Modal Information Extraction from Text, Semi-Structured, and Tabular Data on the Web, " KDD'20: Proceedings of the 26th ACM SIGKDD International Conference on Knowledge Discovery & Data Mining, pp. 3543–3544, August 2020.

[9] S. Zhang and K. Balog, "Web Table Extraction, Retrieval, and Augmentation: A Survey," ACM Transactions on Intelligent Systems and Technology, vol. 11, pp 1–35, April 2020.

[10] L. Theoson and R. Anthony and J. Purnama, "Distance-Measurement-Decision-Making Backend System Using NodeJS, " ICONETSI: Proceedings of the International Conference on Engineering and Information Technology for Sustainable Industry, pp. 1–6, September 2020.

[11] O. Emmanuel, "Effects of Deforestation on Land Degradation", Adebayo Williams (Editor), isbn 978-3-330-34486-0. 2017.

[12] SCITEPRESS - Science and and Technology Publications, Database Design of a Geo-environmental Information System, Proceedings of the 16th International Conference on Enterprise Information Systems. 2014.

[13] , A. Kanukov and P. Ivanov, "IOP Publishing, Geological information database integration into a geographic information modeling system," IOP Conference Series: Materials Science and Engineering, pp.1–6, 2021.

[14] R. Nicholas and J. Weinman and J. Gouwar and A. Shamji, "Deformable Part Models for Automatically Georeferencing Historical Map Images", SIGSPATIAL '19: Proceedings of the 27th ACM SIGSPATIAL International Conference on Advances in Geographic Information Systems, pp. 540—543, November 2019.

[15] A. Agarwal and M. Genesereth, "Extraction and Integration of Web Data by End-Users," International Conference on Information and Knowledge Management, pp. 2405–2410, 2013.

[16] , R. Fayzrakhmanov and E. Sallinger and B. Spencer and T. Furche and G. Gottlob, "Browserless Web Data Extraction: Challenges and Opportunities, " WWW '18: Proceedings of the 2018 World Wide Web Conference, pp. 1095—1104, April 2018.

[17] D. Gong and D. Wang and Y. Peng, "Multimodal Learning for Web Information Extraction," MM '17: Proceedings of the 25th ACM international conference on Multimedia, pp. 288—296, October 2017.

[18] S. Haw and E. Soong, " Performance evaluation on structural mapping choices for data-centric XML documents, " Indonesian Journal of Electrical Engineering and Computer Science, pp. 1539–1550, 2020.

[19] M. Kamdar and M. Musen, "An empirical meta-analysis of the life sciences linked open data on the web." Scientific Data, vol. 8, pp.1–21, January 2021.

[20] M. S. Parvez, K. S. A. Tasneem, S. S. Rajendra and K. R. Bodke, "Analysis Of Different Web Data Extraction Techniques," 2018 International Conference on Smart City and Emerging Technology (ICSCET), 2018, pp. 1–7.

[21] T. Breuer and M. Pest and P. Schaer, "Evaluating Elements of Web-Based Data Enrichment for Pseudo-relevance Feedback Retrieval. " Experimental IR Meets Multilinguality, Multimodality, and Interaction. CLEF 2021. Lecture Notes in Computer Science, vol 12880, pp 53–64.

[22] G. Wenzek et al. "CCNet: Extracting High Quality Monolingual Datasets from Web Crawl Data."Proceedings of the 12th Conference on Language Resources and Evaluation (LREC 2020), pp 4003—4012, May 2020.

[23] T. Alrashed and A. Zhang. "ScrAPIr: Making Web Data APIs Accessible to End Users." CHI '20: Proceedings of the 2020 CHI Conference on Human Factors in Computing Systems, pp. 1—12, April 2020.

[24] M. Rousi et al., "Semantically Enriched Crop Type Classification and Linked Earth Observation Data to Support the Common Agricultural Policy Monitoring, " in IEEE Journal of Selected Topics in Applied Earth Observations and Remote Sensing, vol. 14, pp. 529–552, 2021.

Cross-border Delivery and Web-based Visualization of 3D Buildings

Lassi Lehto and Jaakko Kähkönen
Department of Geoinformatics and Cartography
Finnish Geospatial Research Institute
Masala, Finland
e-mail: lassi.lehto@nls.fi, jaakko.kahkonen@nls.fi

Abstract—**Need for 3D geodata is increasing in various environmental and energy-related applications. This concerns in particular the content theme buildings. Cross-border provision of 3D buildings is thus an important research and development objective, as the challenges related to human settlements tend to traverse physical boundaries and need to be tackled in the international context. The GeoE3 project has been developing a content integration platform for facilitating cross-border access to 3D buildings datasets from five European countries. The approach is based on the utilization of modern standards, like OGC API Features and CityJSON, and applies on-the-fly processing of datasets for improved coverage and harmonization.**

Keywords-3D buildings; cross-border; harmonization; CityJSON, OGC API Features.

I. Introduction

Cross-border provision of 3D geodata is a new and challenging task for the Pan-European Spatial Data Infrastructure development [1]. The provision of nation-wide 3D data is in early stages and related standards are currently in rapid development phase [2]. First examples of genuine cross-border 3D geodata services are just being developed.

GeoE3 project has been working on cross-border interoperable provision of 3D buildings [3]. The project consortium includes National Mapping and Cadastral Agencies (NMCAs) from five European countries: Estonia, Finland, Norway, Spain and The Netherlands. The project has continued for one year and a half and has achieved significant results [4][5]. Although the approach selected by the NMCAs vary drastically from country to country, the GeoE3 project has managed to set up consistent access to 3D buildings from all the participating countries.

The service architecture adopted in the GeoE3 project relies on three-tier model. On the bottom tier, the varying national legacy content provision mechanisms are utilized to get access to the geodata content. On the second tier the GeoE3 data integration platform is responsible for adapting the content encodings and service interfaces to the needs of the modern technologies used on the client side. On the third tier are the client applications making use of the GeoE3 datasets in various identified renewable energy and smart city related use cases.

The Open Geospatial Consortium's new family of service interface standards, called OGC API [6] is the basis of the GeoE3 data integration platform. All the content provision from the platform is based on this set of standard interfaces and the related data encoding specifications. So far, GeoE3 has successfully implemented content access services based on OGC API Features [7] and OGC API Coverages [8] service specifications. In addition, the platform applies OGC API Processes [9] for supplementary on-the-fly processing and OGC API Records [10] for metadata provision. The core software solution used for the integration platforms Python-based computing environment is the OGC API Features reference implementation called pygeoapi [11]. In addition to OGC API Features, the software package supports at least preliminarily all the other needed OGC API standards. Django [12] is used as the Web application framework on the GeoE3 content integration platform and pygeoapi is adapted by the project to run in this framework.

In addition to 3D buildings, the GeoE3 project delivers also 2D buildings, together with rich attribute content. Schema for the building attributes is modelled on the basis of INSPIRE alternative encoding and model simplification rules [13]. GeoE3 is also working with coverage type content themes like Digital Terrain Model (DTM) and Digital Surface Model (DSM). Based on the needs of the selected use cases, some climate-related datasets, like temperature, windspeed and sunshine hours, are also included. These are accessed from the bottom tier as point observations, converted to coverage type data on the platform and provided through OGC API Coverages compliant service points to the client applications.

3D buildings are accesses from various different legacy sources from the bottom level and provided from the integration platform via OGC API Features service end point. According to the general approach adopted in the GeoE3 project, all the available country-specific datasets are configured as individual data collections inside a single OGC API instance. This way a simple but powerful solution for content integration can be achieved. Individual country's dataset can be accessed by querying the appropriate collection. Cross-border data requests are supported naturally with the so called cross-collection query, supported in the OGC API Features standard (Part 3: Filtering and the Common Query Language) [14]. The new CityJSON encoding standard for 3D geodata representation is adopted for the transfer of 3D buildings [15].

The rest of the paper is organised as follows. Section II discusses the solutions used for the provision of 3D building data. Section III describes the approach for delivering 3D buildings via the OGC API Features service interface. In Section IV Web browser-based 3D visualization is discussed. The paper ends with the conclusion in Section V.

II. Delivery Solutions

As the 3D provision of buildings data is in its early stages by the NMCAs, the solutions and selected standards vary significantly from country to country. However, the GeoE3 project has been able to provide full country coverage of 3D buildings in a consistent manner from all the participating five countries. This also involves dynamic, on-the-fly creation of LOD1 building geometries in some cases. 3D buildings are provided via the OGC API Features, Web Feature Service (WFS) or OGC API Processes interface, and are encoded in CityJSON format.

In the case of Estonia and Finland, the approach is quite the same. 3D buildings data are available on the country level as CityGML [16] file downloads. The Estonian dataset covers the whole country. The Finnish 3D buildings dataset at the moment only covers 10 distinct production areas, situated all over the country. The datasets are downloaded to the GeoE3 integration platform and then uploaded to the 3D City DB database [17]. The WFS-compliant service implementation provided by the 3D City DB developers is used to access the contents of the database. Along the adopted principles of the GeoE3 integration platform, the WFS interface is hidden behind an OGC API Features instance, through which the clients will access the 3D buildings using feature ID and BBOX queries.

The Norwegian NMCA, Kartverket, is just about to start the 3D buildings production. An OGC API Processes - compliant on-the-fly process has been developed on the GeoE3 integration platform to provide a temporary solution for the provision of Norwegian 3D buildings. The solution currently only supports feature ID -based queries. When a feature ID comes in to the OGC API Processes instance, the corresponding building is queried from the 2D buildings OGC API Features interface of the GeoE3 platform. From the received feature geometry the Minimum Enclosing Rectangle (MER) of the building is retrieved and the corresponding piece of DTM and DSM are queried. Then DTM and DSM height values inside the area of the building are used to calculate elevation for the building's roof and floor. Finally, the footprint geometry of the building and the derived elevations are used to generate a CityJSON-encoded LOD1 3D model of the building. The process is integrated to the GeoE3 platform so that it can be used as a source for 3D buildings in a similar fashion than other countries' buildings. Input parameters of the OGC API Processes interface include the code of the country from which the building is queried, and the identifier of the building, see Figure 1.

In the case of the Netherlands, the 3D buildings are available for file download readily in the CityJSON format. However, the buildings are packaged into a tiled file structure. Thus, a lot of preprocessing is required to download and integrate the buildings with the GeoE3 platform in a way that facilitates an individual building to be efficiently retrieved. A custom-built database is used on the GeoE3 platform to store the ID of the building, together with the corresponding CityJSON representation of its 3D model. The access interface is currently modelled after the WFS interface's feature ID query.

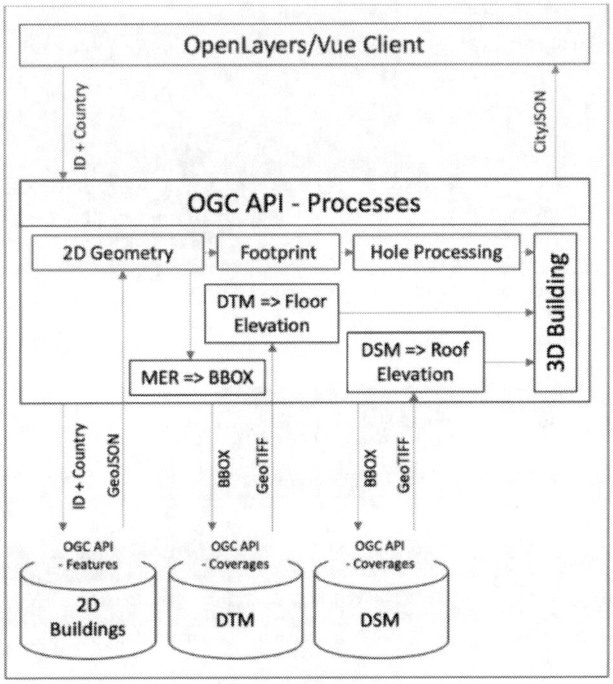

Figure 1. Processing pipeline for the OGC API Processes-based on-the-fly generation of LOD1 category 3D building models on the GeoE3 integration platform.

Spain is a special case among the GeoE3 countries, as it already has a functioning service interface for the 3D buildings available. The service provides access to KML-based representation of the building's 3D model via a feature ID query. So, the interface only supports retrieval of individual buildings. The KML encoding is generated dynamically by the service from a database of floorplans. The resulting 3D model is thus detailed in the internal subdivision of the building, but still represents only LOD1 category 3D modelling. To integrate the Spanish service to the GeoE3 platform, a proxy service was developed for transforming the KML encoding into the CityJSON format. The proxy service publishes to the calling application an interface supporting WFS's feature ID query. Examples of 3D buildings from all the GeoE3 participating countries are presented in Figure 2 (from top to bottom: Finland, Estonia, Norway, The Netherlands, Spain).

III. OGC API Features-based Access

There are several actions going on to define a service interface for accessing wide scale 3D geodata. Many of them

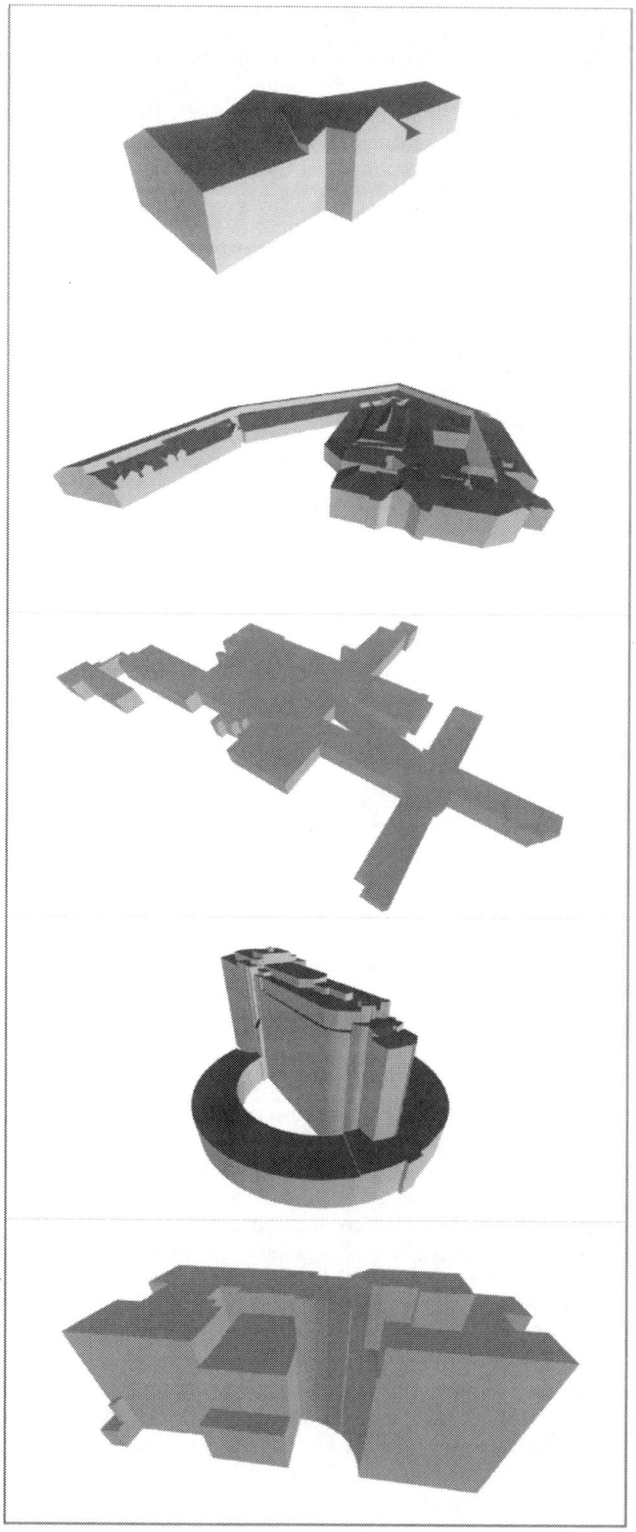

Figure 2. Examples of 3D buildings from all the GeoE3 countries.

focus on efficient streamed delivery of continuous 3D scenes [18]. In GeoE3 the approach to 3D geodata delivery has been kept simple. The idea is to select the area desired for 3D inspection on a 2D basemap, and then request the 3D representation of the whole area in one single query. At the moment the access interface is simply based on the OGC API Features standard, with the format query parameter having value 'cityjson' and the BBOX parameter indicating the area to be requested. The approach is appropriate for conveniently viewing city block level environments. This facilitates general inspection of the whole area with natural 3D controls, and the selection of individual buildings for detailed attribute analysis. At the moment the OGC API Features-based access to 3D buildings is only available for the Finnish and Estonian datasets.

A rich set of attribute information has been added to the 3D building to support the envisaged renewable energy-related use cases. In the case of the Finnish dataset, all attributes available in the corresponding 2D building are first integrated. Then an external service is queried using the building attribute 'externalReference_reference' as the key. Several technical attributes can be added to the building as a result of this query. The climate-related OGC API Coverage services available on the GeoE3 platform are queried next, with the position of the building as the parameter. Three additional parameters, indicating long-period average temperature, windspeed and yearly sunshine hours on the location of the building, can then be added. Finally, the energy certificate register is queried to find out the energy efficiency category of the building. This attribute is added to the building, if available. As a result, the 3D building has a wide set of attributes present, supporting various energy-related analysis scenarios with 3D visualization capabilities (see Figure 3). Similar functionalities will be added to the buildings of other countries once necessary data sources become available.

IV. Web-based 3D Visualization

The 2D mapping functionalities of the GeoE3 platform's user interface rely on use of the OpenLayers library [19]. However, CityJSON and the related software packages have been selected as the solution for 3D visualization needs in the GeoE3 project [20]. All the 3D geodata delivered from the GeoE3 integration platform are currently encoded in CityJSON format. Buildings have varying support on semantic surfaces, depending on the availability of this information in the national datasets. The omission of semantics is partially accounted for by on-the-fly computations in the visualization module (i.e. walls are distinguished from the roof and the floor by their vertical nature). The 3D visualization in the GeoE3 user interface is based on the Vue component 'ThreeJsViewer', part of Ninja [21], developed by the University of Delft [22]. Various helping functionalities have been developed to guide the camera position by mouse movements on the 2D map, potentially considering the elevation information derived from DSM via the GeoE3 platform's OGC API Coverage service. In some cases, the GeoE3 platform also supports 3D viewing of DTM together with the building's 3D model.

Figure 3. City block-level view of the 3D buildings, requested by a BBOX query from the OGC API Features service of the GeoE3 platform (top). Attribute display of the selected building with technical, climate and energy related attributes shown (bottom).

V. Conclusion

The GeoE3 project has been able to develop an advanced content integration platform supporting cross-border access and visualization of 3D buildings. The technical integration across participating countries' 3D data is facilitated by treating individual datasets as collections inside a single OGC API Features service instance. Seamless cross-border queries are supported by applying so-called cross-collection queries of the OGC API Features specification, Part 3. CityJSON is used as the efficient means for transferring and consuming 3D geodata in Web-based user interfaces. Despite the challenges related to varying production mechanisms, 3D building data has been made consistently available from all five participating countries. Various on-the-fly mechanisms have been developed to facilitate the 3D provision of buildings. In particular, an OGC API Processes-compliant process computes LOD1 category building models in real-time from building's 2D footprint and DTM/DSM-derived elevation values.

The work continues to improve the consistency among the countries' datasets and the service interfaces through which they are delivered. For instance, buildings from the Netherlands are to be made available via the OGC API Features interface with support for BBOX queries. All WFS feature ID queries will be replaced by the OGC API Feature interface's Item query. New datasets will be added as they become available – in particular this involves new production areas in Finland. Client application solutions will also be developed for demonstrating the utilization of 3D buildings in further use case scenarios.

Acknowledgment

The GeoE3 project is co-financed by the Connecting Europe Facility (CEF) of the European Union with the grant agreement number INEA/CEF/ICT/A2019/2063390.

The authors wish to acknowledge CSC – IT Center for Science, Finland, for computational resources.

References

[1] F. Biljecki, J. Stoter, H. Ledoux, S. Zlatanova, and A. Çöltekin, "Applications of 3D City Models: State of the Art Review". *ISPRS Int. J. Geo-Inf.* 2015, *4*, pp. 2842-2889. https://doi.org/10.3390/ijgi4042842

[2] OGC, "OGC Advances Standards for the Built Environment and 3D". [Online]. Available from: https://www.ogc.org/domain/built, 2022, [retrieved: May, 2022]

[3] GeoE3, Geospatially Enabled Ecosystem for Europe, GeoE3 Home Page. [Online]. Available from: https://geoe3.eu, 2021, [retrieved: May, 2022]

[4] L. Lehto, J. Kähkönen, J. Reini, T. Aarnio, and R. Tervo, Cross-border and Cross-domain Integration of Content in a European Geospatially Enabled Ecosystem. *GEOProcessing 2021, the Thirteenth International Conference on Advanced Geographic Information Systems, Applications, and Services*, Jul 18-22, 2021, Nice, France, pp. 1-5. ISBN: 978-1-61208-871-6

[5] L. Lehto and J. Kähkönen, OGC API Features HTML-output as a Feature Dashboard, *Abstr. Int. Cartogr. Assoc.*, 3, 176, https://doi.org/10.5194/ica-abs-3-176-2021, 2021, [retrieved: May, 2022]

[6] OGC, OGC API Home Page. [Online]. Available from: https://ogcapi.ogc.org, 2021, [retrieved: May, 2022]

[7] OGC, OGC API – Features Home Page. [Online]. Available from: https://ogcapi.ogc.org/features/, 2022, [retrieved: May, 2022]

[8] OGC, OGC API – Coverages Home Page. [Online]. Available from: https://ogcapi.ogc.org/coverages/, 2022, [retrieved: May, 2022]

[9] OGC, OGC API – Processes Home Page. [Online]. Available from: https://ogcapi.ogc.org/processes/, 2022, [retrieved: May, 2022]

[10] OGC, OGC API – Records Home Page. [Online]. Available from: https://ogcapi.ogc.org/records/, 2022, [retrieved: May, 2022]

[11] T. Kralidis, pygeoapi Home Page. [Online]. Available from: https://pygeoapi.io, 2021, [retrieved: May, 2022]

[12] Django, Django Home Page. [Online]. Available from https://www.djangoproject.com, 2022, [retrieved: May, 2022]

[13] INSPIRE-MIF, INSPIRE Alternative Encoding Model Simplification Rules. [Online]. Available from: https://github.com/INSPIRE-MIF/2017.2/blob/master/model-transformations/TransformationRules.md, 2020, [retrieved: May, 2022]

[14] OGC, "OGC API Features – Part 3: Filtering and the Common Query Language (CQL)". [Online]. Available from https://portal.ogc.org/files/96288, 2020, [retrieved: May, 2022]

[15] H. Ledoux et al. "CityJSON: a compact and easy-to-use encoding of the CityGML data model". *Open geospatial data, softw. stand.* 4, 4 (2019). https://doi.org/10.1186/s40965-019-0064-0

[16] OGC, CityGML Home Page. [Online]. Available from: https://www.ogc.org/standards/citygml, 2012, [retrieved: May, 2022]

[17] Z. Yao et al. 3DCityDB - a 3D geodatabase solution for the management, analysis, and visualization of semantic 3D city models based on CityGML.*Open geospatial data, softw. stand.* 3, 5 (2018). https://doi.org/10.1186/s40965-018-0046-7 [retrieved: May, 2022]

[18] OGC, "Indexed 3D Scene Layers (I3S)". [Online]. Available from: https://www.ogc.org/standards/i3s, 2021, [retrieved: May, 2022]

[19] OpenLayers, OpenLayers Home Page. [Online]. Available from: https://openlayers.org, 2022, [retrieved: May, 2022]

[20] CityJSON, CityJSON Home Page. [Online]. Available from: https://www.cityjson.org, 2021, [retrieved: May, 2022]

[21] S. Vitalis et al. CITYJSON + WEB = NINJA, *ISPRS Annals of Photogrammetry, Remote Sensing and Spatial Information Sciences*, VI-4/W1-2020, pp. 167–173, https://doi.org/10.5194/isprs-annals-VI-4-W1-2020-167-2020, 2020.

[22] TUDelft, TU Delft 3D Geoinformation Home Page. [Online]. Available from: https://3d.bk.tudelft.nl, 2022, [retrieved: May, 2022]

C^2 Spline Quasi-Interpolation To Downscale A Digital Elevation Model

Salah Eddargani
Department of Applied Mathematics
University of Granada
Granada, Spain
email: seddargani@correo.ugr.es

Domingo Barrera, María José Ibáñez
Department of Applied Mathematics
University of Granada
Granada, Spain
emails: {dbarrera,mibanez}@ugr.es

Juan Francisco Reinoso-Gordo
Department of Architectural and
Engineering Graphic Expression,
Universidad de Granada,
Granada, Spain
email: jreinoso@ugr.es

Francisco Javier Ariza-López
Department of Cartographic, Geodesic
and Photogrammetry Engineering,
University of Jaén,
Jaén, Spain
email: fjariza@ujaen.es

***Abstract*— Digital Elevation Models (DEMs) are one of the products delivered by most of the national and regional cartographic agencies of the states. They are discrete representations of a territory and are of undoubted practical importance. Algorithms based on available discrete data make it possible to estimate terrain-related features and perform on DEMs operations of interest. Resampling is one of them (particularly downscaling). Traditional algorithms compute slope and curvature from discrete samples. In this paper a low computational cost spline-based procedure to construct a C^2 continuous surface fitting the data is proposed which will allow to compute slope and curvature. To assess the downscaling quality of the quasi-interpolation-based algorithm, it is proposed two analysis: a) an horizontal displacement computation based on particle image velocimetry and b) a visual analysis for the height error pattern using a threshold parameter**

Keywords-Powell-Sabin triangulation; Bernstein-Bézier representation; data quality; approximating splines; DEM; resampling.

I. INTRODUCTION

Digital Elevation Models (DEMs) are used as the basis for multiple projects concerning Civil Engineering, hydrology, geology and land-use planning. DEM resolution (cell size) depends on the project objective: a geological study will require less resolution than the DEM used to compute the watershed sinking on a small structure crossing a road. Many times there is not a DEM with the appropriate resolution and it is necessary to resample it at smaller or larger scales: an example for the first case occurs when a higher resolution has been used to improve urban flood zones in the absence of denser models [1]; the second occurs when assessing the altimetric accuracy between of a lower resolution DEM versus a higher resolution reference DEM [2]. It is interesting knowing the resampling process quality in the final product: Leon Tan et al. [3] analyze the influence of resampling on the streamflows derived from a DEM. Nevertheless, in most cases, the error introduced by the resampling from a higher resolution to a lower one was left unanalyzed, as indicated in [4]. There are traditional resampling methods but they are not based on continuous functions; they are also weak when computing variables that involve derivatives such as curvature and slope. The quasi-interpolant algorithm we propose solves this problem because the base function is of C^2-continuity.

In Section II we explain the C^2 quasi-interpolant algorithm. The method to assess the algorithm is based on the horizontal displacement computation: a DEM product (DEMpro) is downscaled and assessed versus a DEM reference (DEMref) using the particle image velocimetry technique (Figure 1). A pattern visual analysis is also carried out (Figure 2). Both methods are included in section II. And section III contains the conclusions.

II. METHODOLOGY

The resampling and evaluation algorithm proposal will be made assuming that the pixel size of the DEM_{ref} is XxX m and will be denoted DEM_{refXxX}. The pipeline will be as follow:

1. Upscaling DEM_{refXxX} (Fig. 1): the DEM_{refXxX} is upscaled using the nearest neighbour algorithm to a larger cell size which is called $DEM_{respYxY}$.
2. An approximant surface ($S_{respYxY}$) is fitted to the $DEM_{respYxY}$ by the algorithm Aapx, based on C^2 quasi-interpolation having a good approximation order (Figure 1).
3. Downscaling (Figure 1): Since the definition domain $S_{respYxY}$ is the same as DEM_{refXxX}, $S_{respYxY}$ can be evaluated at the same points that the reference DEM_{refXxX} matrix, from which a homologous

$DEM_{derXxX\_from\_YxY}$ of the same size as DEM_{refXxX} is obtained.

4. The assessment is carried out comparing the DEM_{refXxX} and $DEM_{derXxX\_from\_YxY}$.
5. The A_{apx} planimetric quality is assessed using the [5] method based in particle image velocimetry approach.
6. The altimetric quality is assessed computing the height discrepancy (dh_i) in absolute value and representing in red on a shadow map the cells where dh_i > threshold (Figure 2).

The algorithm A_{apx} constructs, with low computational cost, a spline surface $S_{respYxY}$ that fits the data based on quasi-interpolation in the Bernstein basis. Suppose that the DEM of the terrain under study has an associated decomposition into squares of length h, whose vertices are $v_{i,j}$=(ih,jh), $0 \leq i \leq n$, $0 \leq j \leq m$. Let us define a triangulation by decomposing the square of opposite vertices $v_{i,j}$ and $v_{i+1,j+1}$ into macro-triangles $T_{i,j,1}$=< $v_{i,j}$, $v_{i+1,j}$, $v_{i+1,j+1}$> and $T_{i,j,2}$ =< $v_{i,j}$, $v_{i+1,j+1}$, $v_{i,j+1}$>. The approximating spline will be defined on the subtriangulation obtained by refining $T_{i,j,1}$ and $T_{i,j,2}$ as follows: a Powell-Sabin 6-splits results if the vertices of each triangle are joined with the midpoints of the corresponding opposite sides, intersecting at the barycenter [7]. Each macro-triangle is decomposed into 6 micro-triangles. The restriction of the spline surface to each micro-triangle will be a polynomial of total degree less than or equal to three. Therefore, it can be written as a linear combination of the corresponding ten cubic Bernstein polynomials associated with that micro-triangle. The Bernstein-Bézier coefficients [6] of the constraints must be calculated to get a C^2-continuous surface in such that way that, if the data came from a cubic surface, the approximating spline obtained is itself (exactness on the space of polynomials of degree up most three). Those coefficients will be calculated as linear combinations of DEM values at neighboring points. Their coefficients will provide masks to be computed to ensure C^2continuity and the required exactness.

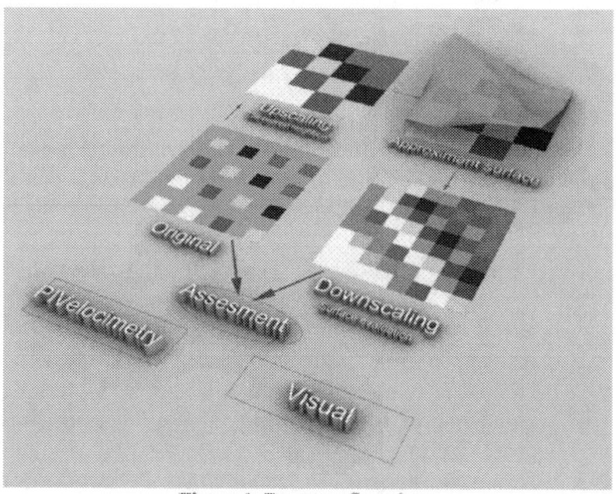

Figure 1: Proccess flowchart.

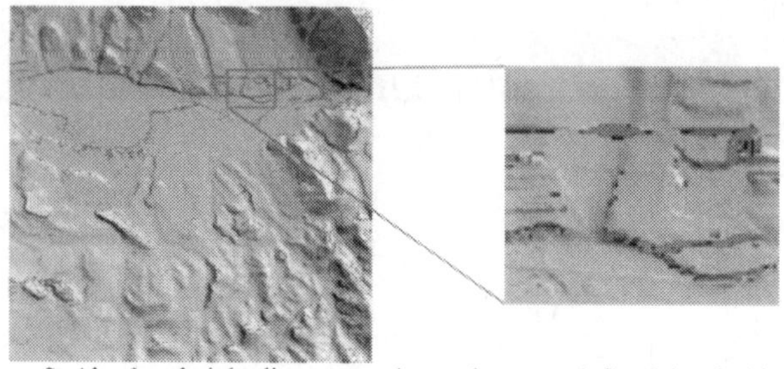

Figure 2: Absolute height discrepancy larger than a predefined threshold.

III. CONCLUSIONS

In this work, it is proposed a new algorithm A_{apx} to get a DEM_{proYxY}, motivated by the necessity to get a downscaled version ($DEM_{derXxX\_from\_YxY}$) The horizontal and vertical accuracy have been assessed comparing it versus a DEM_{refXxX}. It is proposed as well a pipeline to assess the planimetric and altimetric quality. The planimetric quality assessment is innovative because very few cases use the particle image velocimetry approach; It is proposed a graphical threshold approach to inform about the altimetric error which detects pattern where the higher errors occur, e.g., road limits (Figure 2). In future work we will implement the particle image velocimetry algorithm.

ACKNOWLEDGMENT

This work has been financed by the research project "Functional Quality of Digital Elevation Models in Engineering" of the State Agency Research of Spain. PID2019-106195RB-I00/AEI/10.13039/501100011033 (https://coello.ujaen.es/investigacion/web_giic/funquality4dem/).

REFERENCES

[1] J. Shen, F. Tan, "Effects of DEM resolution and resampling technique on building treatment for urban inundation modeling: a case study for the 2016 flooding of the HUST campus in Wuhan," Nat Hazards, vol. 104, pp. 927–957, 2020.

[2] B. Wang, W. Shi, E. Liu, "Robust methods for assessing the accuracy of linear interpolated DEM," Int. J. Appl. Earth Obs. Geoinf., vol. 34, pp. 198–206, 2015.

[3] M. Leong Tan, D. L. Ficklin, B. Dixon, A. L. Ibrahim, Z. Yusop, V. Chaplot, "Impacts of DEM resolution, source, and resampling technique on SWAT-simulated streamflow," Appl. Geogr., vol. 63 pp. 357–368, 2015.

[4] J. L. Mesa-Mingorance, F. J. Ariza-López, "Accuracy Assessment of Digital Elevation Models (DEMs): A Critical Review of Practices of the Past Three Decades," Remote Sens., vol. 12, 2630, 2020.

[5] J. F. Reinoso, C. León, J. Mataix, "Estimating Horizontal Displacement between DEMs by Means of Particle Image Velocimetry Techniques," Remote Sens., vol. 8 (1), 14, 2016.

[6] G. Farin, Curves and Surfaces for CAGD. A practical guide, Fifth Edition, Elsevier, 2002.

[7] M. Powell, M. Sabin, "Piecewise quadratic approximations on triangles," ACM Trans Math Softw, vol. 3, pp. 316–325, 1977

Towards Automatic Inference of Layouts of Traffic Intersections for Smart Cities

Julien A. Vijverberg
Cyclomedia Technology B.V.
Zaltbommel, The Netherlands
email: jvijverberg@cyclomedia.com

Bart J. Beers
Cyclomedia Technology B.V.
Zaltbommel, The Netherlands
email: bbeers@cyclomedia.com

Peter H. N. de With
Dept. of Electrical Engineering
Eindhoven University of Technology
Eindhoven, The Netherlands
email: p.h.n.de.with@tue.nl

***Abstract*—Intersection-topology descriptions can help to improve traffic flow, but currently require significant manual creation effort. This paper describes ongoing work on a combination of algorithms to extract the drive lines across intersections from images and point clouds, captured by a ground-based vehicle. The extraction is based on paint striping and edge-of-road line features, which are clustered in subsequent stages into lane separators for all legs of the intersection. The GEO recall with paint striping is 0.29, and significantly contributes to successfully inferring the junction. However, this score decreases when edge-of-road features are added which is counter-intuitive. We indicate ways to combat this problem and further improve our results.**

Keywords—machine vision; terrain mapping; road transportation.

Figure 1: Colored point cloud data with drive lines (pink) and image recordings (gray circles).

I. Introduction

Analysis of traffic and its infrastructure has gained significant attention in recent years, due to the growth in research on Smart City projects and corresponding themes. For these areas, there has been an continuously increasing focus on a better design of traffic intersections, to improve road safety on those intersections and its users, decrease of travel time and reduction of fuel consumption and related fuel emissions. To this end, new intersection designs have been compared to the current intersection layout using simulations [1]. At the same time, the advent of self-driving cars enforces many manufacturers to increasingly exploit knowledge of the environment to increase the reliability of their algorithms, *i.e.* , sensor-as-a-map [2]. The map data for these applications should include the location of drive lines, to identify signalling that indicates whether changing lanes is acceptable, capture indicated speed limits, etc.

This paper concentrates on generating the drive lines from street-view imagery and point clouds, in order to make accurate descriptions of traffic intersections. We aim at the intended drive lines of the intersection as we are interested in the topology. An example of the input data and drive lines is depicted in Figure 1. The use of drive lines has not been covered yet in most of existing literature, because many publications study modeling of highways, which are mostly straight and often have paint striping (*i.e.* , lane markings) separating all lanes and the normal lanes from the emergency lane (*i.e.* , the shoulder). In contrast, we are generally interested in intersections and their plurality of appearances, up to junctions where paint striping may be absent.

For street-view imagery, some research work [3][4] describes methods to generate intersection layouts, which exploit vehicle detections and their trajectories. For autonomous vehicles, it is considered that such data is available in any case. However, capturing systems specialized for mapping typically have low frame rates and high resolutions, and which do not capture data during non-driving situations to reduce the amount of storage required. The absence of capturing in such situations makes tracking objects and trajectory generation much more difficult and the intersection-layout inference more error-prone.

Other methods detect the paint striping, etc. [5] or the driving lines directly. LaneNet [5] and Gen-LaneNet [6] are proposed networks specialized to detect lanes from images and project them into 3D. These methods do not suggest how to combine the lines across images. Similarly, LaneGraphNet [7] estimates drive lines and directions from the birds-eye view, but does not show yet how to combine the tiles or paint striping. Although Máttyus *et al.* [8] use aerial images and OpenStreetMap as the primary sources for extracting lanes, they propose to construct a Markov Random Field but agree that special considerations are needed for intersections. Zhou *et al.* [9] propose to construct a semantic map and simulate driver behavior using a particle filter to extract drive lines. Initially, this appeared to be overly complex, since it would seem drive lines would follow logical rules based on the geometry of the lane separators, etc.

This paper and its focus on drive lines reports on ongoing research towards an algorithm to generate the intersection layout automatically with intended drive lines. For the algorithm development, data is analyzed from street-view recordings. The proposed research bases the derivation of the drive lines on paint striping and edge-of-road features and investigates their

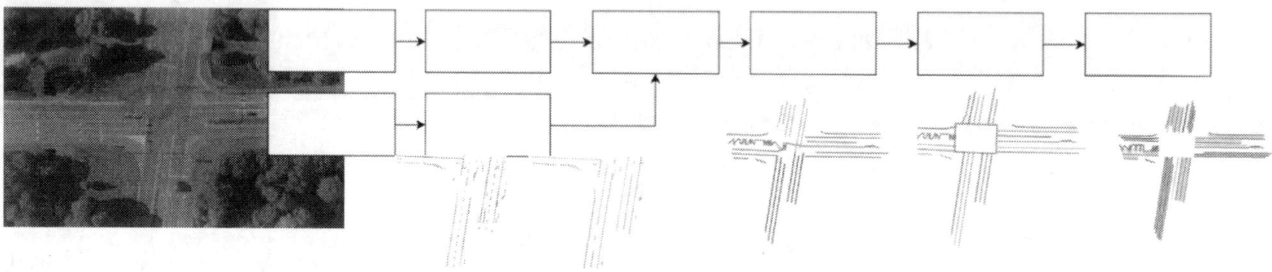

Figure 2: Pipeline flow and intermediate results at several steps in the proposed pipeline.

fusion by manual tuning of the clustering algorithms. This approach should lead to the automated generation of junction topologies, and make those available for traffic guidance and safety control. Thereby, this paper contributes in two ways: (1) an algorithm for automated generation of junction topologies; (2) analysis of the topology detection performance and ways for improving the algorithm in a follow-up development.

This paper is divided as follows. Section II is split into Section II-A, describing the properties of the data and Section II-B proposing a novel drive-line estimation algorithm. The experiments with these methods are described in Section III and visual and numerical results are provided. Section IV presents conclusions.

II. Method

A. Input Data

For the automated generation of junctions, we consider the input system, *i.e.* , the capturing, the image processing and the initial vision processing, as a given.

1) Recordings: The data are captured using a vehicle which is equipped with an omni-directional camera-system using five video cameras, a LiDAR scanner for point clouds and GPS receiver. The capture occurs during the daytime and with relatively good weather. The sensors have been calibrated with respect to each other, such that we can compute the world position for most pixels in the image with high accuracy. The input data comprises vehicle poses, RGB images and point clouds acquired with the LiDAR scanner. An example of a colored point cloud is shown in Figure 1.

2) Front-end Vision: The segmentation is performed by a standard U-Net [10] on the RGB images. Each paint-striping line is projected into the 3D world using the point clouds, *e.g.* , where the horizontal world coordinates are Universal Transverse Mercator coordinates and the third dimension is ellipsoidal height. The result of this step is a list of small 3D line objects. Note that the paint striping intentionally outputs short lines, instead of doing a best guess per image which may yield longer lines and be more consistent. In this way, false positives and true positives are less likely to be merged in a single line and later stages can make decisions per line segment without breaking up these paint-striping lines back into smaller segments. In contrast to paint striping, edge-of-road lines are extracted from polygons with road-surface types [11]. In contrast to [11], we have used an image-segmentation pipeline based on Mask R-CNN [12] with a similar pipeline architecture as the paint-striping pipeline.

B. Proposed Intersection-Inference Algorithm

The proposed intersection-inference algorithm uses the 3D (line) detections of the paint striping and the edge-of-road. The flow of the data is outlined in Figure 2. Note that we did not yet include estimating drive lines across the intersection, since the most common approach using splines [13] is considered of low importance. The following sub-sections will describe the listed algorithmic steps.

1) Per-feature lane-separator clustering: We start with greedy line clustering with the purpose to reduce the amount of lines for the next step. The only features are the distance between the start- and end-points and the angle between the lines.

Highest-Confidence First (HCF) clustering is the main clustering step to both classify all (combined) lines as false or true positive and to determine which lines belong together. This has been applied earlier in multiple object tracking [14]. In this case, given a set of lines $\mathcal{T} = \{T_0, T_1, T_2, ...\}$, we aim at iteratively merging the pair of lines T_i, T_j into the line $T_i \cup T_j$, which reduces an energy function E, specified by

$$\Delta E_{(i,j)} = E\left(T_i, T_j | \mathcal{T}\right) - E\left(T_i \cup T_j | \mathcal{T}\right), \quad (1)$$

where $\Delta E_{(i,j)}$ can be interpreted as a negative log-likelihood and $\Delta E_{(i,j)} < 0$ means the merged line is be more likely than two individual lines. Similar to the tracking application [14], we define separate energy functions for individual features, including the distance, the difference in orientation between two lines, distance between the extrapolated lines, etc.

Another similarity is the energy difference, which can be combined with an energy function, describing the likelihood whether a line is a false positive. Cues to determine the validity of a line include the length, the variance in orientations and the existence of almost parallel lines at approximately the lane width (about 3 meters).

To speed-up the execution of the algorithm, we sub-divide the problem in a spatial hierarchical fashion, cache results $\Delta E_{(i,j)}$, merge batches of lines with similar confidence, and use an R-tree to search for lines.

```
Input: I = {p1, p2, p3, ...}
Result: I'
I'' ← I' ← I;
do
    /* Select point to remove                   */
    p' = arg min_{p∈I'} A(I' − {p}));
    I' ← I'' ;
    I'' ← I' − {p'} ;
    /* Hull decreases significantly?            */
while A(I') < λA(I'');
```

Figure 3: Algorithm to determine the conflict area

2) Combined clustering: During this step, the clustering as described in Section II-B1 is executed on the combined lane separators, albeit with different parameter settings.

3) Approach fitting: At this point, we have a large set of lane separators which are slightly clustered. The goal of this step is to find which approaching roads towards the intersection exist (*approaches*). In addition, we need to determine which lane separators belong to the same approach.

For this fitting, we opt for a RanSaC algorithm [15]. For each iteration, the algorithm randomly selects a (pivot) line. With the selection of all lines on one initial side of the intersection with approximately the same orientation as the pivot line, the approach is fit by projecting all lane separators onto the normal of the pivot line. These lane separators are clustered based on the 1D distance over the line. The clusters that do not lead to sufficiently long lines, are considered false positives for the purpose of the approach fitting. The same method is reused for to find new approaches with the remaining lines until we cannot fit anymore approaches.

To assess the fitting quality between iterations of the algorithm, we compare the length of the lines classified as true and false positives. Moreover, we involve the number of approaches in the comparison, where the a-priori most likely number is 4 and a penalty is given to diverting numbers.

4) Approach-based clustering: Since an estimate of the approach is now available, we can more reliably cluster lane separators, that are distant and could not be merged earlier. This merging is achieved by executing the HCF clustering once again, albeit with different parameter settings.

5) Conflict-area estimation: The conflict area is defined as the area in which the connecting lanes intersect. An initial estimate of the conflict area can be found as the convex hull around the intersection points of the lane separators from different approaches. This initial estimate of the conflict area leads to the creation of outliers. Using the algorithm in Figure 3, this estimate is improved by comparing the convex-hull surface area $A(\mathcal{I})$ of a set of intersection points $\mathcal{I}$ over consecutive iterations.

6) Drive-line extraction: The drive lines are lines fitted between the lane separators, as illustrated in the right-hand part of Figure 2.

TABLE I: QUANTITATIVE COMPARISON TO REPORTED RESULTS OF OTHER METHODS.

	GEO		Topology Accuracy [3]
	recall	precision	
Overall w/o edge-of-road	0.29	0.69	n.a.
Overall with edge-of-road	0.11	0.34	n.a.
He and Balakrishnan [13]	0.821	0.835	n.a.
Zhou *et al.* [9]	n.a.	n.a.	0.8
Geiger *et al.* [3]	n.a.	n.a.	0.92

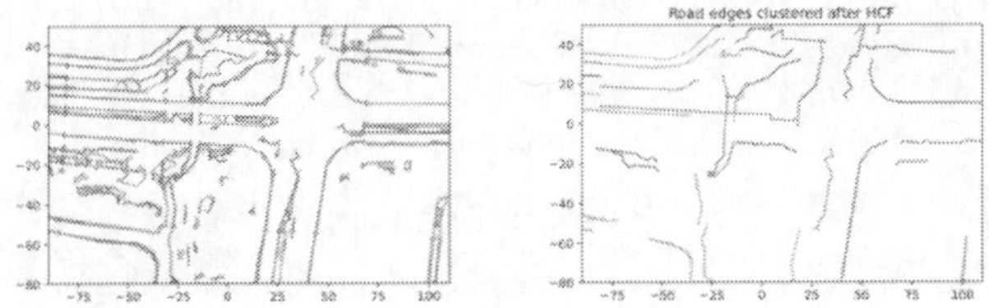

(a) Road edges after greedy (b) Road edges after HCF

Figure 4: Edge-of-road example for the same intersection as depicted in Figure 2, showing high amount of incorrect edges.

III. Experiments

As already mentioned in Section II-B, Figure 2 visualizes some qualitative results for an intersection where paint striping is abundantly present. Figure 4 shows the road edges after greedy clustering (Figure 4a and HCF clustering (Figure 4b). As Figure 4a shows, an important source of noise is caused by the bike lanes surrounding the intersection and passing under the roads for the vehicles. This makes the HCF of the road edges clustering significantly less successful.

Another visual example is shown in Figure 5 in which the sides of the lanes have not been marked by paint striping and the middle of the north-south lane has only been marked for the first 25 meters. The final result is facilitated by false positive paint striping, *e.g.* , the vertical blue line in the top middle lane in Figure 5b. Comparing greedily clustered road edges (Figure 5c to the result of HCF clustering in Figure 5d, it can be observed that many road edges cannot be clustered to significant line features, so that they remain of minor importance and are consequently removed by HCF.

To quantitatively evaluate the proposed algorithm, we use the small dataset with 4 intersections including the intersections depicted in Figure 2 and Figure 5a, but exclude the drive lines across the intersection. These intersections are located in Almelo, the Netherlands and Kingston, Canada. The input data follows the description in Section II-A. The GEO metric [13] is used for comparison, yielding detections scores for the actual drive lines. To compute the GEO metric, we split each line in segments (of say 0.25 m) and match the points of the ground-truth lines and predicted lines. From these matches, one can derive recall and precision. Table I lists the results for all intersections in the above dataset. It is clear that adding edge-of-road yet leads to worse performance compared to using paint striping only, due to its noisy character. Interestingly, He

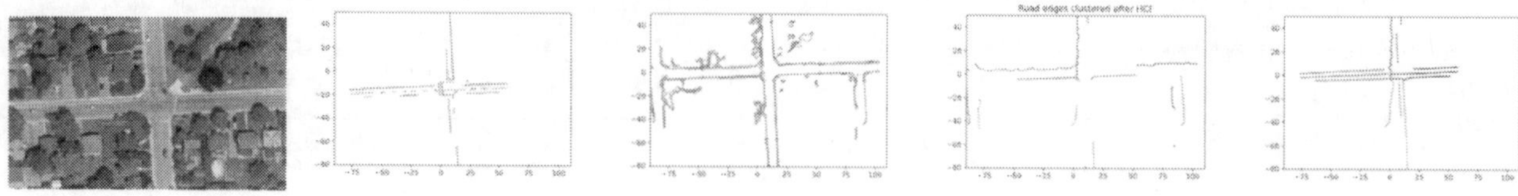

(a) Aerial overview [16] (b) Paint striping (HCF) (c) Edge-of-road (greedy) (d) Edge-of-road (HCF) (e) Approach fit

Figure 5: Intermediate results for paint striping and road edges for an exemplary intersection in Kingston, Ontario, Canada.

and Balakrishnan [13] perform better by directly estimating drive lines from aerial images using the same metrics but a different dataset. Furthermore, Table I also compares our results with other papers albeit with both different datasets and metrics, and hence, only give a global indication.

IV. Conclusion

In this paper, we have presented a combination of algorithms which successfully infers the intersection topology in some cases. Paint striping is evidently an informative cue with which we can successfully infer drive lines. However, our research hypothesis that edge-of-road features would contribute has encountered issues, due to the ability of humans to smoothly integrate a-priori knowledge. This mainly applies to the fine-tuning of the energy function defined in Section II-B1, which is not yet exploited in our algorithmic setting.

We have started our research with a feature exploration on junction topology, to create knowledge on essential features and follow-up directions for finding a good method. After our research, we have found that it is interesting to compare our system, but it is difficult to initially select the preferred method: The algorithm of Zhou *et al.* [9] simulates driver behavior to obtain drive lines, while Zürn *et al.* [7] directly create drive lines without further comparison. Hence, a more detailed comparison between these methods is desired.

Besides this, a significant improvement should be possible by enhancements in the edge-of-road input lines and clustering. The segmentation can become more accurate by improving the annotation quality of the road dataset which has currently noise problems due to projection shifts. Furthermore, the dataset for junctions needs to be significantly enlarged. These last two steps are integrated into our current research.

Acknowledgment

This work has been funded by the Dutch government and supported by ITEA as part of the ITEA3 18036 SMART Mobility Project.

References

[1] P. A. Lopez, M. Behrisch, L. Bieker-Walz, J. Erdmann, Y.-P. Flötteröd, *et al.*, "Microscopic traffic simulation using sumo," *21st Int. Conf. on Intelligent Transportation Systems (ITSC)*, IEEE, pp. 2575–2582, 2018.

[2] J. K. Suhr, J. Jang, D. Min, and H. G. Jung, "Sensor fusion-based low-cost vehicle localization system for complex urban environments," *IEEE Trans. on Intelligent Transportation Systems* vol. 18 no. 5, pp. 1078–1086, 2017, DOI: 10.1109/TITS.2016.2595618.

[3] A. Geiger, M. Lauer, C. Wojek, C. Stiller, and R. Urtasun, "3D traffic scene understanding from movable platforms," *IEEE Trans. on Pattern Analysis and Machine Intelligence* vol. 36 no. 5, pp. 1012–1025, 2013,

[4] A. Meyer, J. Walter, M. Lauer, and C. Stiller, "Anytime lane-level intersection estimation based on trajectories of other traffic participants," *IEEE Intelligent Transportation Systems Conf. (ITSC)*, pp. 3122–3129, 2019.

[5] Z. Wang, W. Ren, and Q. Qiu, *Lanenet: Real-time lane detection networks for autonomous driving*. Available from: https://arxiv.org/pdf/1807.01726.pdf, 2022.05.05.

[6] Y. Guo, G. Chen, P. Zhao, W. Zhang, J. Miao, *et al.*, "Gen-lanenet: A generalized and scalable approach for 3d lane detection," *European Conf. on Computer Vision*, pp. 666–681, 2020.

[7] J. Zürn, J. Vertens, and W. Burgard, "Lane graph estimation for scene understanding in urban driving," *IEEE Robotics and Automation Letters* vol. 6 no. 4, pp. 8615–8622, 2021, DOI: 10.1109/LRA.2021.3111433.

[8] G. Máttyus, S. Wang, S. Fidler, and R. Urtasun, "HD maps: Fine-grained road segmentation by parsing ground and aerial images," *Proceedings of the IEEE Conference on Computer Vision and Pattern Recognition*, pp. 3611–3619, 2016.

[9] Y. Zhou, Y. Takeda, M. Tomizuka, and W. Zhan, "Automatic construction of lane-level hd maps for urban scenes," *IEEE/RSJ Int. Conf. on Intelligent Robots and Systems (IROS)*, IEEE, pp. 6649–6656, 2021.

[10] O. Ronneberger, P. Fischer, and T. Brox, "U-net: Convolutional networks for biomedical image segmentation," *Int. Conf. on Medical Image Computing and Computer-Assisted Intervention*, Springer, pp. 234–241, 2015.

[11] Q. Bai, R. C. Lindenbergh, J. A. Vijverberg, and J. A. P. Guelen, "Road type classification of MLS point clouds using deep learning," *The Int. Arch. of Photogrammetry, Remote Sensing and Spatial Information Sciences* vol. 43, pp. 115–122, 2021,

[12] K. He, G. Gkioxari, P. Dollar, and R. Girshick, "Mask R-CNN," *IEEE Int. Conf. on Computer Vision (ICCV)*, pp. 2980–2988, 2017.

[13] S. He and H. Balakrishnan, "Lane-level street map extraction from aerial imagery," *IEEE/CVF Winter Conf. on Applications of Computer Vision (WACV)*, pp. 1496–1505, 2022. DOI: 10.1109/WACV51458.2022.00156.

[14] J. A. Vijverberg, C. J. Koeleman, and P. H. N. With, de, "Towards real-time and low-latency video object tracking by linking tracklets of incomplete detections," *Proc. of the 10th IEEE Int. Conf. on Advanced Video and Signal Based Surveillance*, pp. 300–305, 2013. DOI: 10.1109/AVSS.2013.6636656.

[15] M. A. Fischler and R. C. Bolles, "Random sample consensus: A paradigm for model fitting with applications to image analysis and automated cartography," *Comm. of the ACM* vol. 24 no. 6, pp. 381–395, 1981,

[16] Google, *Google maps*. Available from: https://www.google.com/maps, 2022.05.05.

Decentralized Swarms Visibility Algorithms in 3D Urban Environments

Oren Gal and Yerach Doytsher
Mapping and Geo-information Engineering
Technion - Israel Institute of Technology
Haifa, Israel
e-mail: orengal@alumni.technion.ac.il

Abstract— **In this paper, we present a unique and efficient visible trajectory planning for aerial swarm using decentralized algorithms in a 3D urban environment. By using SwarmLab environment, we are comparing two decentralized algorithms from the state of the art for the navigation of aerial swarms, Olfati-Saber's and Vasarhelyi's. The first step in our concept is to extract basic geometric shapes. We focus on three basic geometric shapes from point clouds in urban scenes that can appear: planes, cylinders and spheres, extracting these geometric shapes using efficient Random Sample Consensus (RANSAC) algorithms with a high success rate of detection. The second step is a decentralized swarm algorithm for motion planning, demonstrated on drones in urban environment. Our planner includes dynamic and kinematic platform's limitation, generating visible trajectories based on our first step mentioned earlier. We demonstrate our visibility and trajectory planning method in simulations, showing trajectory planning in 3D urban environments for drone's swarm with decentralized algorithms demonstrating performance analysis ,such as order, safety, connectivity and union.**

Keywords-Swarm; Visibility; 3D; Urban environment; Decentralized algorithms.

I. INTRODUCTION

In this paper, we study a fast and efficient visible trajectory planning for drone swarms in a 3D urban environment, based on local point clouds data. Recently, urban scene modeling has become more and more precise, using Terrestrial/ground-based LiDAR on unmanned vehicles to generate point clouds data for modeling roads, signs, lamp posts, buildings, trees and cars. Visibility analysis in complex urban scenes is commonly treated as an approximated feature due to computational complexity.

Our trajectory planning method is based on a two-step visibility analysis in 3D urban environments using predicted visibility from point clouds data. The first step in our unique concept is to extract basic geometric shapes. We focus on three basic geometric shapes from point clouds in urban scenes: planes, cylinders and spheres, extracting these geometric shapes using efficient RANSAC algorithms with a high success rate of detection. The second step include decentralized swarm algorithm for motion planning, demonstrated on drones in urban environment. Our planner includes dynamic and kinematic platform's limitation, generating visible trajectories based on our first step mentioned above. We demonstrate our visibility and trajectory planning method in simulations, showing trajectory planning in 3D urban environments for drone's swarm with decentralized algorithms including performance analysis, such as order, safety, connectivity and union.

Visibility analysis based on this approximated scene prediction is done efficiently, based on our analytic solutions for visibility boundaries. With this capability, we present a local on-line planner generating visible trajectories, exploring the most visible and safe node in the next time step, using our predicted visibility analysis.

For the first time, we propose a solution for decentralized swarm algorithm which takes visibility into account, avoiding obstacles using Velocity Obstacle (VO) search and planning method.

The rest of this paper is organized as follows: In Section II we introduce visibility analysis from point clouds data. In Section III, we introduce fast visibility analysis, and in Section VI we present decentralized swarm algorithm.

II. VISIBILITY ANALYSIS FROM POINT CLOUDS DATA

As mentioned, visibility analysis in complex urban scenes is commonly treated as an approximated feature due to its computational complexity. Recently, urban scene modeling has become more and more exact, using Terrestrial/ground-based LiDAR generating dense point clouds data for modeling roads, signs, lamp posts, buildings, trees and cars. Automatic algorithms detecting basic shapes and their extraction have been studied extensively, and are still a very active research field [2].

In this part, we present a unique concept for predicted and approximated visibility analysis in the next attainable vehicle's state at a one-time step ahead in time, based on local point clouds data which is a partial data set.

We focus on three basic geometric shapes in urban scenes: planes, cylinders and spheres, which are very common and can be used for the majority of urban entities in modeling scenarios. Based on point clouds data generated from the current vehicle's position in state k-1, we extract these geometric shapes using efficient RANSAC algorithms [3] with high success rate detection tested in real point cloud data.

After extraction of these basic geometric shapes from local point clouds data, our unified concept, and our main contribution, focus on the ability to predict and approximate urban scene modeling at the next view point V_k, i.e., at the attainable location of the vehicle in the next time step. Scene prediction is based on the geometric entities and the KF), which is commonly used in dynamic systems for tracking target systems [4][5]. We formulate the geometric shapes as states vectors in a dynamic system and predict the scene structure in the next time step, k.

Based on the predicted scene in the next time step, visibility analysis is carried out from the next view point model [6], which is, of course, an approximated one. As the vehicle reaches the next viewpoint V_k, point clouds data are measured and scene modeling and states vectors are updated, which is an essential for the global swarm visible trajectory planning based on state-of-the-art decentralized algorithms.

A. Shapes Extraction

1) Geometric Shapes:

The urban scene is a very complex one in the matter of modeling applications using LiDAR, and the generated point clouds are very dense. Despite these inherent complications, feature extraction can be made very efficient by using basic geometric shapes. We define three kinds of geometric shapes: planes, cylinders and spheres, with a minimal number of parameters for efficient time computation.

Plane: center point (x,y,z) and unit direction vector from center point.

Cylinder: center point (x,y,z), radius and unit direction vector of the cylinder axis. Cylinder height dimension will be consider later on as part of the simulation.

Sphere: center point (x,y,z), radius and unit direction vector from center point.

2) RANSAC:

The RANSAC [7] is a well-known paradigm, extracting shapes from point clouds using a minimal set of a shape's primitives generated by random drawing in a point clouds set. A minimal set is defined as the smallest number of points required to uniquely define a given type of geometric primitive.

For each of the geometric shapes, points are tested to approximate the primitive of the shape (also known as "score of the shape"). At the end of this iterative process, extracted shapes are generated from the current point clouds data.

Based on the RANSAC concept, the geometric shapes detailed above can be extracted from a given point clouds data set. In order to improve the extraction process and reduce the number of points validating shape detection, we compute the approximated surface normal for each point and test the relevant shapes.

Given a point-clouds $P=\{p_1..p_N\}$ with associated normals $\{n_1..n_N\}$, the output of the RANSAC algorithm is a set of primitive shapes $\{\delta_1..\delta_N\}$ and a set of remaining points $R=P\setminus\{p_{\delta_1}..p_{\delta_N}\}$.

B. Predicted Scene – Kalman Filter

In this part, we present the global KF approach for our discrete dynamic system at the estimated state, k, based on the defined geometric shapes formulation defined in the previous sub-section.

Generally, the Kalman Filter can be described as a filter that consists of three major stages: Predict, Measure, and Update the state vector. The state vector contains different state parameters, and provides an optimal solution for the whole dynamic system [5]. We model our system as a linear one with discrete dynamic model, as described in (1):

$$x_k = F_{k,k-1}x_{k-1} \tag{1}$$

where x is the state vector, F is the transition matrix and k is the state.

The state parameters for all of the geometric shapes are defined with shape center $\vec{s}$, and unit direction vector $\vec{d}$, of the geometric shape, from the current time step and viewpoint to the predicted one.

In each of the current states k, geometric shape center $\overline{s_k}$, is estimated based on the previous update of shape center location $\vec{s}_{k-1}$, and the previous updated unit direction vector $\vec{d}_{k-1}$, multiplied by small arbitrary scalar factor c, described in (2):

$$\vec{s}_k = \vec{s}_{k-1} + c\vec{d}_{k-1} \tag{2}$$

Direction vector $\vec{d}_k$ can be efficiently estimated by extracting the rotation matrix T, between the last two states k, k-1. In case of an inertial system fixed on the vehicle, a rotation matrix can be simply found from the last two states of the vehicle translations in (3):

$$\vec{d}_k = T\vec{d}_{k-1} \tag{3}$$

The 3D rotation matrix T tracks the continuous extracted plans and surfaces to the next viewpoint V_k, making it possible to predict a scene model where one or more of the geometric shapes are cut from current point clouds data in state k-1. The discrete dynamic system can be written as formulated in (4):

$$\begin{bmatrix} \vec{s}_{x_k} \\ \vec{s}_{y_k} \\ \vec{s}_{z_k} \\ \vec{d}_{x_k} \\ \vec{d}_{y_k} \\ \vec{d}_{z_k} \end{bmatrix} = \begin{bmatrix} 1 & 0 & 0 & c & 0 & 0 \\ 0 & 1 & 0 & 0 & c & 0 \\ 0 & 0 & 1 & 0 & 0 & c \\ 0 & 0 & 0 & T_{11} & T_{12} & T_{13} \\ 0 & 0 & 0 & T_{21} & T_{22} & T_{23} \\ 0 & 0 & 0 & T_{31} & T_{32} & T_{33} \end{bmatrix} \begin{bmatrix} \vec{s}_{x_{k-1}} \\ \vec{s}_{y_{k-1}} \\ \vec{s}_{z_{k-1}} \\ \vec{d}_{x_{k-1}} \\ \vec{d}_{y_{k-1}} \\ \vec{d}_{z_{k-1}} \end{bmatrix} \tag{4}$$

where the state vector x is 6×1 vector, and the transition squared matrix is $F_{k,k-1}$. The dynamic system can be extended to additional state variables representing someof the geometric shape parameters such as radius, length etc. We define the dynamic system as the basic one for generic shapes that can be simply modeled with center and direction vector. Sphere radius and cylinder Z boundaries are defined in an additional data structure of the scene entities.

III. Fast and Approximated Visibility Analysis

In this section, we present an analytic analysis of the visibility boundaries of planes, cylinders and spheres for the predicted scene presented in the previous sub-section, which leads to an approximated visibility. For the plane surface, fast and efficient visibility analysis was already presented in [6]. In this part, we extend the previous visibility analysis concept [6] and include cylinders as continuous curves parameterization $C_{clnd}(x, y, z)$.

Cylinder parameterization can be described in (5):

$$C_{Clnd}(x,y,z) = \begin{pmatrix} r\sin(\theta) \\ r\cos(\theta) \\ c \end{pmatrix}_{r=const}, \quad \begin{matrix} 0 \le \theta \le 2\pi \\ c = c+1 \\ 0 \le c \le h_{peds\_max} \end{matrix} \qquad (5)$$

We define the visibility problem in a 3D environment for more complex objects as:

$$C'(x,y)_{z_{const}} \times (C(x,y)_{z_{const}} - V(x_0, y_0, z_0)) = 0 \qquad (6)$$

where 3D model parameterization is $C(x,y)_{z=const}$, and the viewpoint is given as $V(x_0, y_0, z_0)$. Extending the 3D cubic parameterization, we also consider the case of the cylinder. Integrating (5) to (6) yields:

$$\begin{pmatrix} r\cos\theta \\ -r\sin\theta \\ 0 \end{pmatrix} \times \begin{pmatrix} r\sin\theta - V_x \\ r\cos\theta - V_y \\ c - V_z \end{pmatrix} = 0 \qquad (7)$$

$$\theta = \arctan\left(-\frac{-r - \frac{\left(-vy\,r + \sqrt{vx^4 - vx^2 r^2 + vy^2 vx^2}\right) vy}{vx^2 + vy^2}}{vx}, \right.$$
$$\left. \frac{-vy\,r + \sqrt{vx^4 - vx^2 r^2 + vy^2 vx^2}}{vx^2 + vy^2} \right) \qquad (8)$$

As can be noted, these equations are not related to Z axis, and the visibility boundary points are the same for each x-y cylinder profile, as seen in (7), (8).

The visibility statement leads to a complex equation, which does not appear to be a simple computational task. This equation can be efficiently solved by finding where the equation changes its sign and crosses the zero value; we used analytic solution to speed up computation time and to avoid numeric approximations. We generate two values of θ generating two silhouette points in a very short time computation. Based on an analytic solution to the cylinder case, a fast and exact analytic solution can be found for the visibility problem from a viewpoint.

We define the solution presented in (8) as x-y-z coordinates values for the cylinder case as Cylinder Boundary Points (CBP). CBP, defined in (9), are the set of visible silhouette points for a 3D cylinder, as presented in Figure 1:

$$CBP_{i=1..N_{PBP\_bound}=2}(x_0, y_0, z_0) = \begin{bmatrix} x_1, y_1, z_1 \\ x_{N_{PBP\_bound}}, y_{N_{PBP\_bound}}, z_{N_{PBP\_bound}} \end{bmatrix} \qquad (9)$$

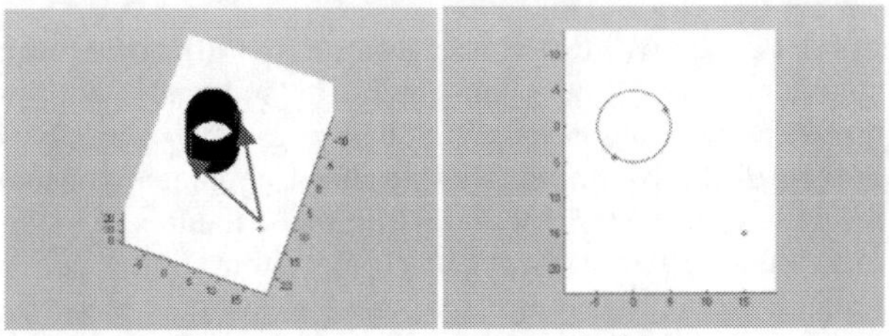

(a) (b)

Figure 1. Cylinder Boundary Points (CBP) using Analytic Solution marked as blue points, Viewpoint Marked in Red: (a) 3D View (Visible Boundaries Marked with Red Arrows); (b) Topside View.

In the same way, sphere parameterization can be described as formulated in (10):

$$C_{Sphere}(x,y,z) = \begin{pmatrix} r\sin\phi\cos\theta \\ r\sin\phi\sin\theta \\ r\cos\phi \end{pmatrix}_{r=const}$$
$$0 \le \phi < \pi$$
$$0 \le \theta < 2\pi \qquad (10)$$

We define the visibility problem in a 3D environment for this object in (11):

$$C'(x,y,z) \times (C(x,y,z) - V(x_0, y_0, z_0)) = 0 \qquad (11)$$

where the 3D model parameterization is $C(x, y, z)$, and the viewpoint is given as $V(x_0, y_0, z_0)$. Integrating (10) to (11) yields:

$$\theta = \arctan\left(\frac{r\sin(\phi)}{v\_y} - \frac{1}{v\_y\,(v\_y^2 + v\_x^2)} \left(v\_x \left(r\sin(\phi)\, v\_x - \sqrt{-v\_y^2 r^2 \sin(\phi)^2 + v\_y^4 + v\_x^2 v\_y^2} \right) \right), \right.$$
$$\left. \frac{r\sin(\phi)\, v\_x - \sqrt{-v\_y^2 r^2 \sin(\phi)^2 + v\_y^4 + v\_x^2 v\_y^2}}{v\_y^2 + v\_x^2} \right) \qquad (12)$$

Where r is defined from sphere parameter, and $V(x_0, y_0, z_0)$ are changes from visibility point along Z axis, as described in (12). The visibility boundary points for a sphere, together with the analytic solutions for planes and cylinders, allow us to compute fast and efficient visibility in a predicted scene from local point cloud data, which are updated in the next state.

This extended visibility analysis concept, integrated with a well-known predicted filter and extraction method, can be implemented in real time applications with point clouds data.

IV. DECENTRALIZED SWARMS TRAJECTORY PLANNING

In this part, we focus on decentralized swarm algorithm with visibility analysis in urban environment as cost function for our trajectory.

For our simulation, we used SwarmLab [10], drone swarm simulator that was implemented and adapted two representative algorithms belonging to the category of decentralized swarming. Decentralized approach can make the system easily scalable and robust to the failures of a single individual. SwarmLab includes algorithm developed by Olfati-Saber [12], who proposes a formal theoretical framework for the design and analysis of swarm algorithms based on potential fields and graph theory.

The second algorithm that was implemented is an adaptation of the recent Vasarhelyi's algorithm [13], defined by the following rules: repulsion to avoid inter-agent collisions, velocity alignment to steer the agents to an average direction, and self-propulsion to match a preferred speed value. In addition, the algorithm includes friction forces that reduce oscillations and ease the implementation on real robots.

In decentralized approaches, one agent's movement is only influenced by local information coming from its neighbors. Neighbors' selection can be operated according to different metrics.

In our work, we adopted these algorithms with visibility analysis as part of swarm's trajectory by leading the swarm to the most visible areas in the scene by the swarm, as presented in the previous section.

Unlike the original SwarmLab simulation where obstacle avoidance is based on simulating the obstacles as virtual agents, we used the Velocity Obstacles [8] local obstacles avoidance method.

This obstacle avoidance method allows us to deal better with swarm behavior and can be more precise and gentler, avoiding obstacles in dense environments.

A. The Planner

As mentioned above, our planner is based on an iterative local planning method, where the swarm is moving to the most visible area. By using RANSAC algorithm, point clouds data are extracted each time step into three possible objects: plane, cylinder and sphere. The scene is formulated as a dynamic system using KF analysis for objects' prediction. The objects are approximated for the next time step, and each safe attainable state that can be explored is set as candidate viewpoint. The cost for each agent is set as total visible surfaces, based on the analytic visibility boundary, where the optimal and safe node is explored for the next time step.

At each time step, the planner computes the next Attainable Velocities (AV). The safe nodes not colliding with objects such as cubes, cylinders and spheres, i.e., nodes outside VO, are explored. Where all nodes are inside VO, a unified analytic solution for time horizon is presented, generating an escape option for these radical cases without affecting visibility analysis. The planner computes the cost for these safe nodes based on predicted visibility and chooses the node with the optimal cost for the next time step. We repeat this procedure while generating the most visible trajectory.

1) Visibility Analysis as Swarm Cost Function

Our swarm direction and movement is guided by minimum invisible parts from viewpoint V to the approximated 3D urban environment model in the next time step, $t + \Delta t$, set by KF after extracting objects from point clouds data using the RANSAC algorithm. The cost function next state is a combination of IRV and ISV, with different weights as functions of the required task.

The cost function presented in (13) is computed for each agent from his current state, considering the agent's future location at the next time step $(x_1(t + \Delta t), x_2(t + \Delta t))$ as viewpoint:

$$w(x(t + \Delta t)) = \alpha \cdot ISV(x(t + \Delta t)) + \beta \cdot IRV(x(t + \Delta t)) \quad (13)$$

where $\propto, \beta$ are coefficients affecting the trajectory's character, as shown in (14). The cost function $w(x(t + \Delta t)$ produces the total sum of invisible parts from the viewpoint to the 3D urban environment.

We divide point invisibility value into Invisible Surfaces Value (ISV) and Invisible Roofs Value (IRV). This classification allows us to plan delicate and accurate trajectories upon demand. We define ISV and IRS as the total sum of the invisible roofs and surfaces (respectively). Invisible Surfaces Value (ISV) of a viewpoint is defined as the total sum of the invisible surfaces of all the objects in a 3D environment, as described in (14):

$$ISV(x_0, y_0, z_0) = \sum_{i=1}^{N_{obj}} IS_{VP_i^{j=1..N_{bound}-1}}^{VP_i^{j=1..N_{bound}-1}} \quad (14)$$

In the same way, we define Invisible Roofs Value (IRV) as the total sum of all the invisible roofs' surfaces, as described in (15):

$$IRV(x_0, y_0, z_0) = \sum_{i=1}^{N_{obj}} IS_{VP_i^{j=N_{bound}}}^{VP_i^{j=N_{bound}}} \quad (15)$$

Extended analysis of the analytic solution for visibility analysis for known 3D urban environments can be found in [6].

V. SIMULATIONS

We implemented the presented algorithm and tested some urban environments on a Intel(R) Core (TM) i5-10210U CPU 2.11 GHz with Matlab. We computed the visible trajectories using our planner, simulating cloud points using Matlab functions.

On the first part, we tested our visibility analysis integrated into decentralized drones swarm algorithms as described above. The workflow of a swarm simulation is summarized in Figure 2, were typical scenario of cylinder objects in our environment can be seen in Figure 3.

In the first case, we tested our algorithm with a relatively large number of agents. As can be seen in Figure 4, thirty agents in the swarm moving forward in straight line, presenting swarm trajectory, distance between the agents during mission, speed and accelerations during movement. The swarm navigates based on modified Olfati-Saber's algorithm where obstacle avoidance implemented by Velocity Obstacles, where agents are simulated by point mass model. Swarm cost function is based on visibility analysis computed each time step as mentioned in the previous section.

In the second case, we tested our algorithm with ten agents in the swarm, so each agent simulated with quadrotor dynamic model. As can be seen in Figure 5, ten agents in the swarm moving forward in straight line with C. Vasarhelyi's etc. algorithm, but visibility analysis and dynamic constraints swift the swarm to the right side. presenting swarm trajectory, distance between the agents. Figure 5 also includes speed and accelerations during movement, performances analysis and total distance to the obstacles during mission.

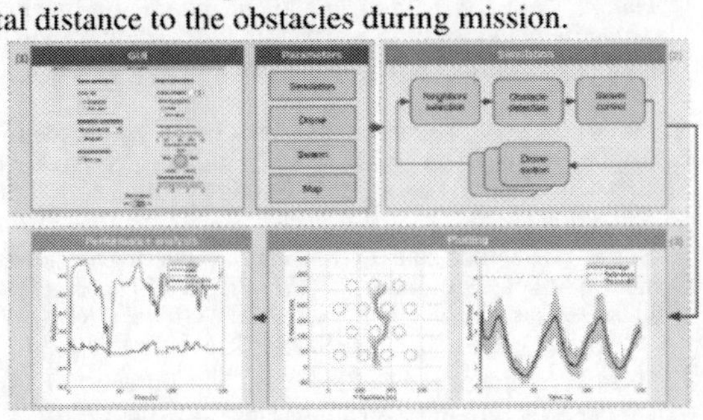

Figure 2. SwarmLab simulation workflow. From the top left, in clockwise order: (1) in the GUI, the user sets the parameters related to the simulation, drone typology, swarm algorithm and environment. (2) the main simulation loop computes control commands for the drones, based on the information of the map and neighboring drones; (3) both real-time and post-simulation (Source [10]).

Order metric captures the correlation of the agents movements and gives an indication about how ordered the flock. Safety metrics, measure the risk of collisions among the swarm agents or between agents and obstacles.

Union metric counts the number of independent subgroups that originates during the simulation.

Connectivity metric defined from the algebraic connectivity of the sensing graph that underlines the considered swarm configuration. Detailed mathematical definitions of these performances' parameters can be found in [11].

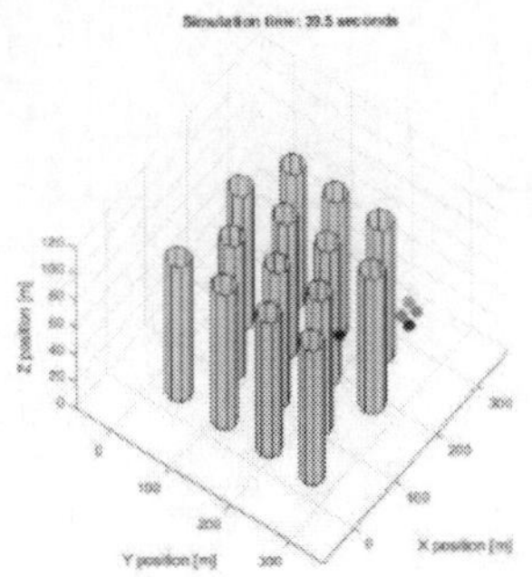

Figure 3. Typical Scenario of Environmmet Obstacles Simulation

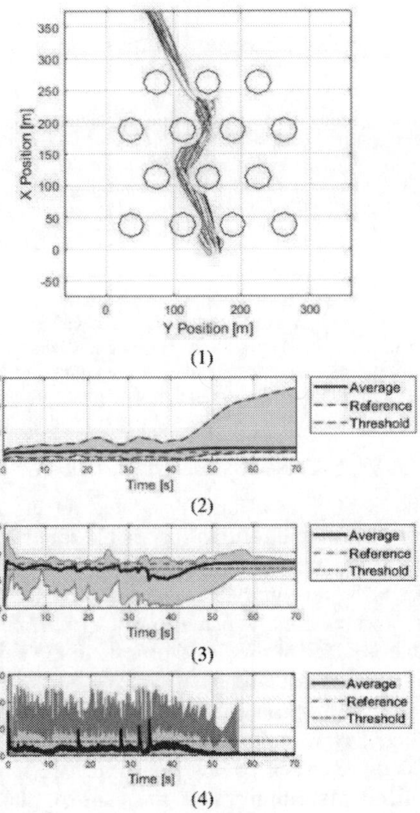

Figure 4. Thirty agents swarm moving forward in straight line using Olfati-Saber's algorithm with visibility analsysis; (1) presenting swarm trajectory; (2) distance between the agents during mission; (3) speed and (4) accelerations during movement.

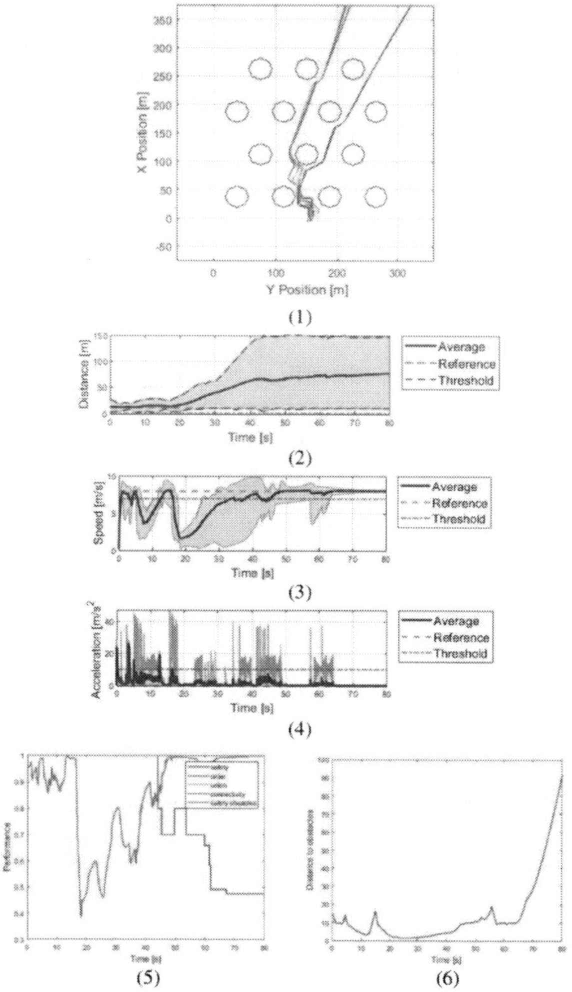

Figure 5. Ten agents swarm moving forward in straight line using Vasarhelyi's algorithm with visibility analsysis, with quadrotor synamic model for agent; (1) presenting swarm trajectory; (2) distance between the agents during mission; (3) speed and (4) accelerations during movement; (5) performances analysis; (6) total distance to the obstacles during mission.

VI. CONCLUSION AND FUTURE WORK

In this research, we have presented an efficient swarm trajectory planning algorithm for visible trajectories in a 3D urban environment.

We extend our analytic visibility analysis method to cylinders and spheres, which allows us to efficiently set the visibility boundary of predicted objects in the next time step. Based on these fast computation capabilities, the on-line planner can approximate the most visible state as part of a decentralized swarm algorithm.

By using SwarmLab environment, we compare two decentralized algorithms from the state of the art for the navigation of aerial swarms, Olfati-Saber's and Vasarhelyi's.

Our planner includes dynamic and kinematic platform's limitation, generating visible trajectories based on our first step mentioned earlier.

We demonstrate our visibility and trajectory planning method in simulations, showing trajectory planning in 3D urban environments for drone's swarm with decentralized algorithms with performance analysis, such as order, safety, connectivity and union.

Further research will focus on advanced geometric shapes, which will allow precise urban environment modeling, facing real-time implementation with on-line data processing from sensors.

REFERENCES

[1] G.Pandey, J.R. McBride, R.M. Eustice, "Ford campus vision and lidar data set." International Journal of Robotics Research, 30(13), pp. 1543-1552, November 2011.

[2] G. Vosselman, B. Gorte, G. Sithole, T. Rabbani. "Recognizing structure in laser scanner point clouds.", The International Archives of the Photogrammetry Remote Sensing and Spatial Information Sciences (IAPRS), 2004, vol. 36, pp. 33–38.

[3] R. Schnabel, R. Wahl, R. Klein, "Efficient RANSAC for Point-Cloud Shape Detection," Computer Graphics Forum, 2007, vol. 26, no.2, pp. 214-226.

[4] R. Kalman. "A new approach to linear filtering and prediction problems.", Transactions of the ASME-Journal of Basic Engineering, 1960, vol. 82, no. 1, pp:35–45.

[5] J. Lee, M. Kim, I. Kweon. "A kalman filter based visual tracking algorithm for an object moving," In IEEE/RSJ Intelligent Robots and Systems, 1995, pp. 342–347.

[6] O. Gal, and Y. Doytsher, "Fast Visibility Analysis in 3D Procedural Modeling Environments," in Proc. of the, 3rd International Conference on Computing for Geospatial Research and Applications, Washington DC, USA, 2012.

[7] H. Boulaassal, T. Landes, P. Grussenmeyer, F. Tarsha- Kurdi. "Automatic segmentation of building facades using terrestrial laser data", The International Archives of the Photogrammetry Remote Sensing and Spatial Information Sciences (IAPRS), 2007, vol. 36, no. 3.

[8] O. Gal, Z. Shiller, E. Rimon, "Efficient and safe on-line motion planning in dynamic environment," in Proceedings of the IEEE International Conference on Robotics and Automation, 2009, pp. 88–93.

[9] Velodyne 2007: Velodyne HDL-64E: A high definition LIDAR sensor for 3D applications. Available at: http://www.velodyne.com/lidar/products/white paper. [Accessed 1/23/2017].

[10] E. Soria, F. Schiano and D. Floreano, "SwarmLab: a Matlab Drone Swarm Simulator," *2020 IEEE/RSJ International Conference on Intelligent Robots and Systems (IROS)*, 2020, pp. 8005-8011, doi: 10.1109/IROS45743.2020.9340854.

[11] E. Soria, F. Schiano, and D. Floreano, "The influence of limited visual sensing on the Reynolds flocking algorithm," IEEE Third International Conference on Robotic Computing (IRC), 2019.

[12] R. Olfati-Saber, "Flocking for Multi-Agent Dynamic Systems: Algo-rithms and Theory," IEEE Transactions on Automatic Control, vol. 51, no. 3, pp. 401–420, 2006.

[13] G. V´as´arhelyi, C. Vir´agh, G. Somorjai, T. Nepusz, A. E. Eiben, and T. Vicsek, "Optimized flocking of autonomous drones in confined environments," Science Robotics, vol. 3, no. 20, 2018.

Generating a Pseudo Resident Registration Register by Using Open Data

Dominik Visca, Max Hoppe, Pascal Neis
Department of Technology
Mainz University of Applied Sciences
Mainz, Germany
dominik.visca@hs-mainz.de, max.hoppe@hs-mainz.de, pascal.neis@hs-mainz.de

Abstract— **The paper offers a possibility for a (partial) reconstruction of a resident registration dataset combining and linking open (geo-) data with respect to data protection regulations. Here, a method is proposed that simulates a building-level georeferenced resident registration register as a pseudo-derivative. Understood as a potential supplement for research projects, the increasing relevance and discussion of datasets for analyzing individual dynamics on a small scale is taken up with easy-to-generate datasets without facing data protection issues. Complete reconstruction and disaggregation are not possible due to anonymization techniques and data available, but further improvements are conceivable with the latest census and additional open data. This procedure thus reflects trends of Urban-Geo to expand and better visualize small-scale demographic analyses, and also highlights the potential value of opening up register data to science.**

Keywords-Resident registration register; disaggregation; census data; open data; register-based research

I. INTRODUCTION

Public sector data (federal, state, local) are essential sources for small-scale analyses. However, data from statistical offices are usually aggregated at the municipal level or higher. These numbers do not provide an adequate framework for answering many critical questions in science and society, as it is impossible to conclude individual dynamics from aggregated data [1]. Therefore, applicability is limited. Especially in Social Sciences, the need for combined datasets for modeling research questions on a preferably small-scale level, e.g. for the investigation of local inequalities, of lifestyles or the residential location choice of certain groups, is in high demand [2]. As a consequence, also under the impression of the Corona pandemic, the discussion about opening up register data for research is very present.

A large number of private companies offer micro geographic data variables that are used in the commercial sector, e.g. to analyze customer potential, for target-group-specific advertising campaigns, or for location and branch network planning. Some of these variables are available at an address level, but at least at the level of settlement units or urban neighborhoods. They contain information on household sizes and household type, but also derived indicators on social status, income classes or purchasing power [3]. However, the underlying methods used by private companies to produce fee-based micro geographic data are generally not revealed. For scientific work, this means a limitation in terms of in-depth quality control. Therefore, transparent methods are needed being compatible with the requirements of data protection and yet flexible enough for modeling different research questions as well as other applications [2].

In compliance with data protection regulations and within concessions to quality, timeliness, and data resilience, expedient solutions for observations below the community level can be offered as a potential complement for research projects. This paper discusses a method for a (partial) reconstruction of a building-level georeferenced resident registration register using open data for the use as a small-scale geomonitoring based on demographic analyses.

Before the method is outlined in Section III, the paper introduces background and challenges regarding register-based research and resident registration data in Section II. In Section IV, results for a test area are discussed and evaluated. The paper ends in Section V with a conclusion and an outlook regarding potentially available data in the future.

II. BACKGROUND AND CHALLENGES

In Germany, certain information about residents is held in a register covered by the German Federal Registration Act (Bundesmeldegesetz, BMG). Currently, the registration authorities have to keep 19 attributes and 11 details for individuals who are required to register. Among the address, it contains information like date of birth, gender, or when moving in and out. The initial law dates back from May 3, 2013, and entered into force on November 1, 2015 [BGBl. I, 2015]. With this legislation, the federal government used its exclusive legislative competence, which was transferred to the state as part of a federalism reform. Affecting federal states now only have regulatory authority if they are explicitly entitled [4]. To its legally defined extent, the resident registration register is neither made for science nor a source for small-scale geomonitoring [5]. However, the overall positive effects of register-based research are reflected, for example, in Recital 157 of the EU General Data Protection Regulation [2016] (GDPR): "By coupling information from registries, researchers can obtain new knowledge of great value with regard to widespread medical conditions such as cardiovascular disease, cancer, and depression. On the basis of registries, research results can be enhanced as they draw on a larger population. Within social science, research on the basis of registries enables researchers to obtain essential knowledge about the long-term correlation of a number of social conditions such as unemployment and education with other life conditions. "

For example, Othengrafen, Linda, and Greinke [6] discuss the potential of resident registration data concerning multilocality in rural areas. Schmoigl and König [7] point out the value of opening register data to science if regulated using three examples from different fields. Also highlighting the need of population data with a fine spatial resolution, Pajares, Muñoz Nieto, Meng and Wulfhorst [8] propose an approach to hybrid population disaggregation using open and widely available data. As reference data for comparison, they use information from a resident registration register.

Emphasizing a more detailed spatial observation in terms of a small-scale geomonitoring, Schaffert and Höcht [5] draw attention to the possibilities of resident registration data. By assigning geocoordinates to data, referred to as georeferencing or geocoding, spatial observations can be related to each other. At the same time, concrete analyses such as calculations of geographical distances between points or a more precise determination of supply needs and land consumption become possible [5][9].

Initially, addresses held in resident registration data allow buildings to be referenced. They do not necessarily consist of personal data with concern to the GDPR [9]. However, the assignment of an address to a single building could become critical if only one person inhabits the building. The identity of this individual might then be revealed [9]. In case geocoded address data are combined with further information (e.g., simple survey data without name reference), it is crucial to pay attention to data protection, as the spatial location poses a re-identification risk or may allow de-anonymization of individuals [9][10]. This difficulty is also mentioned by producers of German official statistics working on integrating statistical and spatial data: The more small-scale statistical data are provided and illustrated, the problem of detection risk becomes more relevant [11]. With regard, Section 16 of the Federal Statistics Act (2016) states that individual data on personal and factual circumstances must be kept secret resp. that re-identification of individuals is prohibited.

III. METHOD AND PROCEDURE

Attributes to be kept in resident registration registers are listed in Section 3 of the BMG. Due to privacy and data regulations, a complete reconstruction of a resident registration register using open data is impossible since attributes such as names, ID card numbers, or tax IDs are not available. With some loss of information, other attributes can be reconstructed. For example, open data offers age classes instead of using the date of birth as listed. But focusing on geomonitoring based on demographic analyses, a complete reconstruction is not necessary. For the method presented here, open data of the 2011 Census [12] and free-to-use geodata from OpenStreetMap [13] will be utilized. Table 1 shows an overview of attributes relevant to demographic analyses that are kept in resident registration registers and the data sources used as underlying input for deriving.

TABLE I. RELEVANT ATTRIBUTES AND THEIR DERIVATION FROM OPEN DATA

Attribute	Open Data Source
Date of birth	2011 Census (age groups)
Current address	OpenStreetMap
Indication, whether spouse or life partner exists	2011 Census (family types)
Indication, whether minor children exist	2011 Census (family types)

Small-scale, localized results of the 2011 Census are available in statistical tables for linking to a geographic grid system. These new data sets were only made possible by a 2013 amendment to the Federal Statistics Act (Bundesstatistikgesetz, BStatG). They are not available for all information collected in the 2011 Census [14]. To assign data geographically, it is necessary to use a corresponding grid dataset.

The Federal Agency for Cartography and Geodesy (Bundesamt für Kartographie und Geodäsie, BKG) provides geographic grids in different spatial resolutions. According to INSPIRE implementing regulations regarding interoperability of spatial data sets and services [15], a georeferenced ETRS89-LAEA 100m grid is decisive for using with 2011 Census data. But not all attributes of the 2011 Census are available within a spatially resolved 100m grid system. Available data can be accessed through a web portal that provides what are called "grid cell-based results" for "population," "demographics," "families," "households," "buildings," and "housing." Handed as CSV tables, this data can then be joined to geographic grids by assigning the ID [16].

An overview of all single processing steps generating a resident registration register from open data can be seen in Figure 1. The area for which a derived resident registration register is to be generated can be bounded by a polygon. First, this area is intersected with all census grid cell data. Then, attributes contained are linked to the grid cells. Structurally, the table for "population" is different from others. Result tables for "demographics," "families," "households," "buildings," and "dwellings" contain a separate row for each existing characteristic value of each characteristic per grid cell. Tables need to be pivoted to enable a 1:1 join between grid cells and result tables. In conclusion, tables now contain one row for each grid cell and one column for each existing combination of the characteristic and characteristic value. In contrast, the result table "population" contains for each grid cell a column with the population number of the respective cell, which eliminates the need for preprocessing.

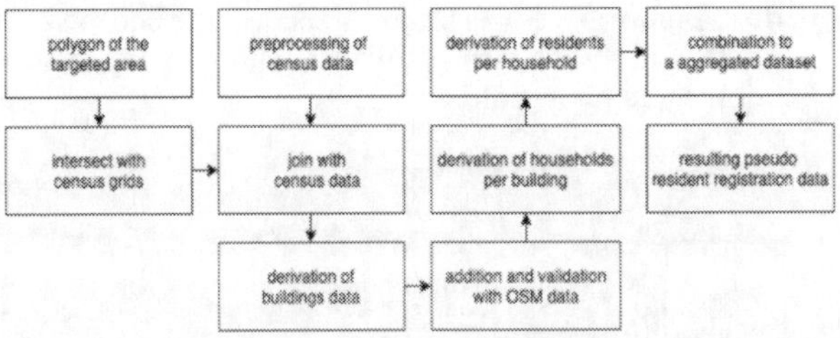

Figure 1. Schematic illustration for all single processing steps

Next, datasets of the grid cell-based results are linked to the geographic grid cells based on their grid ID. It is essential to ensure that the geographic grid is projected correctly, as the grid ID is derived from the respective cell coordinates [17]. An assignment to the 2011 census results is only possible when applying an ETRS89-LAEA projection for the geographical grids. As for further processing, all single cells of the geographic grid are the decisive spatial reference unit. I.e., the following work steps take place for each grid cell individually. The result of each iteration leads to a complete data set (see Figure 2). A data structure is filled for each iteration of the following processing steps. The grid ID is passed as metadata and spatial reference information to the data structure. After that, the total number of buildings and households are transferred from the linked tables. This serves as a control panel.

The census grid cell-based results' building type (size) attribute, which describes the building type e.g. "detached single house" or "apartment building", served as a critical comparison feature for the OpenStreetMap dataset. This attribute classifies, among other things, whether buildings are single-family or multi-family houses. The summed number of buildings per attribute constitutes the total population of residentially inhabited buildings in a grid cell. Single buildings are enriched with address information from OpenStreetMap. For this purpose, the Overpass API tool is used to extract addresses from a spatially bounded area, i.e., the extent within the current grid cell [18]. In addition to spatial bounding, the Overpass Query Language (Overpass QL) also allows thematic selection based on OpenStreetMap's data model and tagging guidelines [18]. In OpenStreetMap, buildings are provided as *way* to which thematic information such as the address or the type of a building is kept in the form of *tags*. As a result of free editability, incorrect or missing data can be part of OpenStreetMap datasets [19]. Sometimes, address information is not attached to a building polygon but to a point object within the building polygon. Therefore, *address tags* of all *nodes* and *landuse* tags of all *ways* in respective grid cells are also requested. Data sets with an *amenity* tag or an incompatible *landuse* value (i.e., other than residential or settlement area) are filtered out, meaning commercially used buildings are not considered. This allows more accurate matching of buildings listed in the census dataset, containing only buildings with (partial) residential occupancy [20].

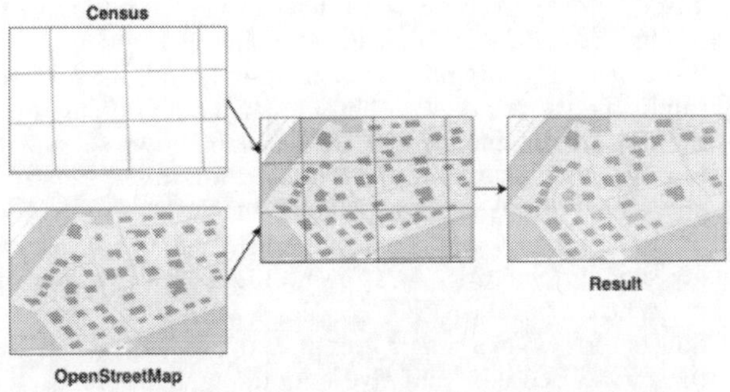

Figure 2. Derivation of the pseudo-derivative, © OpenStreetMap contributors

If possible, the assignment of address data from OpenStreetMap and building information within the census datasets proceeds via building types, otherwise randomized. Based on the building type and the census data attribute "number of apartments in the building," apartments or households are distributed across the buildings. The population of households is founded on the summed households belonging to the characteristic "type of private household," to which adequate factual data of the characteristic "size of private household" was assigned in each case. In this way, households with a corresponding number of individuals are assigned to a building. A classification of whether the household members are adults or children is done by the household type, i.e., "single-person household" or "couples with children." Afterward, a certain number of people datasets are generated for each household according to the household size attribute. These are assigned to appropriate age classes from the census data. After successful iteration, the final cell data structure is added to a comprehensive data set.

IV. EVALUATION AND DISCUSSSION

The method presented here was applied to the city of Herborn as a test area (Germany, state of Hesse) shown in Figure 3. The area covers an area of approximately 4.52 km2 with 257 residential grid cells. 1,992 houses were derived and enriched with attributes relevant for demographic analyses.

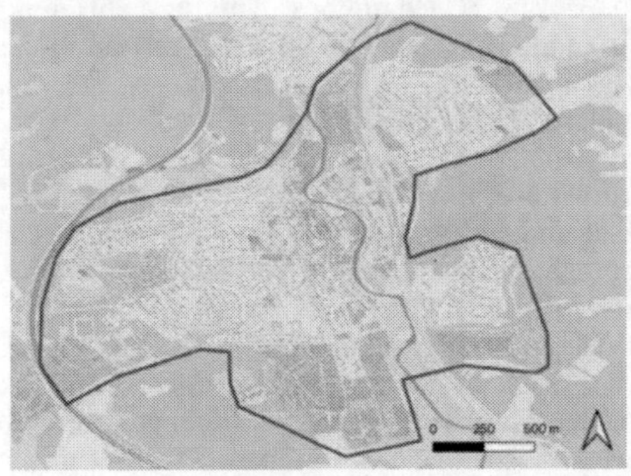

Figure 3. Overview across the test area of the city of Herborn, © OpenStreetMap contributors.

Figure 4 shows a classification by building type (size) based on the census data. All nine residential buildings listed in OpenStreetMap were detected within the grid cell, eight of them as a single-family (marked in red) and one as a multi-family house (marked in blue). A manual comparison with the keys maintained in OpenStreetMap shows seven single-family and two multi-family houses for this area. A field check also reveals a corresponding result.

In total, 25 residents are distributed across twelve households in this grid cell. More specifically, three households consist of couples with one child, two households with a single parent and one child, two single-person households, and five couples with no children. For each resident, the characteristics listed in Table 1 are available. The grid cell shown is characterized by its relatively homogeneous settlement structure. This is a factor of a high level of coherence between Census and OpenStreetMap data. However, this needs further investigation.

Figure 4. Classification result by building type (size), © OpenStreetMap contributors.

Parts of the census dataset suggest two additional residential buildings for this grid cell, a fact interesting to point out. The anonymization technique underlying the production of census data leads to a scenario in which summations across different characteristics will not necessarily produce identical results [20]. Summing up, all expressions of the characteristic "building type (size)" returns only 1,805 buildings. This is a difference of about 9%. In total, 161 of the 257 grid cells, meaning almost 63 %, showed a deviation with a mean value of 1.75 buildings and a standard deviation of 0.89 of these two characteristics, which can vary either positively or negatively. These deviations are also found for other attributes of the census data set and put a theoretically achievable accuracy of the disaggregation into perspective. As such, it also fulfills the purpose of the SAFE (Secure anonymization for individual data) technique for anonymization [20]. Figure 5 below shows a result of an anonymization technique. According to OpenStreetMap, the grid cell contains four buildings; the census dataset indicates 76 inhabitants, but any information on buildings or households is missing. An in situ field comparison shows the existence of three multi-story buildings with elderly residences and a school building (left part of Figure 5). So far, the method described here cannot account for these 76 residents without information on buildings and households.

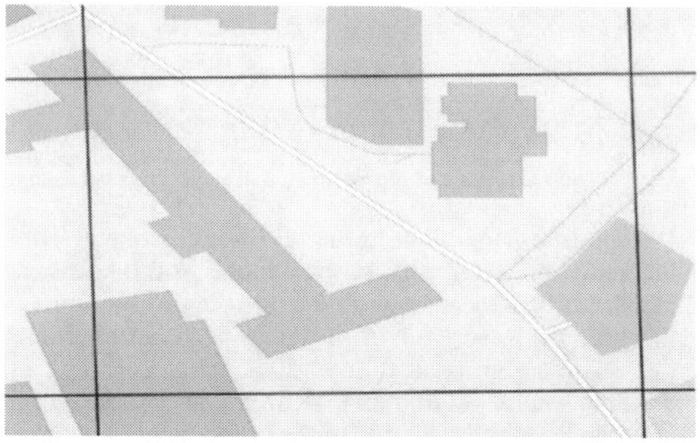

Figure 5. Lack of mapping due to anonymization of census data, © OpenStreetMap contributors

Furthermore, the results of the presented method correlate with the address completeness in OpenStreetMap. The selected test area shows a medium to good completeness of about 71 % in relation to the official real estate cadastre (Amtliches Liegenschaftskatasterinformationssystem, ALKIS). Building-related accuracy is expected to be marginal for areas with low address completeness. Additionally, the timeliness of the datasets also affects the results. While the census dataset reflects the state of 2011, OpenStreetMap tends to contain a continuously updated dataset. Depending on urban dynamics and population fluctuations, smaller or larger deviations are expected. In addition, the intended area of application must also be taken into account. As mentioned above, both of these factors need to be investigated in more detail in a follow-up study.

V. CONCLUSION AND OUTLOOK

This paper proposes a method that generates a georeferenced resident registration register at a building level as a pseudo-derivative based on openly available spatial and public-statistical data. Complete reconstruction and disaggregation of the census data is not possible due to the anonymization techniques but is usually not necessary for research purposes. In this case, addresses were assigned to demographic characteristics with relevant age classes. The accuracy of the assignment can be improved by considering additional census data characteristics, OpenStreetMap tags, and different open data sets. The census dataset offers other attributes such as gender, religious affiliation, or citizenship. This can increase the applicability of the pseudo-derivative. The lack of internal consistency of the census data caused by the underlying SAFE-anonymization technique and the data quality of OpenStreetMap requires a more comprehensive evaluation of the quality of the dataset generated by the method outlined.

Regarding the 2022 Census in Germany, it is possible to continue providing easy-to-generate datasets for research purposes without facing data protection issues. Looking at ways of enriching or combining data, the German government's open data strategy published in 2021 [21] gives reason to expect that more data from public administrations will be made available and that its quality will steadily improve. In addition, the availability of previously inaccessible data from the economy, science, and civil society is expected to increase. The State of Hesse, or rather the Hessian Administration for Land Management and Geoinformation (Hessische Verwaltung für Bodenmanagement und Geoinformation, HVBG), where the method presented here was applied using the example of the city of Herborn, has also been making additional free geodata available since 2022.02.01 [22]. The products of the real estate cadastre, the state measurement, and the real estate valuation are made available via the store component, the download center, as Web Map Service (WMS) and Web Feature Service (WFS). The data is continuously updated and permanently available.

The Council for Social and Economic Data (Rat für Sozial- und Wirtschaftsdaten, RatSWD) [23] also recommends in a position paper for the 20th legislative period of the German Bundestag to facilitate access to register and administrative data for scientific purposes. An envisaged Research Data Act is intended to strengthen science in Germany and open up research into socially relevant issues, even in politically sensitive areas.

ACKNOWLEDGMENT

The work on this article was done as part of the project "Spatial Intelligence for the Integrated Care of Seniors in Rural Neighborhoods (RAFVINIERT)", which is funded by the Carl Zeiss Foundation in the program "Transfer - Intelligent Solutions for an Aging Society".

REFERENCES

[1] W. Redaktion, „Registry Research: Opportunities, Risks, and Challenges," Wirtschaft Und Gesellschaft, vol. 46(3), pp. 315–328, November 2020.

[2] B. Heldt and D. Heinrichs, „Using the 2011 Census to model households' residential location choices under conditions of secrecy," Zeitschrift für amtliche Statistik Berlin Brandenburg, pp. 29-33, 2017.

[3] A. Milbert and S. Fina, „Small town research methods: definitions, data, and spatial analysis," in A. Steinführer, L. Porsche and M. Sondermann (Eds.), Compendium of Small Town Research, pp. 24-49, Hannover: Forschungsberichte der ARL 16, 2021.

[4] E. Ehmann, Dealing with Data from Population Registers Correctly, 3rd ed., Stuttgart: Boorberg, 2017.

[5] M. Schaffert and V. Höcht, „Geocoded Data from Population Registers as a Source for Needs-Based Planning in Rural Municipalities and Regions," Raumforschung und Raumordnung, vol. 76(5), pp. 421–35, 2018.

[6] F. Othengrafen, L. Linda and L. Greinke, Temporary arrivals and absences in rural areas: effects of multilocal lifestyles on land and society. Wiesbaden, Wiesbaden: Springer Fachmedien, 2021.

[7] R. König and L. Schmoigl, „Successful Registry Research in Austria. What additional value does the regulated opening of registry data generate for scientific research? A presentation based on three examples," Österreichisches Institut für Wirtschaftsforschung (WIFO) und Institut für höhere Studien (IHS), pp. 1-16, 2020.

[8] E. Pajares, R. Muñoz Nieto, L. Meng and G. Wulfhorst, "Population Disaggregation on the Building Level Based on Outdated Census Data", ISPRS Int. J. Geo-Inf., 10(10), 662, pp. 1-21, 2021, doi.org/10.3390/ijgi10100662.

[9] S. Müller, "Spatial Linking of Georeferenced Survey Data with Geospatial Data: Opportunities, Challenges, and Practical Recommendations," in U. Jensen, S. Netscher and K. Weller, Research Data Management of Social Science Survey Data, pp. 211-29, Barbara Budrich, 2019.

[10] M. Van Der Meer, F. Meissner, M. Merten and D. Münderlein, "Development and Potentials of Digital Spatial Research. Ethical Issues and Impulses for University Teaching," RaumPlanung, vol. 2/3(196), pp. 20–27, 2018.

[11] S. Schnorr-Bäcker and M. Etienne, "Challenges and Possible Solutions in Combining Statistical and Spatial Data from the Perspective of Federal Statistics," Stadtforschung und Statistik: Zeitschrift des Verbandes Deutscher Städtestatistiker, vol. 3(1), pp. 63–69, 2018.

[12] Statistische Ämter des Bundes und der Länder. Zensus 2011. [Online]. Available from: https://www.zensus2011.de/ [retrieved: 04.2022].

[13] OpenStreetMap. OpenStreetMap. [Online]. Available from: https://www.openstreetmap.org [retrieved: 04.2022].

[14] M. Neutze, „Grid-based Evaluations of the 2011 Census," Stadtforschung und Statistik, pp. 64-67, February 2015.

[15] COMMISSION REGULATION (EU) No 1089/2010 of 23 November 2010 Implementing Directive 2007/2/EC of the European Parliament and of the Council as Regards Interoperability of Spatial Data Sets and Services. [Online]. Available from: https://eur-lex.europa.eu/eli/reg/2010/1089 [retrieved: 04.2022].

[16] Statistische Ämter des Bundes und der Länder. Results of the 2011 Census for Download - Extended. [Online]. Available from: https://www.zensus2011.de/DE/Home/Aktuelles/DemografischeGrunddaten.html [retrieved: 04.2022].

[17] Bundesamt für Kartographie und Geodäsie. Documentation. Geographic Grids for Germany. GeoGrid. [Online]. Available from: https://sg.geodatenzentrum.de/web_public/gdz/dokumentation/deu/geogitter.pdf [retrieved: 04.2022].

[18] R.M. Olbricht, "Data Retrieval for Small Spatial Regions in OpenStreetMap," in J. Jokar Arsanjani, A. Zipf, P. Mooney, M. Helbich, Eds. OpenStreetMap in GIScience. Lecture Notes in Geoinformation and Cartography, pp. 101-122. 2015.

[19] P. Neis and D. Zielstra, "Recent Developments and Future Trends in Volunteered Geographic Information Research: The Case of OpenStreetMap," Future Internet, vol. 6, pp. 76-106, 2014.

[20] Statistische Ämter des Bundes und der Länder. 2011 Census. Methods and Procedures. [Online]. Available from: https://www.zensus2011.de/SharedDocs/Downloads/DE/Publikationen/Aufsaetze_Archiv/2015_06_MethodenUndVerfahren.pdf;jsessionid=48260D25A514027445F421D903862F47.live422?__blob=publicationFile&v=2 [retrieved: 04.2022].

[21] Bundesministerium des Innern, für Bau und Heimat. Open Data Strategy of the Federal Government.

[22] Hessische Verwaltung für Bodenmanagement und Geoinformation. Introduction of Open Data by 2022.02.01 [Online]. Available from: https://hvbg.hessen.de/open-data [retrieved: 04.2022].

[23] Rat für Sozial- und Wirtschaftsdaten. RatSWD Position Paper on the Federal Government's Data Strategy.

Building an Open Personal Trajectory Repository

Ville Mäkinen, Anna Brauer, Juha Oksanen
Department of Geoinformatics and Cartography
Finnish Geospatial Research Institute FGI, National Land Survey of Finland
Otaniemi, Espoo, Finland
email: ville.p.makinen@nls.fi, anna.brauer@nls.fi, juha.oksanen@nls.fi

Abstract—**Portable Global Navigation Satellite System (GNSS) -enabled devices enable gathering comprehensive personal trajectory data about the movement of citizens. Such data would be extremely useful for example improving the cyclability of cities. On the other hand, the data is personal and can reveal surprisingly large amount of personal information. To develop robust privacy-aware and utility-preserving methods to obfuscate personal trajectory data, we are faced with the problem that no comprehensive data sets exist that is needed to conduct such studies. Therefore, we are designing an open trajectory repository where citizens can donate their data for science. The main challenges are 1) how to motivate citizens to contribute and 2) how can we share the trajectory data back to participants and to society while respecting the participants' privacy.**

Keywords-privacy; microtrajectory; open data.

I. Introduction

Portable GNSS-enabled devices have become ubiquitous in modern society [1]. In principle, these devices enable gathering accurate location data of citizens. Such data could be used for example to assess the flow of cycling traffic, and thus be used to improve the cyclability of cities [2]. Efforts to mitigate climate change are needed and especially in cities, where transportation accounts for a large amount of greenhouse emissions [3], supporting cycling is an important way to help in this battle.

When used for tracking, smartphones and other GNSS-enabled devices usually record their location every few seconds. This results into accurate personal trajectories (consecutive (x, y, z, t) points) that can reveal surprisingly large amount of information about their carriers [4], especially when linked to other data sets [5]. Sharing such trajectories openly thus compromises the participants' privacy. This has been acknowledged in the EU's General Data Protection Regulation (GDPR). One unfortunate outcome of the regulation is that it has made the access and usage of personal location data practically impossible for anyone other than the companies who collect the data. Usually, only heavily aggregated data is available (e.g., Strava heat maps [6]), whose utility compared to the original data is considerably reduced.

We think that the current situation is unbearable. In the GeoPrivacy project, we are studying methods that would enable the use of personal trajectories while respecting the privacy of their owners. More precisely, we are studying how personal trajectories could be processed so that their utility remains high while their potential to violate owners' privacy is hindered. One problem we are facing is that there are almost no personal trajectory data sets that can be used to conduct such studies. To tackle this, we opted to build an open trajectory donation service, where volunteers can donate their trajectory for science.

The rest of the paper discusses the various issues we have so far faced when designing and building such a service. Section II highlights the previous research relevant to this work. Section III summarizes our previous study about the citizens' motivation to participate. Sections IV and V present the methodology that we have developed for this work and possible data sets that could be produced. The sections VI and VII contain detailed implementation details of the service and potential issues. Finally, section VIII contains the conclusion that we have drawn.

II. Previous Work

Anonymization of databases have been studied extensively and numerous privacy protection concepts have been devised, for example k-anonymity [7] and l-diversity [8]. Research has been conducted also specifically with spatio-temporal data, but often the developed methods are applicable for relatively coarse data, such as phone location data from mobile operators [9]. The methods that are applicable to GNSS trajectories often require the data set to be dense. For example, in [10] the trajectories are translated closer to each other to achieve a specific (k, δ)-anonymity. In addition, the presented methods seem to be developed mainly for a fixed set of trajectories. Applying such methods to constantly growing data sets may pose additional issues.

There are some studies about anonymization of individual trajectories. For example, truncating the trajectories from their endpoints has been studied in [11]. However, the method does not consider the environment of the trajectory in any way, which in turn can lead to unnecessary utility loss.

As mentioned, open personal GNSS trajectory data sets are scarce. The only publicly available data set we are aware of is the GeoLife data set [12] which contains ~17000 trajectories recorded by 178 individuals in Beijing, China.

We are aware of the Bike Data Project [13], in which cycling data has been gathered. However, they seem to publish only aggregations of the donated trajectories.

These findings support our hypothesis that more open personal GNSS trajectory data would boost the development of privacy-preserving publication methods of such data.

III. How to Motivate Participants?

The obvious first question is: is there anybody who might be interested in donating their movement data, and what are their motivations to do so? We conducted an online questionnaire to map citizens' thoughts and opinions on the topic. The survey was targeted to Finnish citizens. The results of the survey suggest that the general attitude towards donating personal trajectory data to an open data repository is positive [14]. At the same time, the participants seemed to be aware of the privacy issues. The most important motivators seemed to be the possibility to help to improve pedestrian and cycling lanes, and to participate in scientific research. These findings gave us confidence to proceed with the plan.

The results also indicate that the most important doubts the participants had about such service are related to revelation of personal information and to what the data will be used for. These tell us that it will be important to build the service in such a way that the users can trust the service.

IV. Privacy-Aware Trajectory Processing

A naive method to anonymize personal trajectory data is to simply replace the subjects' personal information with a pseudo-identifier that is unique to each participant. This approach is valid only if there is no other data that the trajectories can be compared to. With external data, for example the known location of an individual at a certain time, a matching trajectory can be linked to the individual. This in turn may reveal for example the home or the workplace, or any other sensitive location, by inspecting the trajectories with the same pseudo-identifier. Removing the pseudo-identifier may make this harder. However, people's movement behavior, for example the mode of transportation (walking or cycling speed) can help narrow down the possible trajectories that belong to the same individual. Also, people are likely to use the same device/application for recording their movement, which may introduce some identifiable information to the trajectories (average accuracy, systematic errors).

One method to counter these threats is to publish only aggregations of the trajectories. An example of this approach are the heat maps by Strava [6]. A more utility-preserving method is to aggregate attributes for example to the segments of the street network of the area [2]. These and similar methods are the most privacy-respecting ones. At the same time, they reduce the utility of the data considerably.

Often the sensitive locations of the trajectories are the endpoints and stay points, i.e., locations where the trajectory spends a considerable amount of time. These can be at the endpoints of the trajectory (user forgets to turn the tracking off after arriving at the destination) or somewhere in the middle (stop at red lights, a quick stop at a shop). We have studied a method to truncate trajectories in such a way that sensitive locations (endpoints and stay points) can be narrowed down only to a group of locations nearby the real location [15]. This approach mitigates some of the threats but leaves (possibly most) parts of the trajectories untouched.

V. Possible Open Data Products

A. Aggregated data sets

Aggregation is commonly used and somewhat "safe" method to publish sensitive data. We have considered to publish two different aggregated data sets. The first one is an aggregation to a regular grid with coarse enough grid size. The second one consists of deriving various attributes from the trajectories and aggregating them onto the segments of the underlying street network, like in [2].

B. Obfuscated trajectories

Publishing even parts of the raw trajectories must be done with extreme care, as the data is personal. We are planning to use the method in [15] as a basis, but further process the trajectories to obfuscate for the exact temporal information. In addition, we have considered resampling the trajectories to a uniform time resolution to make distinguishing them from one another more difficult. This list is not exhaustive and studying and developing new methods in this context is at the focus of our research.

VI. Implementation Details

We aim to keep the implementation of the service simple. It will consist of a Vue.js frontend and a Django backend. In addition, there will be an off-line data storage where the original trajectories are stored (Figure 1). The most interesting and important questions are related to processing the trajectory data and management of the possible open data products.

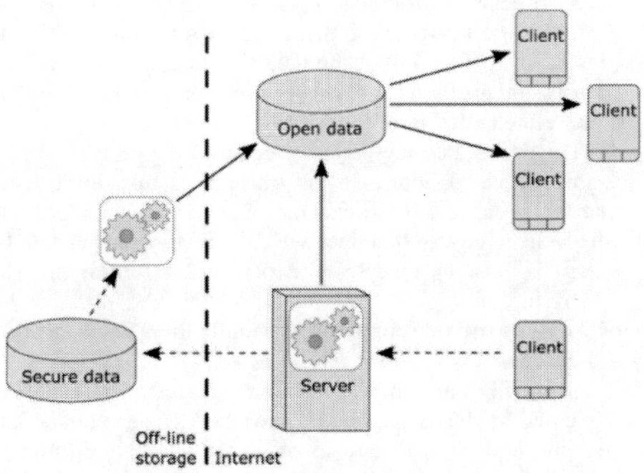

Figure 1. Schematic representation of the architechture of the service. The arrows indicate the data flow (dash dotted: original data, solid: anonymized data).

We argued above that data aggregation is the safest way to publish sensitive spatial data. However, when new trajectories are donated (or some existing ones deleted), we must have all the previous data available to recalculate the aggregations. This is not a problem here since the motivation for us to set up the service is to collect trajectory data. However, we do not want to store the original data on the server that is connected to the internet. A more responsible way is to store the original trajectories on the previously mentioned off-line storage and upload recalculated aggregations to the server when needed. In this scenario, the raw data exists on the backend only for a moment when data is donated but before it has been transferred to the secure storage.

Another option we have mentioned is to publish obfuscated individual trajectories without any further aggregation. In this scenario there is no need to store the original data because there is no need to recalculate any aggregations. It would be possible to perform the trajectory obfuscation on the client-side, and the user could see the results and decide trajectory-wise whether they are happy with the results before donating. In a "production" version of the service this is an interesting approach, because it reduces the role of the trusted party that now stores the original sensitive data. In the first phase of the implementation, we will have a hybrid version of this idea: the data will be uploaded to the backend for processing, but the results are sent back to the user for inspection, and only after explicitly consenting are the results stored permanently in the service.

It should be noted that if we want the participants to be able to request to remove their data, there must be a way to link the obfuscated trajectories to their accounts. Using a pseudo-identifier is the simplest option. More privacy-conserving way is to use a unique identifier for each trajectory and an index that is not public.

VII. Identified Issues

Aggregated data products have the least privacy issues. Still, care must be taken so that no individual trajectories can be seen or deduced from the data. This can be achieved by filtering out grid cells or street segments that contain less than a predefined number of trajectories.

The obfuscated raw trajectories are more problematic. It is impossible to obfuscate the trajectories in a bulletproof manner, because it is always possible to devise another more comprehensive external data set that the trajectories can be linked against to reveal some personal information. The underlying question is: is a trajectory that is obfuscated in a certain way still personal data? Currently there does not seem to be a clear answer for this.

Originally our plan was to make releases of the database that could be stored indefinitely and used as a benchmark data sets in scientific research. However, the GDPR's right to be forgotten raises concerns whether this is feasible.

The service we have described here is designed mainly for collecting data for research. Even though one of the motivators that was identified in the questionnaire was the ability to improve pedestrian and cycling lanes, we are aware that we are not likely to be able to affect the city planning during this project.

We are also facing the chicken and the egg problem. One of the goals for setting up the service is to gather personal trajectory data that can be used to develop more robust obfuscation methods. At the same time, robust and well-tested obfuscation methods would increase the trust to the service and possibly attract more users.

One big reason for the success and popularity of the existing tracking applications is the ease of use. Having to use a separate service to manually upload data will inevitably drive away potential motivated users. Having a dedicated app for our service might attract more users and should be kept in mind for further development. However, for a relatively small research project such things are big investments. In the first phase we will concentrate on making the user experience of the service as smooth as possible without compromising security.

It might be possible for the user to allow the service to access a third-party service and download data automatically from there. Questions that rise immediately are a) is such use in accordance with the terms of use of the third-party service and b) is it possible to download the original trajectory data programmatically. Usually, it is possible at least for users to download all their data from a service. Developing the import functionality of such data exports from a few popular services may be more cost-effective, given that the trajectory data is provided in a format that can be read for example by the common open-source libraries.

VIII. Conclusions

The higher goal of the project is to advance the use of ever-growing personal location data for the common good without compromising the privacy of the individuals. The results from the questionnaire suggest that there is willingness in general to participate in such an endeavor. Acquiring the trust of potential participants is of paramount importance. We will try to accomplish that by being 100% transparent with the goals of the service, the methods used, and the possible privacy threats. In practice, these must be communicated to the participants as clearly as possible, in plain language, for example when we ask for their consent to donate data.

We acknowledge that it is entirely possible that there is no "universal" privacy-preserving obfuscation method for personal trajectories, but instead a suitable aggregation must be done case by case. Even in that case, the different aggregations must be generated and published with a thought. Generating and delivering aggregations carelessly may lead into a situation where different aggregations can be combined to reveal more information that what was originally intended.

The results from the research in the GeoPrivacy project will provide more insight into this area as well.

We consider the service that we are building as a test case of a more official service that would be maintained for example by city officials. That would enable a natural connection between the donation service and city planning, make it easier to provide feedback back to the citizens and thus motivate more people to participate.

ACKNOWLEDGMENT

The project is funded by the Finnish Cultural Foundation. We made use of geocomputing platform provided by the Open Geospatial Information Infrastructure for Research (Geoportti, urn:nbn:fi:research-infras-2016072513) funded by the Academy of Finland, CSC – IT Center for Science, and other Geoportti consortium members.

REFERENCES

[1] N. Bento, "Calling for change? Innovation, diffusion, and the energy impacts of global mobile telephony," Energy Research & Social Science, pp. 84–100, 2016.

[2] A. Brauer, V. Mäkinen, and J. Oksanen, "Characterizing cycling traffic fluency using big mobile activity tracking data," Computers, Environment and Urban Systems, vol. 85, 101553, Jan. 2021, doi:10.1016/j.compenvurbsys.2020.101553.

[3] L. Chapman, "Transport and Climate change: a review", Journal of Transport Geography, vol. 15, pp. 354–367, 2007, doi:10.1016/j.jtrangeo.2006.11.008.

[4] C. Song, Z. Qu, N. Blumm, and A.-B. Barabási, "Limits of Predictability in Human Mobility,", Science, vol. 327, pp. 1018–1021, Feb. 2010, doi:10.1126/science.1177170.

[5] O. Goga et al., "Exploiting Innocuous Activity for Correlating Users Across Sites" in The 22nd International conference on World Wide Web, WWW'13, May 2013, Rio de Janeiro, Brazil. pp.447-458, doi:10.1145/2488388.2488428

[6] Strava, "Global Heatmap", 2022, https://www.strava.com/heatmap [retrieved: 05, 2022].

[7] L. Sweeney, "k-anonymity: A model for protecting privacy", International Journal of Uncertainty, Fuzziness and Knowledge-Based Systems vol. 10(5), pp. 557–570, 2002.

[8] A. Machanavajjhala, J. Gehrke, D. Kifer, and M. Venkitasubramaniam, "l-diversity: privacy beyond k-anonymity", ACM Transactions on Knowledge Discovery from Data, vol. 1(1), pp. 3, 2007.

[9] M. Gramaglia, M. Fiore, A. Furno, and R. Stanica, "GLOVE: Towards Privacy-Preserving Publishing of Record-Level-Truthful Mobile Phone Trajectories", ACM/IMS Transactions on Data Science, vol. 2(3), pp. 1–36, 2021.

[10] O. Abul, F. Bonchi, and M. Nanni, "Never Walk Alone: Uncertainty for Anonymity in Moving Objects Databases", 2008 IEEE 24th International Conference on Data Engineering, 2008, pp. 376-385.

[11] J. Krumm, "Inference Attacks on Location Tracks". In: LaMarca, A., Langheinrich, M., Truong, K.N. (eds) Pervasive Computing. Pervasive 2007. Lecture Notes in Computer Science, vol 4480. Springer, Berlin, Heidelberg.

[12] Y. Zheng, H. Fu, X. Xie, W.-Y. Ma, and Q. Li, "Geolife GPS trajectory dataset – User Guide", https://www.microsoft.com/en-us/research/publication/geolife-gps-trajectory-dataset-user-guide/ [retrieved: 05, 2022].

[13] Bike Data Project, https://www.bikedataproject.org/ [retrieved: 05, 2022].

[14] V. Jokinen, V. Mäkinen, A. Brauer, and J. Oksanen, "Would citizens contribute their personal location data to an open database? Preliminary results from a survey", in Basiri, A., Gartner, G., & Huang, H. (Eds.). (2021). LBS 2021: Proceedings of the 16th International Conference on Location Based Services, doi:10.34726/1741.

[15] A. Brauer, A. Forsch, V. Mäkinen, J. Oksanen, and J.-H. Haunert, "My home is my secret: concealing sensitive locations by context-aware trajectory truncation", International Journal of Geographical Information Science, in press.

Creating a Holocene-prehistoric Inventory of Volcanological Features Groups

Towards Sustainable Multi-disciplinary Context Integration in Prehistory and Archaeology Based on the Methodology of Coherent Conceptual Knowledge Contextualisation

Claus-Peter Rückemann
Westfälische Wilhelms-Universität Münster (WWU), Germany;
Unabhängiges Deutsches Institut für Multi-disziplinäre Forschung (DIMF), Germany;
Leibniz Universität Hannover, Germany
Email: ruckema@uni-muenster.de

Abstract—**This paper presents research on a practical solution for geoscientific inventories based on conceptual contextualisation. The goal of this research is the creation of a practical Holocene-prehistoric inventory of worldwide volcanological features groups, coherently integrating multi-disciplinary conceptual knowledge. The focus is a sustainable multi-disciplinary integration of knowledge contexts, especially from prehistory and archaeology, which further enables coherent conceptual knowledge contextualisation and georeferenced symbolic representation. This paper provides implementations and realisations of the coherent conceptual knowledge and the methodological component integration. The resulting inventory is illustrated by excerpts of two features groups based on a conceptual knowledge result matrix. Future research will address the resulting Holocene-prehistoric inventory of worldwide volcanological features, continuous development of resources and integration and coherent conceptual knowledge contextualisation with prehistorical and archaeological knowledge resources.**

***Keywords*–Prehistory; Holocene; Coherent Multi-disciplinary Conceptual Knowledge Integration; CKRI; CRI Framework.**

I. Introduction

The goal of this research is the creation of a practical Holocene-prehistoric inventory of worldwide volcanological features groups, integrating arbitrary coherent conceptual knowledge. The target is a sustainable multi-disciplinary integration of knowledge contexts, especially from prehistory and archaeology, which further enables a coherent conceptual knowledge contextualisation and georeferenced symbolic representation. The approach conforms with information science fundaments and universal knowledge, which enable an integration of the required components from methodologies to realisations for knowledge representations of realia and abstract contexts [1], considering that many facets of knowledge, including prehistory, need to be continuously acquired and reviewed [2]. Creating contextualisation requires to coherently integrate multi-disciplinary knowledge and to enable symbolic representations, e.g., integrating chorological and chronological contexts. Realisations need to integrate a wide range of components as required from participating disciplines, e.g., for dynamical processing, geoprocessing, spatial contextualisation. Implementation and realisation based on the methodology of coherent conceptual knowledge contextualisation requires the integration of standardised, modular components required for task within participating disciplines. This research employs knowledge resources, data sources, and Points of Interest (PoI), especially Knowledge Resources (KR) focussing on volcanological features, prehistory, and archaeology.

Therefore, two major reference implementations were deployed for implementation, realisation, and continuous further development. The coherent knowledge resources and the practical realisation are fully based on the main implementations of the prehistory-protohistory and archaeology Conceptual Knowledge Reference Implementation (CKRI) [3] and the Component Reference Implementations (CRI) framework [4]. CKRI provides the knowledge framework, including multi-disciplinary contexts of natural sciences and humanities [5]. CRI provides the required component groups and components for the implementation and realisation of all the procedural modules. The component and workflow procedure related research for this inventory is in focus of multi-disciplinary research groups and matter to be reported in separate publications. Many aspects of knowledge [6], including meaning, can be described using knowledge complements supporting a modern definition of knowledge [7] and subsequent component instrumentation, e.g., considering factual, conceptual, procedural, metacognitive, and structural knowledge. Knowledge complements are a means of understanding and targeting new insight, e.g., enabling advanced contextualisation, integration, analysis, synthesis, innovation, prospection, and documentation. Regarding knowledge, it should be taken for granted, that scientific members of any disciplines nowerdays continuously practice and train themselves in development and practical employment of methods, algorithms, and components as required by their disciplines and keep track with how to integrate methods. The reference implementations are part of the developments and provide sustainable, flexible, and efficient fundaments for solutions targeting the creation of coherent multi-disciplinary conceptual knowledge contextualisation.

The rest of this paper is organised as follows. Section II presents the methodological implementation and realisation with the CKRI references and the respective component integration for this research. Section III shows the resulting inventory, the knowledge integration results, and excerpts of the created volcanological features groups of the inventory. Section IV provides a compact discussion of the results regarding the coherent conceptual knowledge integration. Section V summarises lessons learned, conclusions, and future work.

II. Methodological implementation and realisation

Implementation and realisation are based on the CKRI reference implementation [3], and respective contextualisation. Components outside the core scope of this knowledge focussed geoscientific, prehistoric, and archaeological research are employed and can be extended via the CRI frame reference implementations [4]. Both provide sustainable fundaments for highest levels of reproducibility and standardisation.

A. Resulting coherent conceptual knowledge implementation

Universally consistent multi-disciplinary conceptual knowledge is based on the Conceptual Knowledge Reference Implementation (CKRI) [3] and implemented via UDC code references for demonstration, spanning the main tables [8] shown in Table I.

TABLE I. CKRI IMPLEMENTATION OF COHERENT CONCEPTUAL KNOWLEDGE CONTEXTUALISATION; MAIN TABLES (EXCERPT).

Code / Sign Ref.	*Verbal Description (EN)*
UDC:0	Science and Knowledge. Organization. Computer Science. Information. Documentation. Librarianship. Institutions. Publications
UDC:1	Philosophy. Psychology
UDC:2	Religion. Theology
UDC:3	Social Sciences
UDC:5	Mathematics. Natural Sciences
UDC:52	Astronomy. Astrophysics. Space research. Geodesy
UDC:53	Physics
UDC:539	Physical nature of matter
UDC:54	Chemistry. Crystallography. Mineralogy
UDC:55	Earth Sciences. Geological sciences
UDC:550.3	Geophysics
UDC:551	General geology. Meteorology. Climatology. Historical geology. Stratigraphy. Palaeogeography
UDC:551.21	Vulcanicity. Vulcanism. Volcanoes. Eruptive phenomena. Eruptions
UDC:551.2...	Fumaroles. Solfataras. Geysers. Hot springs. Mofettes. Carbon dioxide vents. Soffioni
UDC:551.44	Speleology. Caves. Fissures. Underground waters
UDC:551.46	Physical oceanography. Submarine topography. Ocean floor
UDC:551.7	Historical geology. Stratigraphy
UDC:551.8	Palaeogeography
UDC:56	Palaeontology
UDC:6	Applied Sciences. Medicine, Technology
UDC:7	The Arts. Entertainment. Sport
UDC:8	Linguistics. Literature
UDC:9	Geography. Biography. History
UDC:902	Archaeology
UDC:903	Prehistory. Prehistoric remains, artefacts, antiquities
UDC:904	Cultural remains of historical times

The CKRI is provided in development stage editions, prehistory-protohistory and archaeology E.0.4.6, natural sciences E.0.2.8). Table II shows an excerpt of consistent multi-disciplinary conceptual knowledge based on UDC code references spanning auxiliary tables [9].

TABLE II. CKRI IMPLEMENTATION OF COHERENT CONCEPTUAL KNOWLEDGE CONTEXTUALISATION; AUXILIARY TABLES (EXCERPT).

Code / Sign Ref.	*Verbal Description (EN)*
UDC (1/9)	Common auxiliaries of place
UDC:(23)	Above sea level. Surface relief. Above ground generally. Mountains
UDC:"..."	Common auxiliaries of time.
UDC:"6"	Geological, archaeological and cultural time divisions
UDC:"62"	Cenozoic (Cainozoic). Neozoic (70 MYBP - present)
UDC:"63"	Archaeological, prehistoric, protohistoric periods and ages

The CKRI implementations provide the fundament for the coherent multi-disciplinary knowledge based integration and the realisations of the methodological component integration.

B. Resulting methodological component integration

Integration components, reflecting standards and sustainable modules are based on the major groups of the Component Reference Implementations (CRI) frame [4]. The CRI framework is provided in development stage edition E.0.3.7. The ten major CRI component groups were integrated for the implementation and realisation of the practical Holocene-prehistoric inventory of volcanological features groups, especially:

1) Conceptual knowledge frameworks.
2) Conceptual knowledge base.
3) Integration of scientific reference frameworks.
4) Formalisation.
5) Methodologies and workflows integration.
6) Prehistory Knowledge Resources.
7) Natural Sciences Knowledge Resources.
8) Inherent representation groups.
9) Scientific context parametrisation.
10) Structures and symbolic representation.

Focus is on the contextualisation and conceptual knowledge framework, its development, and its flexibility of integration with advanced components. Relevant pre-existing and ongoing component developments addressing knowledge with multi-disciplinary KR have been summarised [10]. Integration of components and procedural realisations are out of scope here but subject of research in respective fields. Procedural realisations will therefore be published separately.

The exact components for the implementation and realisation of the practical Holocene-prehistoric inventory of volcanological features groups are given in the next sections.

III. RESULTING INVENTORY

The following sections provide illustrative object entity examples of the new practical Holocene-prehistoric inventory of volcanological features groups as implemented and realised integrating the aforementioned reference implementations.

A. Resulting coherent conceptual knowledge integration

Table III shows an excerpt of the result matrix of Holocene-prehistoric volcanological features groups. The result matrix includes conceptual knowledge view groups [11] based on CKRI references [3], factual knowledge from the Knowledge Resources objects, and respective country codes.

The coherent conceptual knowledge integration enables a multi-disciplinary conceptual knowledge integration. This case demonstrates an integration of Holocene-prehistoric volcanological features, geoscientific knowledge, and spatial knowledge. Any further knowledge can be coherently integrated, e.g., prehistoric and archaeological knowledge.

The result matrices reflect the key assets with the CRI framework [4] to realise the inventory and symbolic representations and to enable a continuous development.

B. Resulting symbolic representation of features groups

Figure 1 shows a resulting symbolic representation of a volcanological features group, strato volcano, as based on the coherent conceptual knowledge integration. Generated representations include integrated CKRI references, projection of topographic and bathymetric results, and further knowledge for respective areas. Figure 2 shows a resulting symbolic

TABLE III. RESULT MATRIX OF HOLOCENE-PREHISTORIC VOLCANOLOGICAL FEATURES GROUPS (EXCERPT). THE RESULT MATRIX INCLUDES CONCEPTUAL KNOWLEDGE VIEW GROUPS [11] (CKRI), KNOWLEDGE RESOURCES OBJECTS, AND COUNTRY CODES (EXCERPT).

Conceptual Knowledge View Group	*Knowledge Resources Object*	*Country Code*
CKRI: UDC:551.21,550.3,(23),STRATO_VOLCANO;"62"...	Agua de Pau	PT
CKRI: UDC:551.21,550.3,(23),STRATO_VOLCANO;"62"...	Alngey	RU
CKRI: UDC:551.21,550.3,(23),STRATO_VOLCANO;"62"...	Azuma	JP
CKRI: UDC:551.21,550.3,(23),STRATO_VOLCANO;"62"...	Hekla	IS
CKRI: UDC:551.21,550.3,(23),STRATO_VOLCANO;"62"...	...	...
CKRI: UDC:551.2...,551.21,550.3,(23),...MAARS_FEATURES;"62"...	Cerro Tujle	CL
CKRI: UDC:551.2...,551.21,550.3,(23),...MAARS_FEATURES;"62"...	Suoh	ID
CKRI: UDC:551.2...,551.21,550.3,(23),...MAARS_FEATURES;"62"...	Ukinrek Maars	US
CKRI: UDC:551.2...,551.21,550.3,(23),...MAARS_FEATURES;"62"...	West Eifel Volcanic Field	DE
CKRI: UDC:551.2...,551.21,550.3,(23),...MAARS_FEATURES;"62"...	...	...

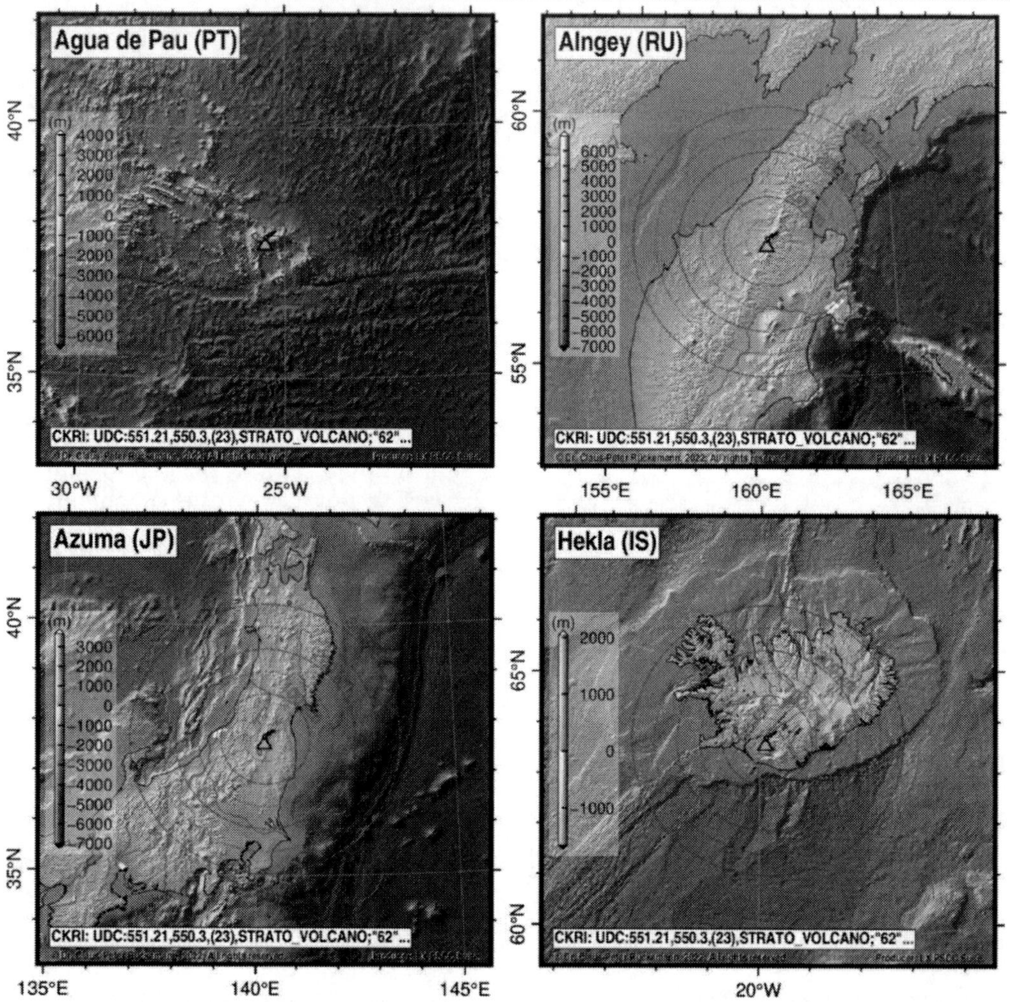

Figure 1. Resulting symbolic representation of a volcanological features group (strato volcano) based on coherent conceptual knowledge integration (excerpt). Generated representations include integrated CKRI references, projection of topographic and bathymetric results, and further knowledge for respective areas.

representation of a volcanological features group, maars, as based on the coherent conceptual knowledge integration. The resulting symbolic representations reflect the coherent conceptual knowledge (CKRI, UDC references) and topographic and bathymetric knowledge (CRI components). Projection for all representations is Lambert Azimuthal Equal Area. Ellipsoid is World Geodetic System 84 (WGS-84). The conceptual knowledge references correspond with the symbolism, e.g., automatic assignment of symbols, e.g., volcano symbols or different colours for different volcanological features groups.

These features groups integrate topographic and bathymetric knowledge, for example. Here, available multi-disciplinary knowledge can be used for contextualisation, e.g., representing characteristics, physical properties, plate tectonics, soil, and age. The conceptual knowledge view groups of object entities of Holocene-prehistoric volcanological features groups correspond with the result matrix (Table III). Entities of each features group refer to any further available volcanological knowledge, e.g., factual knowledge. In these excerpts, the symbolic representations include the calculated object labels, calculated

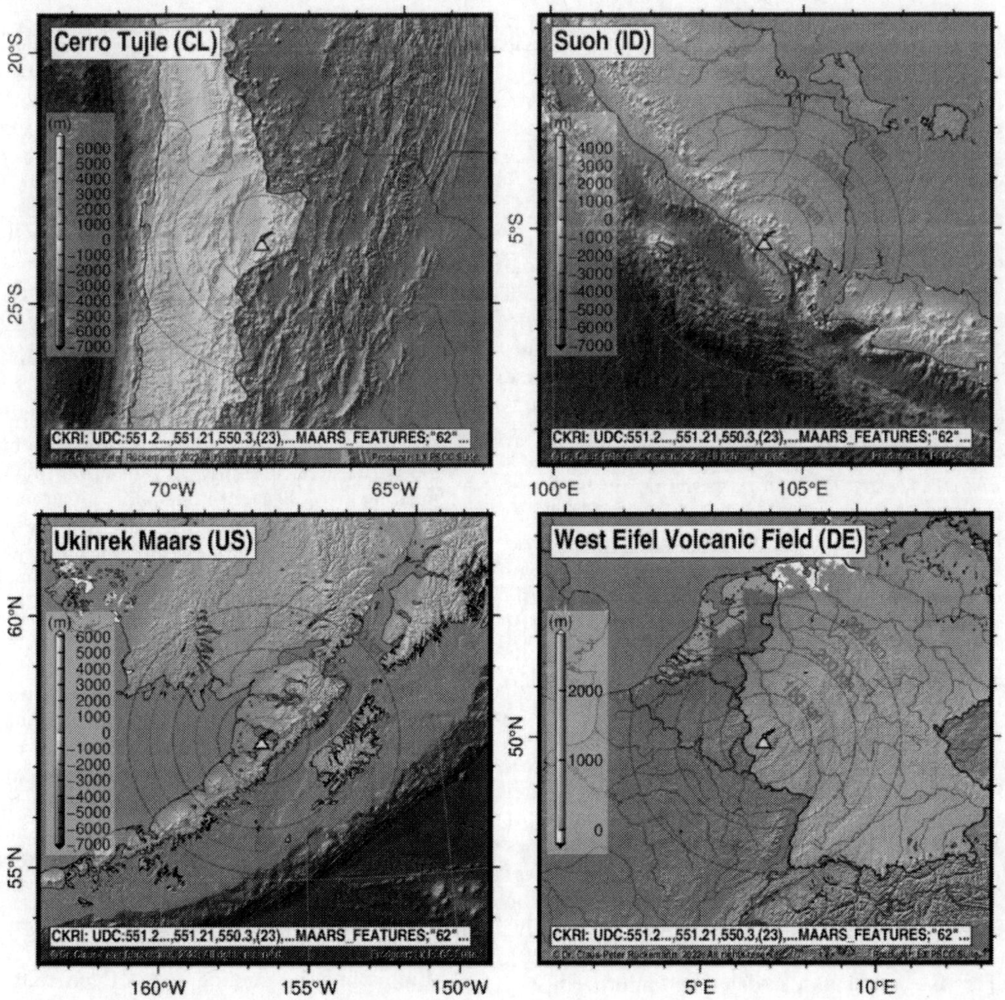

Figure 2. Resulting symbolic representation of a volcanological features group (maars) based on coherent conceptual knowledge integration (excerpt). Generated representations include integrated CKRI references, projection of topographic and bathymetric results, and further knowledge for respective areas.

country codes, distance markers up to 300 km in 50 km steps, and calculated country height range of bathymetry/topography.

The generated symbolic representations can integrate most recent knowledge (e.g., factual, conceptual, procedural, metacognitive, structural) contributed by disciplines and can therefore consider multi-disciplinary results and findings in order to create conceptual knowledge references and new insight.

IV. Components Integrated for Implementation and Realisation

The following passages give a compact overview of major component implementations and development integrated with this research. More detailed, comprehensive discussion and examples regarding fundaments are available with the references on methodology, contextualisation, and conceptual knowledge.

The created and further developed reference implementations of conceptual knowledge frameworks (this research major references in Tables I and II) are used with the implementation and realisation *KR* [10].

Conceptual knowledge base is The *Universal Decimal Classification (UDC)* [11], a general plan for knowledge classification, providing an analytico-synthetic and *faceted* classification, designed for subject description and indexing of content of information resources *irrespective of the carrier, form, format, and language*. UDC-based references for demonstration are taken from the multi-lingual UDC summary [11] released by the UDC Consortium, Creative Commons license [12].

Relevant scientific practices, frameworks, and standards from disciplines and contexts are integrated with the Knowledge Resources, e.g., here details regarding volcanological features [13], chronologies, spatial information, and Volcanic Explosivity Index (VEI) [14].

All integration components, for all disciplines, require an *explicit and continuous formalisation* [15] *process*. The formalisation includes computation model support, e.g., *parallelisation standards, OpenMP* [16], Reg Exp patterns, e.g., *Perl Compatible Regular Expressions (PCRE)* [17].

Methodologies for creating and utilising methods include model processing, remote sensing, spatial mapping, high information densities, and visualisation. Respective contextualisation of (prehistoric) scenarios should each be done under specific (prehistoric) conditions, especially supported by state-of-the-art methods, e.g., spatial operations, triangulation, gradient computation, and projection.

The symbolic representation of the contextualisation can

be done with a wide range of methods, algorithms, and available components, e.g., via LX Professional Scientific Content-Context-Suite (LX PSCC Suite) deploying the Generic Mapping Tools (GMT) [18] for visualisation.

Prehistoric objects and contexts are taken from *The Prehistory and Archaeology Knowledge Archive (PAKA)*, in continuous development for more than three decades [19] and is released by DIMF [20].

Several coherent systems of major natural sciences' context object groups from *KR realisations* have been implemented, especially Knowledge Resources focussing on volcanological features [14] deployed with in depth contextualisation [13] and with a wide range [11] of contexts [10] and structures [21].

The contextualisation for the inventory can employ state-of-the-art results from many disciplines, e.g., context from the natural sciences resources, integrating their inherent representation and common utilisation, e.g., *points, polygons, lines, Digital Elevation Model (DEM), Digital Terrain Model (DTM), and Digital Surface Model (DSM) representations* sources, e.g., from *satellites*, Unmanned Aerial Vehicles (UAV), *z-value representations, distance representations, area representations, raster, vector, binary*, and *non-binary data*. Employed resources are High Resolution (HR) (Space) Shuttle Radar Topography Mission (SRTM) [22] data fusion [23], HR Digital Chart of the World (DCW) [24], and Global Self-consistent Hierarchical High-resolution Geography (GSHHG) [25]. SRTM was produced under the National Aeronautics and Space Administration (NASA) Making Earth System Data Records for Use in Research Environments (MEaSUREs) program. The Land Processed Distributed Active Archive Center (LPDAAC), USA [26], operates as a partnership between the U.S. Geological Survey (USGS) and the National Aeronautics and Space Administration (NASA), USA, and is a component of NASA's Earth Observing System Data and Information System (EOSDIS). Resources are released by NASA and JPL Jet Propulsion Laboratory (JPL), USA, data [27] and site [28]. SRTM15 Plus [23] is continuously updated and improved [22].

Scientific *context parametrisation of prehistoric targets* can use the overall insight from all disciplines, e.g., parametrising algorithms and creating palaeolandscapes.

Structure is an organisation of interrelated entities in a material or non-material object or system [21]. Structure is essential in logic as it carries unique information. Structure means features and facilities. There are merely higher and lower facility levels of how structures can be addressed, which result from structure levels. Structure can, for example, be addressed by logic, names, references, address labels, pointers, fuzzy methods, phonetic methods. The deployment of long-term universal structure and data standards is essential. Relevant examples of sustainable implementations are *NetCDF* [29] based standards, including advanced features, hybrid structure integration, and parallel computing support (*PnetCDF*) and generic multi-dimensional table data, standard xyz files, universal source and text based structure and code representations.

V. Discussion

Implementation and realisation provide a coherent conceptual contextualisation and a seamlessly coherent conceptual knowledge integration with any available knowledge resources. The practical Holocene-prehistoric inventory of volcanological features groups shows important characteristics for multi-disciplinary knowledge space, e.g.:

- Coherent conceptual knowledge integration.
- Selection and coherent integration of resources.
- Flexible criteria for knowledge integration.
- High level of knowledge consistency.
- High level of reproducibility for workflows and results.
- Automated and semi-automated workflow creation.
- Consequent multi-language support (e.g., UDC).
- Deployment of structural knowledge.
- Deployment of available processing and filtering.
- Spatial integration and processing.
- Georeferencing, generic components and results.

Characteristics for component space are, e.g.:

- Dynamical integration of resources and workflows.
- Arbitrary numbers of contextualisation results.
- Flexible creation of workflows and parallelisation.
- Scalable realisation, e.g., parallelisation models.

Knowledge and its complements are interrelated with possible structures and the organisation of knowledge, which contributes to the facilities, which can be parametrised and deployed, e.g., flexibility of data locality and parallelisation. The reference implementation supports parallelisation, e.g., embarrassingly parallel procedures, e.g., via OpenMP [16] and job parallel procedures. The CRI framework components allow efficient parallelisations for any part of workflows and resources, e.g., parallel computation, processing, and generation of frames from satellite data including parallel deployment of Knowledge Resources for multi-dimensional model creation.

Each set of component integration can range from a few to millions of entities for each result group and in consequence millions of symbolic representations for integrated contexts. In the case of the practical Holocene-prehistoric inventory of volcanological features groups we create about 500–1000 basic object entity sets per context.

VI. Conclusion

Employing the methodology of coherent conceptual knowledge classification for developing a coherent context integration in prehistory and archaeology proved efficient and sustainable. The goal of creating a practical Holocene-prehistoric inventory of worldwide volcanological features groups based on the CKRI and CRI framework was successful achieved and allows further coherent contextualisation with knowledge resources, especially for the integration and contextualisation of multi-disciplinary research in prehistory, archaeology, natural sciences, and humanities.

Future work will address the resulting and continuously further developed Holocene-prehistoric inventory of worldwide volcanological features, continuous resources development, coherent conceptual knowledge contextualisation and integration with prehistorical and archaeological knowledge resources, including further georeferencing and spatial processing.

Acknowledgements

This ongoing research is supported by scientific organisations and individuals. We are grateful to the "Knowledge in Motion" (KiM) long-term project, Unabhängiges Deutsches Institut für Multi-disziplinäre Forschung (DIMF), for partially funding this research, implementation, case studies, and publication under grants D2019F1P04998, D2020F1P05228, D2022F1P05308, and D2022F1P05312. and to its senior scientific members and members of the permanent commission of the science council, especially to Dr. Friedrich Hülsmann, Gottfried Wilhelm Leibniz Bibliothek (GWLB) Hannover, to Dipl.-Biol. Birgit Gersbeck-Schierholz, Leibniz Universität Hannover for fruitful discussion, inspiration, and practical multi-disciplinary contextualisation and case studies. We are grateful to Dipl.-Geogr. Burkhard Hentzschel and Dipl.-Ing. Eckhard Dunkhorst, Minden, Germany, for prolific discussion and exchange of practical spatial, UAV, and context scenarios. We are grateful to Dipl.-Ing. Hans-Günther Müller, Göttingen, Germany, for providing specialised, manufactured high end computation and storage solutions. We are grateful to The Science and High Performance Supercomputing Centre (SHPSC) for long-term support. / DIMF-PIID-DF98_007; URL: https://scienceparagon.de/cpr .

REFERENCES

[1] C.-P. Rückemann, "From Knowledge and Meaning Towards Knowledge Pattern Matching: Processing and Developing Knowledge Objects Targeting Geoscientific Context and Georeferencing," in Proc. GEOProcessing 2020, November 21–25, 2020, Valencia, Spain, 2020, pp. 36–41, ISSN: 2308-393X, ISBN-13: 978-1-61208-762-7.

[2] R. Gleser, Zu den erkenntnistheoretischen Grundlagen der Prähistorischen Archäologie. Leiden, 2021, 2021, (title in English: On the Epistemological Fundaments of Prehistorical Archaeology), in: M. Renger, S.-M. Rothermund, S. Schreiber, and A. Veling (Eds.), Theorie, Archäologie, Reflexion. Kontroversen und Ansätze im deutschsprachigen Diskurs, (in print).

[3] C.-P. Rückemann, "Towards Conceptual Knowledge Reference Implementations for Context Integration and Contextualisation of Prehistory's and Natural Sciences' Multi-disciplinary Contexts," International Journal on Advances in Systems and Measurements, vol. 14, no. 1&2, 2021, pp. 113–124, ISSN: 1942-261x, LCCN: 2008212470 (Library of Congress), URL: http://www.iariajournals.org/systems_and_measurements [accessed: 2022-04-23].

[4] C.-P. Rückemann, "Towards a Component Reference Implementations Frame for Achieving Multi-disciplinary Coherent Conceptual and Chorological Contextualisation in Prehistory and Prehistoric Archaeology," International Journal on Advances in Systems and Measurements, vol. 14, no. 1&2, 2021, pp. 103–112, ISSN: 1942-261x, LCCN: 2008212470 (Library of Congress), URL: http://www.iariajournals.org/systems_and_measurements [accessed: 2022-04-23].

[5] C.-P. Rückemann, "The Information Science Paragon: Allow Knowledge to Prevail, from Prehistory to Future – Approaches to Universality, Consistency, and Long-term Sustainability," The International Journal "Information Models and Analyses" (IJ IMA), vol. 9, no. 3, 2020, pp. 203–226, Markov, K. (ed.), ISSN: 1314-6416 (print), Submitted accepted article: November 18, 2020, Publication date: August 17, 2021, URL: http://www.foibg.com/ijima/vol09/ijima09-03-p01.pdf [accessed: 2022-04-23].

[6] L. W. Anderson and D. R. Krathwohl, Eds., A Taxonomy for Learning, Teaching, and Assessing: A Revision of Bloom's Taxonomy of Educational Objectives. Allyn & Bacon, Boston, MA (Pearson Education Group), USA, 2001, ISBN: 978-0801319037.

[7] C.-P. Rückemann, F. Hülsmann, B. Gersbeck-Schierholz, P. Skurowski, and M. Staniszewski, Knowledge and Computing. Post-Summit Results, Delegates' Summit: Best Practice and Definitions of Knowledge and Computing, Sept. 23, 2015, The Fifth Symp. on Adv. Comp. and Inf. in Natural and Applied Sciences (SACINAS), The 13th Int. Conf. of Num. Analysis and Appl. Math. (ICNAAM), Sept. 23–29, 2015, Rhodes, Greece, 2015, pp. 1–7, DOI: 10.15488/3409.

[8] "UDC Summary Linked Data, Main Tables," 2022, Universal Decimal Classification (UDC), UDC Consortium, URL: https://udcdata.info/078887 [accessed: 2022-04-23].

[9] "UDC Summary Linked Data, Auxiliary Tables," 2022, Universal Decimal Classification (UDC), UDC Consortium, URL: https://udcdata.info/ [accessed: 2022-04-23].

[10] C.-P. Rückemann, "Prehistory's and Natural Sciences' Multi-disciplinary Contexts: Contextualisation and Context Integration Based on Universal Conceptual Knowledge," in Proc. INFOCOMP 2020, May 30 – June 3, 2021, Valencia, Spain, 2021, ISSN: 2308-3484, ISBN: 978-1-61208-865-5.

[11] "Multilingual Universal Decimal Classification Summary," 2012, UDC Consortium, 2012, Web resource, v. 1.1. The Hague: UDC Consortium (UDCC Publication No. 088), URL: http://www.udcc.org/udcsummary/php/index.php [accessed: 2022-04-23].

[12] "Creative Commons Attribution Share Alike 3.0 license," 2012, URL: http://creativecommons.org/licenses/by-sa/3.0/ [accessed: 2022-04-23], (first release 2009, subsequent update 2012).

[13] C.-P. Rückemann, "Long-term Sustainable Knowledge Classification with Scientific Computing: The Multi-disciplinary View on Natural Sciences and Humanities," International Journal on Advances in Software, vol. 7, no. 1&2, 2014, pp. 302–317, ISSN: 1942-2628.

[14] C.-P. Rückemann, "Cognostics and Knowledge Used With Dynamical Processing," International Journal on Advances in Software, vol. 8, no. 3&4, 2015, pp. 361–376, ISSN: 1942-2628, LCCN: 2008212462 (Library of Congress), URL: http://www.iariajournals.org/software/ [accessed: 2022-04-23].

[15] C.-P. Rückemann, R. Pavani, B. Gersbeck-Schierholz, A. Tsitsipas, L. Schubert, F. Hülsmann, O. Lau, and M. Hofmeister, Best Practice and Definitions of Formalisation and Formalism. Post-Summit Results, Delegates' Summit: The Ninth Symp. on Adv. Comp. and Inf. in Natural and Applied Sciences (SACINAS), The 17th Int. Conf. of Num. Analysis and Appl. Math. (ICNAAM), Sept. 23–28, 2019, Rhodes, Greece, 2019, DOI: 10.15488/5241.

[16] L. Dagum and R. Menon, "OpenMP: an industry standard API for shared-memory programming," Computational Science & Engineering, (IEEE), vol. 5, no. 1, 1998, pp. 46–55.

[17] "Perl Compatible Regular Expressions (PCRE)," 2021, URL: https://www.pcre.org/ [accessed: 2022-04-23].

[18] P. Wessel, W. H. F. Smith, R. Scharroo, J. Luis, and F. Wobbe, "The Generic Mapping Tools (GMT)," 2020, URL: http://www.generic-mapping-tools.org/ [accessed: 2022-04-23], URL: http://gmt.soest.hawaii.edu/ [accessed: 2022-04-23].

[19] C.-P. Rückemann, "Information Science and Inter-disciplinary Long-term Strategies – Key to Insight, Consistency, and Sustainability: Conceptual Knowledge Reference Methodology Spanning Prehistory, Archaeology, Natural Sciences, and Humanities," International Tutorial, DataSys Congress 2020, Sept. 27 – Oct. 1, 2020, Lisbon, Portugal, 2020, URL: http://www.iaria.org/conferences2020/ProgramINFOCOMP20.html [accessed: 2022-04-23].

[20] "The Prehistory and Archaeology Knowledge Archive (PAKA) license," 2021, (release 2021), Unabhängiges Deutsches Institut für Multidisziplinäre Forschung (DIMF): All rights reserved. Rights retain to the contributing creators.

[21] C.-P. Rückemann, "The Impact of Information Science Accompanied Structural Information on Computation of Knowledge Pattern Matching and Processing: A Prehistory, Archaeology, Natural Sciences, and Humanities Conceptual Integration Perspective," in Proc. INFOCOMP 2020, Sept. 27 – Oct. 1, 2020, Lisbon, Portugal, 2020, ISBN: 978-1-61208-807-5, URL: http://www.thinkmind.org/index.php?view=article&articleid=infocomp_2020_1_10_60015 [accessed: 2022-04-23].

[22] B. Tozer, D. T. Sandwell, W. H. F. Smith, C. Olson, J. R. Beale, and P. Wessel, "Global Bathymetry and Topography at 15 Arc Sec: SRTM15+," Earth and Space Science, vol. 6, no. 10, Oct. 2019, pp. 1847–1864, ISSN: 2333-5084, DOI: 10.1029/2019EA000658.

[23] C. L. Olson, J. J. Becker, and D. T. Sandwell, "SRTM15_PLUS: Data fusion of Shuttle Radar Topography Mission (SRTM) land topography with measured and estimated seafloor topography," (NCEI Accession 0150537), National Centers for Environmental Information (NCEI), NOAA, 2016.

[24] P. Wessel, "DCW for GMT 6 or later," 2022, URL: http://www.soest.hawaii.edu/pwessel/dcw/ [accessed: 2022-04-23].

[25] P. Wessel, "GSHHG," 2017, URL: http://www.soest.hawaii.edu/pwessel/gshhg/ [accessed: 2022-04-23].

[26] "Land Processed Distributed Active Archive Center," 2022, LP DAAC, URL: https://lpdaac.usgs.gov/ [accessed: 2022-04-23].

[27] "U.S. Releases Enhanced Shuttle Land Elevation Data," 2014, JPL, September 23, 2014, URL: https://www.jpl.nasa.gov/news/us-releases-enhanced-shuttle-land-elevation-data [accessed: 2022-04-23].

[28] "U.S. Releases Enhanced Shuttle Land Elevation Data, Official NASA SRTM Site," 2014, Australia, September 23, 2014, URL: https://www2.jpl.nasa.gov/srtm/ [accessed: 2022-04-23].

[29] "Network Common Data Form (NetCDF)," 2021, DOI: 10.5065/D6H70CW6, URL: http://www.unidata.ucar.edu/software/netcdf/ [accessed: 2022-04-23].

Use of UAV-Based RGB Imagery and Vegetation Index for Early Detection of the Rabies of Chickpeas

Lorena Parra[1, 2], Barbara Stefanutti, David Mostaza-Colado[1], Jose F. Marin[3], Jaime Lloret[2], and Pedro V. Mauri[1]
[1]Instituto Madrileño de Investigación y Desarrollo Rural, Agrario y Alimentario (IMIDRA), Finca "El Encin", A-2, Km 38, 2, 28805 Alcalá de Henares, Madrid, Spain
[2] Instituto de Investigación para la Gestión Integrada de Zonas Costeras Universitat Politècnica de València, Valencia, Spain
[3] Area verde MG Projects SL. C/ Oña, 43 28933 Madrid, Spain
Email: loparbo@doctor.upv.es, barbara.stefanutti@madrid.org, david.mostaza@madrid.org, jmarin@areaverde.es, jlloret@dcom.upv.es, and pedro.mauri@madrid.org

Abstract—**Rainfed crops rarely include the application of phytosanitary products due to the high cost of their application and the reduced rentability of crops. Nonetheless, if diseases are early detected, phytosanitary application costs are heavily reduced. This paper presents a method of detecting rabies in chickpeas based on true-colour images gathered from drones. The methodology consists of applying a series of vegetation indexes and filters. In the proposed method, applied to several images, we include the detection of areas affected by rabies of chickpea but also their differentiation from other areas with lower vigour. The developed approach is tested with images obtained in different soil types and gathered at diverse flying heights. As vegetation indexes, we used well-known vegetation indexes and specific vegetation indexes developed for chickpeas. To evaluate the accuracy of the proposed methodology, the number and percentage of true positives and false positives are assessed. Moreover, a verification is done using a different picture in order to evaluate if the methodology might be applied in other scenarios. The results of the initial test and the verification test offer a number of true positives higher than 85%. Thus, we can affirm that the proposed methodology can be useful for the differentiation between areas affected by rabies of chickpea and areas with low vigour due to the passing of machinery.**

Keywords-plant disease; aggregation; image processing; legume; biotic stress; crop

I. INTRODUCTION

Chickpea is a legume crop with a high percentage of protein, which can help to reduce the dependence on meat. Spain is the main producer of chickpea in Europe. Nonetheless, the cultivation of chickpeas has declined in recent decades. As indicated by the Lonja de Sevilla, the main problems are the following: (i) Lack of support via Common Agrarian Policy, (ii) Little Research (little use of certified seed), (iii) Technical difficulties in crop management (high presence of weeds, diseases, such as rabies and harvesting problems) and (iv) Obstacles in marketing. The technical difficulties of crop management are the most important for farmers and those that can be solved by means of new technologies. Of these difficulties, the detection of weeds [1] and plants affected by diseases [2] are vital in chickpea cultivation and other crops. Among the chickpea diseases, rabies of the chickpea is one of the most problematic ones, causing a decrease in production and even the death of the plant.

The use of a remote sensing approach is pointed out as one of the best methodologies for evaluating plant features. In other crops, the use of remote sensing for detecting plant diseases is common. According to [3], the most studied diseases are fungal diseases. They are generally studied in cereals such as wheat, rice and maise, followed by soya. No study evaluated the use of hyperspectral images in chickpeas or other rainfed legumes. In [4], a large collection of Vegetation Indexes (VI) developed by different authors for diverse crops is presented. The authors indicate that VI are highly correlated at plot level with the presence of plant diseases. Focusing on VI, RGB images are reported as adequate for cotton, sugar beet, grapefruit, and tobacco [5]. Although hyperspectral images provide more information than RGB images, the elevated cost of hyperspectral cameras precludes its use for real solutions.

The main problem of applying VI to identify the areas to be treated is that we can find other zones characterised by low vigour in the fields, which can be confused with zones affected by rabies. These zones are usually the areas that have been stepped on by a tractor when entering to apply treatments. If the areas are not correctly differentiated, phytosanitary products will be wasted, increasing the treatment's cost and efficiency.

The aim of this paper is to evaluate the use of RGB images taken by Unmanned Aerial Vehicle (UAV) to identify areas affected by rabies in different fields. The images have been taken at different heights and included affected and unaffected areas. The entire process includes the application of the VI (testing up to 5 different VI) and the use of different tools for image processing, such as aggregation or reclassification tools. Simple tools are selected to avoid the use of artificial inteligence or complex tools. This, ensures that the methodology can be applied in the fields in real time. Thus, the Unmanned Aerial Vehicle (UAV) will be able to identify the areas to be treated and apply the treatment at the same time.

The rest of the paper is structured as follows; Section II outline the related work and the gap in the current solutions. The proposal is described in Section III. Section IV details the material and methods used in this research. The results and main discussion are presented in Section V. Finally, the conclusion and future work are summarised in Section VI.

II. Related Work

This section summarises the existing proposals for identifying diseases or abiotic stress in plants using RGB images and the existing VI developed for chickpeas.

Regarding the use of RGB images to identify plant diseases, we can find a limited number of examples. More examples of using the RGB data to evaluate abiotic stress.

In 2019, Marc Sancho-Adamson et al. [6], showed the use of RGB-based VI for evaluating the effects of VerticilliumWilt of olive. The authors used the following VI: Green Area (GA), Greener Area (GGA), normalised green-red difference index and triangular greenness index. Their results indicate that GA was the one with the strongest correlations between the VI and chlorophyll and carotenoid extractions to identify the diseases. Nonetheless, the VI was applied in pictures done in the laboratory, not in the field.

Another example of the application of RGB indexes to identify plat diseases was published in 2021 by Arturo Yee-Rendon [7]. In their paper, the authors pointed out the possibility of using RGB-based VI for detecting tobacco mosaic virus and pepper huasteco yellow vein Virus in jalapeño pepper plants. New VI was proposed and evaluated. The authors combine the VI with a convolutional neural network to identify the affected leaves in their proposal. Their results indicate that the VI with better accuracy was the normalised green–blue vegetation index, which combines the green and the blue bands.

In 2021, Brenon Diennevam Souza Barbosa et al. [8], assess the use of RGB images for monitoring a coffee farm. A total of 9 VI were used and correlated with the obtained Leaf Area Index (LAI). Results indicate that the index that best correlates with the LAI varies along the different phenological stages of the crop. Salima Yousfi et al. in 2022 [9] present the use of RGB-based VI for evaluating the hydric stress in turfgrasses. GA and GGA were used to assess the stress of the plants. Their results indicate that RGB-based VI obtained from aerial images explains the hydric stress of the plants better than terrestrial indexes, even better than the Normalised Difference Vegetation Index (NDVI). The NDVI is a well-known VI that uses not only the RGB data but also the information of infrared light.

Finally, a few examples of VI applied for chickpeas monitoring can be found. Particularly, in the case of RGB indexes, only two papers have been published. In the first example, the VI was used to differentiate soil from vegetation in order to assess the degree of establishment of different legumes, including lentils and chickpea [10]. In the second example, a tailored VI including a series of thresholds is used to differentiate species of legumes in intercropping. The included species were chickpea, lentil and ervil. The results of [11] pointed out that chickpea was the species that was easier to differentiate.

As far as we know, no paper has shown the use of RGB-based VI to identify chickpea's rabies nor to differentiate regions affected by the disease and the pass of machinery. Moreover, no example of RGB-based VI applied in the field is found. Thus, the methodology presented in this paper can be considered an advance over state of the art.

III. Proposal

In this section, we outline the proposal developed in the paper. We will describe why the proposed methodology is the most suitable approach for the problem.

The problem indicated in the introduction is differentiating areas affected by rabies of chickpea from areas with lower vigour due to the passing of machinery. Our proposal is to develop a methodology that allows an UAV to apply it in real-time to smartly decide the areas to be treated with the phytosanitary product. The aim is to minimise the application of phytosanitary products treating only the area affected by the disease and its surroundings. Thus, it is essential to differentiate the areas in which crop has low vigour due to the rabies of the chickpea from the areas with low vigour due to the machinery, which does not need any treatment.

Figure 1 shows an example of a picture in which, manually, we have differentiated the areas with low vigour and their cause. The proposed approach is depicted in Figure 2, in which we represent the whole process to minimise the use of phytosanitary products. Applying the phytosanitary product to the affected area it is possible to reduce the cost and environmental impact of the treatment without minimizing its effectivity. Traditionally, the phytosanitary product is applied to the whole plot.

Figure 1. Example of areas with low vigour.

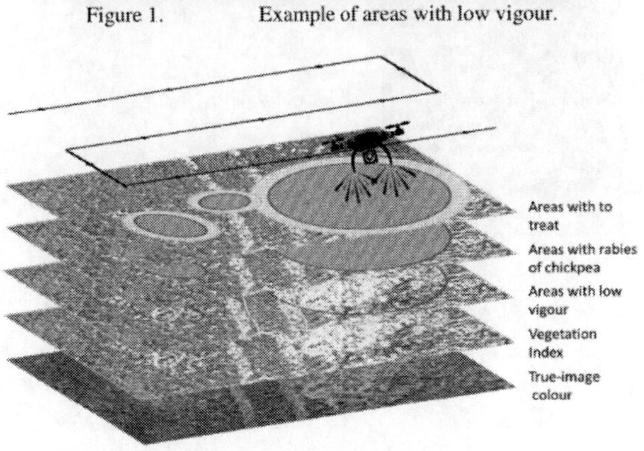

Figure 2. Representation of proposal.

IV. Material and Methods

A. *Studied area*

The study area is located in the autonomous community of Castilla la Mancha (Spain), in the municipality of Trijueque (40º46'45"N, 2º59'2"W) at an approximate altitude of 1,000 m.a.s.l. The location of the studied area in Spain and the detailed image of the studied fields can be seen in Figure 3 a) and Figure 3 b). The studied area is composed of two production fields in which chickpea is grown. Different crop densities characterise the plots due to different soils. Plots are located on a plain close to a highway.

Pictures were gathered on 25 May 2021 in cloudless sky conditions (clouds covered less than 20% of the sky). This ensures the light condition for picture collection.

B. *Studied crop*

In the studied plots, chickpeas are in the reproductive stage. More specifically, chickpea was in the phenologic state R6, with the seeds starting their formation in the pods. The plants have an approximate height of about 40 cm. The plats belong to a variety of chickpea with small seeds.

At different points of the plots, it is possible to identify areas affected by rabies of chickpeas. Those areas can be seen in Figure 4. In addition to the affected areas, the use of agricultural machinery in the early stages has affected the correct development of plants.

C. *AUV details*

The images are taken by a drone (Parrot Bebop 2) that uses an RGB and thermal camera (FLIR ONE Pro thermal – RGB camera). In the present study, only the information from the RGB camera is used. Figure 5 depicts the data gathering process.

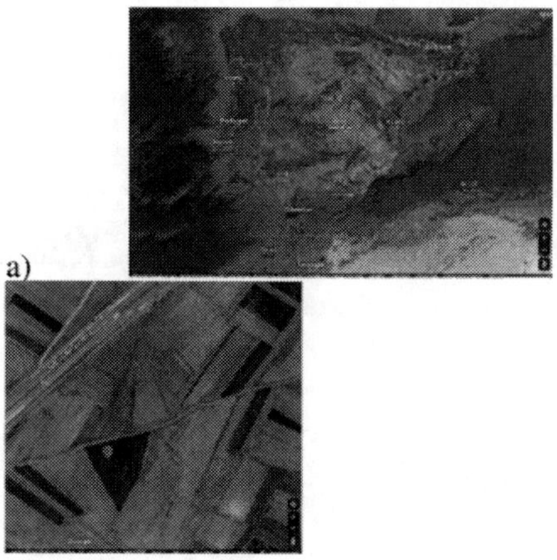

a) b)

Figure 3. Location of the studied area, a) location in the Iberian Peninsula and b) image of the fields.

Figure 4. Terrestrial picture of the studied area.

Figure 5. Picture during data collection.

D. *Image processing*

The pictures were taken at a height of 8 to 10 m above the ground. The images are subsequently processed mathematically to identify the areas with low vigour, differentiating the areas affected by rabies from the areas affected by the passage of a tractor. In Figure 1, we can see an example of the images taken. In each of the images, the tractor pass (on the left of the image) and the area affected by rabies (on the right of the image) are identified.

The problem that we need to solve is the possible false positives caused by the tractor tread area. It is expected that when applying the VI, both the areas affected by rabies and the areas trampled by the tractor will give similar results.

The process used with the images to identify areas with low vigour and differences between areas affected by rabies or by the passage of a tractor is broken down into the following elements: (i) Application of the VI (created for this case), (ii) Tools to differentiate false positives from the machinery pass, and (iii) Aggregation techniques and mathematical operations between bands. The process is summarized in Figure 6.

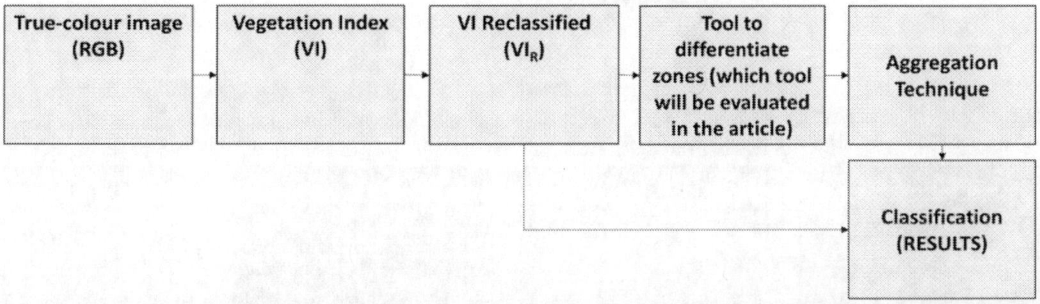

Figure 6. Block diagram of the followed process, including the most relevant tools (VI, reclassification and aggregation technique).

V. Evaluation of Results and discussion

In this section, we analyse the results of the proposed methodology and the selected values for each of the conducted steps. Moreover, we display the code of the used tools.

A. *Followed process*

Figure 7 shows the results of the processes followed to identify the areas affected by rabies. An example of the raster obtained working with the image taken at 10 m is shown in each block diagram.

As VI, we have evaluated the use of well-known VI as well as analysed the generation of tailored VI. The use of existing VI does not offer good results compared with the proposed VI. Among the proposed VI, five different VI were considered. Being the VI indicated in (1), the one with better results. Three of the proposed VI are based on blue and green bands (B3 and B2), another VI is based on red and green bands (B1 and B2), and the last one on the three bands (B1, B2 and B3). The VI with better results is the one based on the combination of the three bands.

Another relevant finding of this paper is that the "Thin" tool was the one that allowed the differentiation of the areas with low vigour due to the machinery from the areas affected by rabies of chickpea. The differentiation is done based on the different shapes of affected areas (round for rabies of chickpea and linear for the machinery). This tool was selected among different spatial analyst tools. Other tools tested in this paper included Boundary clean, Expand, Nibble, and Shrink. Nonetheless, none of these tools has proven to be as accurate as of the Thin tool.

We can identify it at the end of the block diagram. As a result, a raster in which combines the AIVR and ATIVRR (see (2)), the red spots indicate the area in which rabies of chickpea appear. The area in grey is discarded due to the fine tool since it indicates that the shape of the area cannot be considered as an area affected by rabies of the chickpea for the given flying height and camera.

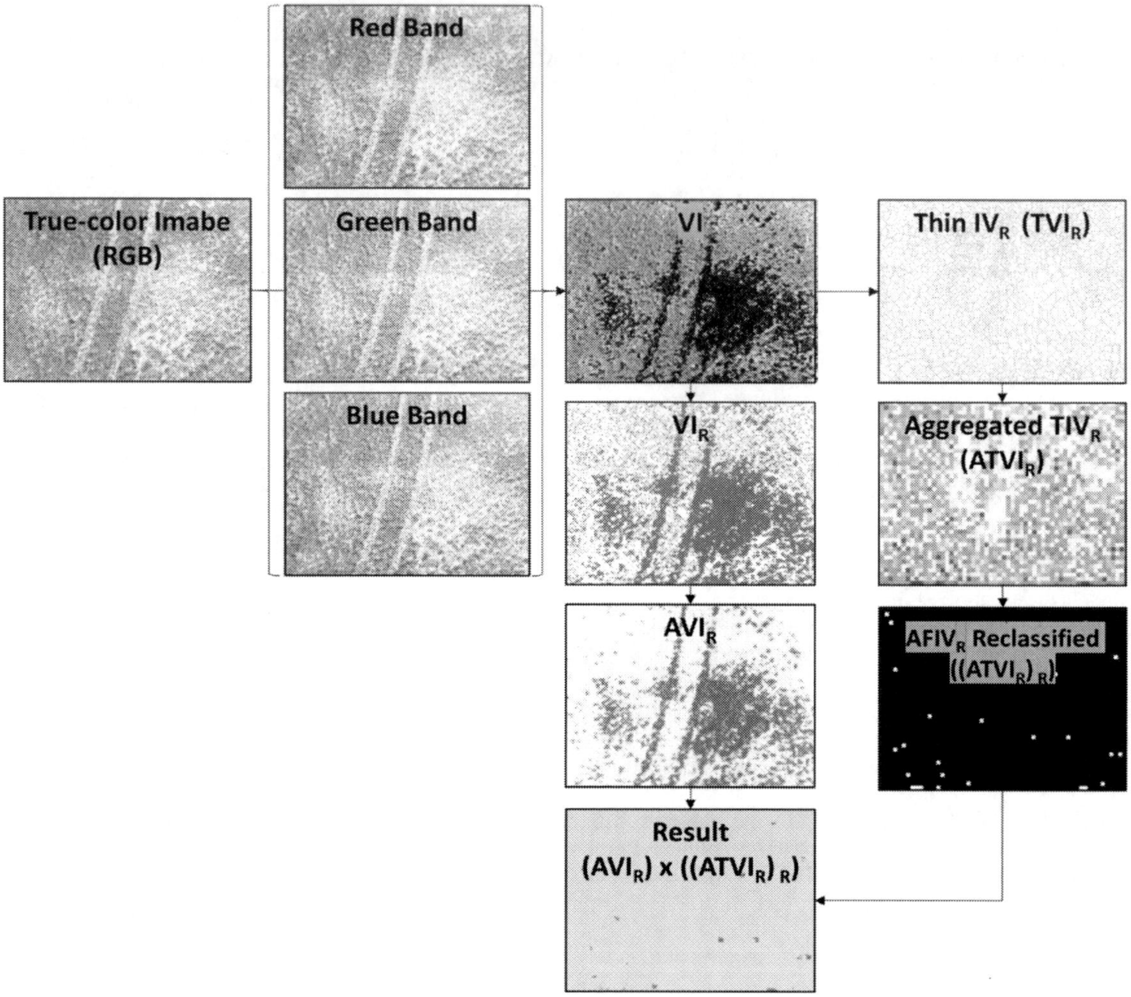

Figure 7. Results of each step until reaching the result.

B. *Code and values for selected code*

Following the process described in Figure 7, we detail the included code. The first code to be described is used for the reclassification of VI to generate the VIR. This code can be seen in Figure 8. The selected ranges do not need to be adapted if the proposed methodology is applied under different conditions.

In the next step, the use of the Thin tool is defined in Figrue 9. In this case, the selected parameters were round since the results are more accurate than with sharp and 50 as the maximum thickness in pixels. The number of maximum thickness should be reconsidered for other scenarios in which the pixel size changes, such as for using another flying height or a camera with a different resolution.

The Aggregation processes for both IVR and ATVIR are defined in Figrue 10. The aggregation method (mean for IVR and summation for ATVIR) should not be modified. Nonetheless, the cell size should be reconsidered and adapted for other scenarios.

Code 1

```
# Code for Reclassify Operation (I)
import arcpy
from arcpy import env
from arcpy.sa import *
env.workspace = "C:/sapyexamples/data"
outReclass1 = Reclassify("VI", "Value",
RemapRange([[0,1,1],[1,255,2]]))
outReclass1.save("C:/sapyexamples/output/VIR")
```

Figure 8. Code for reclassify operation (i)

Code 2:

```
# Code for Thin
import arcpy
from arcpy import env
from arcpy.sa import *
env.workspace = "C:/sapyexamples/data"
thinOut = Thin("VIR","ZERO", "FILTER","ROUND",50)
thinOut.save("c:/sapyexamples/output/FIVR")
```

Figure 9. Code for thin operation

Code 3:

```
# Code for Aggregate Operation
import arcpy
from arcpy import env
from arcpy.sa import *
env.workspace = "C:/sapyexamples/data"
outAggreg = Aggregate("IVR", 5, "MEAN",
"TRUNCATE", "DATA")
outAggreg.save("C:/sapyexamples/output/AVIR")
outAggreg = Aggregate("TAVIR", 25, "SUMMATION",
"TRUNCATE", "DATA")
outAggreg.save("C:/sapyexamples/output/ATAVIR")
```

Figure 10. Code for Aggregate Operation

Finally, Figure 11 presents the reclassification of ATVIR. Again, no modification of this code is needed for different scenarios. The selected values for the aggregation are the ones that allow the assigment of pixel value = 1 in the result of the methodology when the area has rabies of chickpea.

Code 4:

```
# Code for Reclassify Operation (II)
import arcpy
from arcpy import env
from arcpy.sa import *
env.workspace = "C:/sapyexamples/data"
outReclass1 = Reclassify("AFIVR", "Value",
RemapRange([[0,1],[0,255,0]]))
outReclass1.save("C:/sapyexamples/output/VIR")
```

Figure 11. Code for reclassify operation (ii).

(1)

(2)

C. Accuracy of obtained results and verification

The proposed methodology makes it possible to identify the areas affected by rabies in 100% of the cases. After removing the positives that are on the edge of the photograph, there are 85.7% true positives versus 14.3% false positives. In the verification of the methodology, using a different picture, we identify 100% of affected areas by rabies of chickpea. In this case, we have 88.2% of true positives and 11.8% of false positives. The results in terms of true positives and false positives are summarised in Table 1.

TABLE I. SUMMARY OF RESULTS AND VERIFICATION

	Accuracy		
	N° of positive pixels	***True positives***	***False positives***
Test	7	6 (85.7 %)	1 (14.3 %)
Verification	17	15 (88.2 %)	2 (11.8 %)

A correct classification percentage of 80% is within what is expected in this type of case, especially for preliminary results [11]. The precision is lower than in other articles in which more advanced classification techniques are used, in which case the precision is close to 90% [12]. There are cases in which these advanced classification techniques have a precision of less than 80% [13].

D. Dicussion

The obtained accuracy, in the verification is aligned with accuracies found in other similar models [10 and 11].

Existing approaches to solve the identification of fungic diseases focused on machine learning are designed for other crops such as cotton [14], wheat [15], maize [16], oilseed rape [17] or strawberry [18], amon oghers. Nonetheless, it is not possible to fairly compare the results since the accuracy of the methodologies are calculated in a whyde range of forms (confusion matrices, R2 of the correlation, etc).

Only one paper has been found in which the detection of fungic disease in chickpea is analyzed [19] Nevertheless, in [19] the authors do not offer the accuracy of the disease detection, results are referred to productivity. Another example of use of remote sensing in chickpea, aimed to detect water stress, obtained accuracies between 72 % and 83 %. In a posterior study, using convolutional neural network [21], the maximum accuracy reached 96%. The accuracy of porposed method is aligned with existing accuracies in proposals for chickpea.

The main limitation of the proposed methodology is the use of RGB images. Probably, if infrared informtionis included the differentiation will be easier. However, to maintain the methodology as simple as possible and to avoid using high-cost resources, RGB images are the sole information source.

VI. CONCLUSION

In the presented work, we have evaluated a methodology to identify areas affected by rabies capable of not giving false positives in the areas through which agricultural machinery has passed. It is a preliminary methodology that will be evaluated within the framework of the GO TecnoGAR and Valvagar-Dron Guardes projects in the years 2022 and 2023.

In the future, it is hoped that this information will be combined with specific treatments that will reduce the number of phytosanitary products used to treat large areas. Similar methodologies will also be used to identify weeds.

ACKNOWLEDGMENT

This research was partially funded by the "Programa Estatal de I+D+i Orientada a los Retos de la Sociedad, en el marco del Plan Estatal de Investigación Científica y Técnica y de Innovación 2017–2020" (Project code: PID2020-114467RR-C31 and PID2020-114467RR-C33), and by

"Proyectos de innovación de interés general por grupos operativos de la Asociación Europea para la Innovación en materia de productividad y sostenibilidad agrícolas (AEI-Agri)" in the framework "Programa Nacional de Desarrollo Rural 2014–2020", GO TECNOGAR, and by Comunidad de Madrid, through IMIDRA" FP22-ValvaGAR.

References

[1] J. Gai, L. Tang, L., and B. L. Steward, "Automated crop plant detection based on the fusion of color and depth images for robotic weed control," Journal of Field Robotics, vol. 37, no. 1, pp. 35-52, 2020.

[2] J. D. Pujari, R. Yakkundimath, and A. S. Byadgi, "Image processing based detection of fungal diseases in plants," Procedia Computer Science, vol. 46, pp. 1802-1808, 2015.

[3] N. Zhang, et al., "A review of advanced technologies and development for hyperspectral-based plant disease detection in the past three decades," Remote Sensing, vol. 12, no. 19, pp. 3188, 2020.

[4] J. Zhang, et al., "Monitoring plant diseases and pests through remote sensing technology: A review," Computers and Electronics in Agriculture, vol. 165, pp. 104943, 2019.

[5] N. K.Gogoi, B. Deka, and L. C. Bora, "Remote sensing and its use in detection and monitoring plant diseases: A review, " Agricultural Reviews, vol. 39, no. 4, pp. 307-313, 2018.

[6] M. Sancho-Adamson, M. I. Trillas, J. Bort, J. A. Fernandez-Gallego, and J. Romanyà, "Use of RGB vegetation indexes in assessing early effects of Verticillium wilt of olive in asymptomatic plants in high and low fertility scenarios," Remote Sensing, vol. 11, no. 6, pp. 607, 2019.

[7] A. Yee-Rendon, I. Torres-Pacheco, A. S. Trujillo-Lopez, K. P. Romero-Bringas, and J. R. Millan-Almaraz, "Analysis of New RGB Vegetation Indices for PHYVV and TMV Identification in Jalapeño Pepper (Capsicum annuum) Leaves Using CNNs-Based Model," Plants, vol. 10, no. 10, pp. 1977, 2021

[8] B. D. S. Barbosa, et al. "Application of RGB Images Obtained by UAV in Coffee Farming," Remote Sensing, vol. 13, no. 12, pp. 2397, 2021.

[9] S. Yousfi, J. Marín, L. Parra, J. Lloret, and P. V. Mauri, "Remote sensing devices as key methods in the advanced turfgrass phenotyping under different water regimes," Agricultural Water Management, vol. 266, pp. 107581, 2022.

[10] L. Parra, et al., "Drone RGB images as a reliable information source to determine legumes establishment success," Drones, vol. 5, no. 3, pp. 79, 2021.

[11] L. Parra, D. Mostaza-Colado, J. F. Marin, P. V. Mauri, and J. Lloret, "Methodology to Differentiate Legume Species in Intercropping Agroecosystems Based on UAV with RGB Camera," Electronics, vol. 11, no. 4, pp. 609, 2022.

[12] Z. Iqbal, et al. "An automated detection and classification of citrus plant diseases using image processing techniques: A review," Comput. Electron. Agr., vol. 153, pp. 12-32, 2018.

[13] J. Boulent, S. Foucher, J. Théau, and P. L. St-Charles, "Convolutional neural networks for the automatic identification of plant diseases," Frontiers in plant science, vol. 10, pp. 941, 2019.

[14] T. Wang, J. A. Thomasson, C. Yang, T. Isakeit, and R. L. Nichols, "Automatic classification of cotton root rot disease based on UAV remote sensing," Remote Sensing, vol. 12, no. 8, pp. 1310, 2020.

[15] U. Shafi, et al. "Wheat rust disease detection techniques: a technical perspective," Journal of Plant Diseases and Protection, pp. 1-16, 2022.

[16] A. Loladze, F. A. Rodrigues Jr, F. Toledo, F. San Vicente, B. Gérard, and M. P. Boddupalli, "Application of remote sensing for phenotyping tar spot complex resistance in maize," Frontiers in Plant Science, vol. 10, pp. 552, 2019.

[17] F. Cao, et al. "Fast detection of sclerotinia sclerotiorum on oilseed rape leaves using low-altitude remote sensing technology," Sensors, vol. 18, no. 12, pp. 4464, 2018.

[18] Q. Liu, et al. "Information fusion of hyperspectral imaging and electronic nose for evaluation of fungal contamination in strawberries during decay," Postharvest Biol. Technol., vol. 153, pp. 152–160, 2019.

[19] C. Zhang, W. Chen, and S. Sankaran, "High-throughput field phenotyping of Ascochyta blight disease severity in chickpea," Crop Protection, vol.125, pp. 104885, 2019.

[20] S. Azimi, T. Kaur, and T. K. Gandhi, "Water stress identification in chickpea plant shoot images using deep learning," The 17th India Council International Conference (INDICON), Delhi, India, 10-13 Decembre 2020, pp. 1-7.

[21] S. Azimi, T. Kaur, and T. K. Gandhi, "BAT optimized CNN model identifies water stress in chickpea plant shoot images," In the 25th International Conference on Pattern Recognition (ICPR), Milano, Italy, 10-15 January 2021 pp. 8500-8506.

International Academy, Research,
and Industry Association (IARIA)
412 Derby Way
Wilmington, DE 19810

ISBN 978-1-7138-6950-4

CURRAN ASSOCIATES INC.
proceedings.com